IN THE NAME OF **ALLAH**

Beacon of Guidance on the Heights of Eloquence

Nahj al-Balaghah: Translation and Commentary

Ayatollah Naser Makarem Shirazi

By: Ayatollah Naser Makarem Shirazi

In Collaboration with a Body of Scholars from the Islamic Seminary School of Qom

English Translation by:
Morteza Bassirian

Design by:
Mohammad Hossein Moayyedi

ISBN: 978-1-922583-63-5

Lantern Publications
info@lanternpublications.com
www.lanternpublications.com

Ordering Information:
Quantity sales. Special discounts are available on quantity purchases by corporations, associations, and others. For details, contact the distributor at the address below.

Shia Books Australia
www.shiabooks.com.au
info@shiabooks.com.au

ISBN: 978-1-922583-63-5

First Edition

Translated from the original text in Farsi entitled:
پیام امام امیرالمؤمنین علیه‌السلام (Payām-i Imām Amīr al-Mu'minīn (a))

Acknowledgments

We would like to extend our gratitude to a number of individuals who helped in the publication of this volume. We would like to thank Ali Mahdavi, Mohammad Asem Ahmadi, Ahmad Abbasi and Hasan Haeritabar for their contribution to the preparation of the present volume for publication.

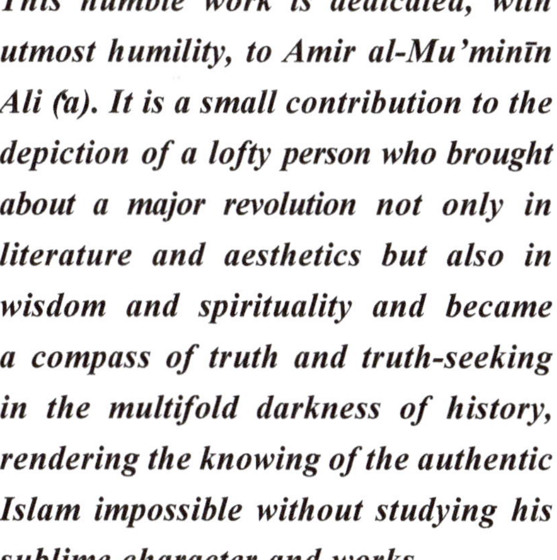

This humble work is dedicated, with utmost humility, to Amir al-Mu'minīn Ali (ʿa). It is a small contribution to the depiction of a lofty person who brought about a major revolution not only in literature and aesthetics but also in wisdom and spirituality and became a compass of truth and truth-seeking in the multifold darkness of history, rendering the knowing of the authentic Islam impossible without studying his sublime character and works.

CONTENTS

Foreword

As human beings, we know by intuition that there is more to us than meets the physical eye. As far as the physical aspect of our own existence and that of the natural world is concerned, we are able to study them and gain more knowledge of them through empirical research. However, when it comes to our non-physical spiritual aspect, we are unable to directly observe and study its attributes, hence the path to learning about it seems blocked at first sight. However, in order to compensate for this shortcoming of human beings, Allah_ Glory to Him_ chose the most virtuous and righteous ones among them to act as His Messengers and deliver to them, among other sorts of knowledge, knowledge regarding the spiritual aspect of their existence and His created spiritual realm.

But as human beings, Divinely-sent Prophets would live their lives and then pass away, leaving the important job of passing on this vital knowledge to later generations of mankind to their successors. As the last and the most comprehensive Divinely-sent religion, Islamic knowledge, its laws, and its spiritual teachings needed to be communicated to later generations after the demise of the Prophet Muhammad (ṣ), a job that was entrusted to his rightful successor, Amir al-Mu'minīn Ali ('a).

As the "Leader of Believers" [the literal translation of his title "Amir al-Mu'minīn"], Imam Ali ('a) carried out his duty perfectly by relating the Prophet's teachings (which were essentially Revealed teachings) to people in different ways and on a myriad of occasions. He would impart that knowledge to people individually, in his public sermons, and through letters that he wrote to various people. A few centuries after his martyrdom, the renowned Muslim scholar and literary figure, Abū al-Ḥassan Muḥammad bin al-Ḥussayn bin Musa, also known as "al-Sharīf al-Raḍī" [or al-Sayyid al-Raḍī] compiled the most eloquent parts of the Imam's sayings into a book which he chose to call "Nahj al-Balāgah" [which literally translates into English as "The Path to Eloquence"].

Initially, Sayyid al-Raḍī's aim was merely to compile and present those of the Imam's words which enjoyed supreme eloquence and displayed his unparalleled literary genius. However, in so doing, he also left a legacy for mankind of the most enlightening and soul-shaking spiritual and moral teachings by Imam Ali ('a), presented in his sermons, letters, and aphorisms. Indeed, the title "Beacon of Guidance on the Heights of Eloquence" has been chosen for the present series to capture both of these amazing dimensions of the book "Nahj al-Balāghah" and also the unmatched position of the one to whom these amazing words belong.

The present series includes both the English translation of the Nahj al-Balāghah and also the translation of an invaluable commentary written on the book by the great Shi'a authority, Ayatollah Makarem Shirazi.

The decision regarding launching the project for this translation was twofold: due to the lack of a dependable and accurate English translation of the Nahj al-Balāghah and also a total lack of any translations of the commentaries written on the book, it was decided that action needed to be taken in this regard.

Initially, a team of experts studied the existing commentaries of the book and, due to its distinguishing characteristics_ including its easy language and minimum use of technical terminologies_ they concluded that the book "Payām-i-Imām Amir al-Mu'minīn ('a)" written as a commentary on the Nahj al-Balāghah was the most suitable choice for translation into English.

The supreme mastery of the author over various Islamic sciences needed to write such a commentary, and his deep understanding of the teachings latent within the rather concisely expressed contents of the Nahj al-Balāghah were but a few of the reasons why this specific commentary was chosen for translation.

During the course of translation of the work, the translator of the work, Mr. Morteza Bassirian, had several meetings with Ayatollah Makarem Shirazi, the author of the original Farsi commentary, in order to double check with him the points which needed extra attention in translation.

Several hours of discussion and debate were also held with several other experts, including experts in the Arabic language and literature, Islamic philosophy, Islamic jurisprudence [Fiqh], and Theology in order to choose the best English equivalents for the Islamic concepts which might not be very familiar to the English speaking audience.

After the process of translation of the work was completed, the English translation underwent a triple process of technical editing, proofreading, and technical transliteration of Arabic names and concepts by a number of respectable editors and proofreaders. It is noteworthy that the English translation of the verses of the Quran mentioned in the Nahj al-Balāghah were adopted from the English translation of the Quran by the same translator, translated for the publication of the office of Ayatollah Makarem Shirazi.

Indeed, carrying out such a massive project could not be done by a single person as it required expertise in several areas of science and knowledge, only one of which is translation. The present series is the result of the contributions of a group of translation and English language and literature experts, scientists, and Islamic scholars to whom we are indebted for the completion of this grand work. Although we are not able to name all of those involved in this project here, we would like to name a few of them who contributed the most to the work.

First of all, we would like to extend our most profound gratitude to Mr. Morteza Bassirian who did the job of translating into English one of the most exquisite literary works and greatest books of spiritual teachings in the world, along with its commentary.

Our thanks are also due to H.I Sheikh Qasem Muhammadi the supervisor of the project.

We acknowledge that no published work, regardless of how much effort and energy has been invested in it to be error-free, is actually free of errors and our work is no exception. Therefore, we would humbly ask all experts to contact us at international@makarem.ir regarding any mistakes or errors that they might come across in the work.

Finally, we hope that this series serves as a beacon of guidance, in the darkness of this world, for whoever chooses to embark on the journey of going through its teachings.

Institute for Compiling and Publishing the Works of Ayatollah Makarem Shirazi, International Dep.

The Reason behind the Writing of This Book

The Nahj al-Balāghah has been called "the great treasure chest of Islamic teachings", "the most sublime of resources for spiritual education of mankind", "the best reference for self-discipline and self-purification", as well as "the most effective book of instructions for building a healthy, pure and proud society".

Yet, these facts about the Nahj al-Balāghah can only be understood by those who have read it at least once from cover to cover. Only by reading this book carefully will one be able to realize that it is such an invaluable work and that even though a great deal has been said and written about it, it is not still nearly enough to do justice to it.

Much like many others who take a special interest in this book, I had also studied various parts of it that I needed to study. Yet, on Khordād 15 of the year 1342, I was arrested and imprisoned, together with a number of other Muslim clerics and scholars, by the despotic regime of the Shāh of Iran.

When we first entered the prison, we were treated rather harshly by both the warden and the guards for the first few days so much so that we were not even permitted to have books in our cells to read. However, due to the pressure of the public opinion, they gradually alleviated the pressure on us, and therefore my fellow scholars and I were able to ask some of our friends to send us some books to study in prison.

The first book that I asked for was the Nahj al-Balāghah, as I deemed it the best time to study the entire book thoroughly without being preoccupied with any other business. I was particularly lucky, as I was able to carefully and closely study and reflect upon the second section of the book [i.e. Imam Ali's letters, and the ethical and political directives to various people]. It was at that time that I realized that the Nahj al-Balāghah was far greater than we thought it was.

When I got the chance to properly contemplate the Nahj al-Balāghah, I found myself overwhelmed by an ocean of knowledge which dealt with the most important material and spiritual issues of human life. The book appeared to me like a vast and deep ocean full of treasures which would throw its jewels ashore with each of its waves, bringing all who set foot on its shores tremendous spiritual and material benefits. Yet, those who dare to plunge into its depths will gain the most benefits of all.

It was also then that I understood what the people who were unaware of it were missing; such people would resort to various less significant sources for acquiring knowledge, while the greatest source of knowledge was here within their reach!

One of the peculiarities of the Nahj al-Balāghah, much like its main source of knowledge, the Quran, is that unlike all other resources on various political and moral schools of thought which become obsolescent overtime, its teachings are still very rigorous in terms of their intellectual and rational basis. Thus, although these words were uttered some 14 centuries ago by Imam Ali ('a), they seem as if they were spoken recently and were meant for the present era or even the future. It is therefore befitting for those who seek the truth, the ones who seek to gain more knowledge of Allah, as well as those who are in pursuit of a better way of life to pay the tomb of al-Sayyid al-Raḍī[1] a visit so that they can pay tribute to that great man. Indeed, he made a great contribution not only to the Muslim community, but to mankind as a whole by compiling and editing such a precious collection of Imam Ali's words and teachings.

Much has been said and written about the Nahj al-Balāghah, yet it still does not seem nearly enough to reveal the significance of the teachings that it contains. Therefore, we will stop this introduction and go straight to the heart of the matter, i.e. the present book and its characteristics.

During the past several centuries of the Islamic era, a great many commentaries have been written on the Nahj al-Balāghah, and numerous great scholars, both in the past and during the contemporary era, have made great attempts to unravel the mysteries and secrets within this book. Nevertheless, regardless of their great efforts, the Nahj al-Balāghah still remains arguably the most unexplored source of knowledge for mankind. Unfortunately, even many Muslims do not

1. The great Shi'a scholar who gathered and compiled the words of Imam Ali ('a) into a single book which he called the Nahj al-Balāghah.

know anything about this book; this is a fact which indicates the need for further exploring this book in order to understand it and help others understand its teachings as well.

This need is felt to a greater extent at the present time period, considering the complicated problems which have ravaged the human world. These include the emergence of various baseless and destructive spiritual schools and the open and all-out warfare waged by materialists and imperialists against morality, piety, righteousness and human virtues in order to achieve their illegitimate goals and further their selfish interests.

Under the current circumstances of the world, more attention needs to be paid to the Nahj al-Balāghah and its teachings if a way out of our problems is to be found. More collaborative research needs to be conducted on the teachings of this great book in order to find solutions to the spiritual and material problems of mankind, both on personal and social levels. Furthermore, certain strategies need to be drawn up, based on the teachings of the Nahj al-Balāghah, in order to effectively combat the ruinous schools of thought which are destroying the very foundations of morality in the human world.

Thank God, a group of my good friends and I had the chance to write the books Tafsīr-e Nemūneh and Payām-e Quran, which had a great influence on both the scientific communities as well as the ordinary people who love the Quran.

Therefore, based on our successful experience in writing commentaries on the Quran, a group of scholars believed that it was now time to attend to the Nahj al-Balāghah and its teachings. They insisted that we needed to write a commentary on the Nahj al-Balāghah in the same way we had written our Quranic exegeses, using the past experiences to prepare a much better and more robust scientific work.

But there were a lot of obstacles on our way, including the everyday occupations of us all; but then I thought that I was losing the valuable time and that, despite all the problems that we had, we needed to accomplish this great work. Therefore, putting our trust in Allah and asking the great soul of Imam Ali ('a) to pray for us, we made the final decision to begin writing a comprehensive commentary on the Nahj al-Balāghah.

We first drew up the general plan for writing the book and some of my old friends along with some new ones, all of whom were prominent scholars, promised to lend me a hand in completing this work. The decision was made to write a new and comprehensive commentary on the Nahj al-Balāghah with a focus on issues that people face in our contemporary era in order to solve our current ideological and social problems. We also decided to draw upon the ideas of the past scholars who had written commentaries on this great book, but at the same time, to incorporate some novel approaches and perspectives into our exploration of its lofty teachings.

We began writing the new commentary on Rajab 13, 1413, on the blessed birth anniversary of Imam Ali ('a). At the outset, the process of writing the book was rather slow and it took us three long years just to finish the first volume of the book, but we knew that any high-quality scientific work needed to be done with utmost care and we also knew that this process would be slow in the beginning.

But, thank God, the process of writing the book accelerated over time and we hoped that it would become even faster as we further mastered the work. Yet, the mountainous waves of knowledge in the Nahj al-Balāghah would prevent us from writing commentaries as quickly as we wanted to; it was now clear to us that we were up against a huge ocean of intricate knowledge, the analysis of which proved to be an extremely daunting task.

In any case, we will not explain the process of writing this book, i.e. how the commentaries presented in this book were written with utmost care and precision, and we will leave the task of assessing our work to the knowledgeable and interested readers. We would also like to ask all the experts and scholars to send us their ideas if they feel that there are shortcomings anywhere in this book or that there are points which need to be added to it to make it a more perfect commentary.

In the end, we pray to Allah, who gave us the opportunity to complete this work, to grant all the people the opportunity to delve into the teachings of the Nahj al-Balāghah and draw great benefits from this precious book.

The Islamic Seminary School of Qom,
Nāṣer Makārem Shīrāzī
Rabīʿ al-Thānī 3, 1417 AH
Mordād 29, 1375 SH
August 19, 1996.

Al-Sayyid al-Raḍī, the Author Who Compiled the Nahj al-Balāghah

All Muslim historians unanimously believe that al-Sayyid al-Raḍī was born in 359 Ah in Baghdād. His parents called him Muḥammad but he later became known as al-Sharīf al-Raḍī or Dhū al-Ḥasabayn. His mother, Fāṭimah, was the daughter of Ḥusayn ibn Abī-Muḥammad Uṭrūsh, a descendant of Imam Ali ('a).[1] She was a virtuous and pious woman, about whom al-Sayyid al-Raḍī composed a poem, a part of which reads:

"If all mothers were virtuous and righteous like you,
Children would be in no need of fathers [for upbringing]!"[2]

His father, Ḥusayn ibn Mūsā,[3] was a descendant of Imam Mūsā al-Kāẓim ('a) and he was held in such high esteem both by the Abbasid and Buyid governments that Abū Naṣr Bahā' al-Dīn [a ruler of Buyid dynasty] nicknamed him "Al-Ṭāhir al-Awḥad" [meaning "the singularly righteous one"].

Abū Aḥmad, the father of al-Raḍī, was appointed the head of the Ṭālibīyīn[4] five times and he passed away while he was still the chief and head of that group. Thus, al-Sayyid al-Raḍī was born to a great father and mother and belonged to a noble family; this was why he was given a great upbringing and he showed virtue and greatness even when he was still a child.

The late 'Allāmah al-Amīnī has written the following about al-Sayyid al-Raḍī:

Al-Sayyid al-Raḍī was one of the most prominent figures among the descendants of the Prophet (ṣ) and those of the Infallible Imams ('a); he was a great scholar, hadith expert, and Arabic literary figure, as

1. The list of the maternal ancestors of al-Sayyid al-Raḍī is as follows [starting with his mother]: Fāṭimah daughter of Ḥusayn son of Muḥammad al-Ḥasan al-Uṭrūsh son of Ali son of al-Ḥasan son of Ali son of 'Umar son of Ali ibn Abī Ṭālib ('a).

2. Cited from the introduction of the booklet published in commemoration of al-'Allāmah al-Sharīf al-Raḍī.

3. The list of the paternal ancestors of al-Sayyid al-Raḍī is as follows [starting with his father]: Abū Aḥmad al-Ḥusayn son of Mūsā son of Muḥammad son of Mūsā son of Ibrāhīm son of Imam Mūsā al-Kāẓim ('a).

4. The Ṭālibīyīn were a group of the prominent Muslim figures who were all the descendants of Abū Ṭālib.

well as an avid supporter of Islam, the Shi'a school, and the religious teachings.

He was an example in all that he inherited from his pure ancestors; he possessed encyclopedic knowledge in various fields, he was a truly spiritual person, a man of keen insight, a highbrow and abstemious person, and a decorous man of noble descent.

He was a descendant of the Prophet (ṣ) and a progeny of Imam Ali ('a); he had inherited his grandeur from the lady Fāṭimah al-Zahrā' ('a) and his magnanimity and eminence from Imam al-Kāẓim ('a). He also possessed numerous other virtues and merits which cannot all be contained in this book.[1]

Al-'Allāmah al-Amīnī then goes on to list the names of forty books on the life, personality, and works of al-Sayyid al-Raḍī, and then adds the following:

The accounts of his great virtues and lofty character qualities can be found in a book of 112 pages that al-'Allāmah al-Shaykh 'Abd al-Ḥusayn al-Ḥillī has written as an introduction to the fifth section of his Quranic exegesis. Furthermore, a detailed account of his great personality and merits can be found in a book written by the renowned scholar Zakī Mubārak, i.e. 'Abqarīyah al-Raḍī, which is a book of two voluminous volumes. But before these two, al-'Allāmah al-Shaykh Muḥammad Riḍa Kāshif al-Qiṭā' had also written a book on the life, virtues, and works of al-Sayyid al-Raḍī.

The Masters and Teachers of al-Sayyid al-Raḍī

In his book, Al-Ghadīr, al-'Allāmah al-Amīnī has listed fourteen great scholars with whom al-Raḍī studied, some of whom are the following:

1. Abū Sa'īd Ḥasan ibn 'Abdullāh ibn Marzbān al-Naḥwī, also known as al-Sīrāfī [deceased, 368 AH.]. Al-Sayyid al-Raḍī studied Arabic grammar and syntax under him when he was still not ten years of age.
2. Abū 'Alī Ḥasan ibn Aḥmad al-Fārsī, a distinguished Arabic syntax expert [deceased, 377 AH.].
3. Hārūn ibn Mūsā.
4. Abū Yaḥyā 'Abd al-Raḥīm ibn Muḥammad, also known as Ibn

1. Al-Ghadīr, vol. 4, p. 181.

Nubātah, a skilled and famous orator [deceased, 394 Ah.].
5. Qāzī 'Abd al-Jabbār, a well-known Shāfi'ī and Mu'tazilī scholar.
6. But perhaps the greatest master of al-Sayyid al-Raḍī was the illustrious and prominent Shi'a scholar, jurist, hadith expert, and theologian, al-Shaykh al-Mufīd. The story of how al-Raḍī and his brother al-Murtaḍā came to be students of al-Shaykh al-Mufīd is an interesting one.

The author of the book Al-Darajāt al-Rafī'ah has narrated this story as follows: One night, al-Shaykh al-Mufīd had a dream, in which he saw the lady Fāṭimah al-Zahrā' ('a) entering the Masjid al-Karkh neighborhood [an old neighborhood in Baghdad] while holding the hands of her two little sons, Imam al-Ḥasan ('a) and Imam al-Ḥusayn ('a). She then came to al-Shaykh al-Mufīd and brought her two sons forward and said: "O' Shaykh! Teach these two sons of mine Islamic jurisprudence [i.e. Fiqh]!

Al-Shaykh al-Mufīd was startled awake, astonished by his dream; the next morning, he went to the mosque, like always, to begin teaching his Fiqh course there. Before long, he saw Fāṭimah, the mother of al-Sayyid al-Raḍī and al-Sayyid al-Murtaḍā, enter the mosque with her maids while she was holding the hands of her two small sons. When al-Shaykh al-Mufīd saw her, he got up out of respect for her and greeted her.

Then Fāṭimah addressed the Shaykh, saying, "O' Shaykh! These two are my sons; I have brought them here so that you may teach them the Islamic jurisprudence [i.e. Fiqh]!"

Suddenly, al-Mufīd remembered the dream he had had the night before and he burst into tears and told Fāṭimah about his dream. This was how al-Raḍī and al-Murtaḍā came to be students of al-Mufīd; al-Shaykh al-Mufīd gave a lot of attention to the education of those two boys and Allah also favored them by opening the gates of knowledge and virtues to them. As history suggests, those two brothers later became two of the greatest Shi'a scholars and wrote a large number of worthwhile scholarly books.

It is noteworthy that this story has also been related by Ibn Abī al-Ḥadīd in his commentary on the Nahj al-Balāghah [vol. 1, p. 41].

The Students of al-Sayyid al-Raḍī

A large number of outstanding Shi'a and Sunni scholars studied the Islamic Traditions under al-Sayyid al-Raḍī and related traditions from him. Al-'Allāmah al-Amīnī has listed 9 of the most prominent scholars who were students of al-Sayyid al-Raḍī. Among the most prominent scholars who related Islamic traditions from al-Raḍī were his great brother, al-Sayyid al-Murtaḍā and the leading Shi'a scholar and religious authority, al-Shaykh Abū Ja'far Muḥammad ibn Ḥasan al-Ṭūsī.

One of the major feats of al-Sayyid al-Raḍī which he accomplished through painstaking effort was the establishment of a boarding Islamic seminary school. He opened this school for Islamic seminary students to live and study there and he named it "Dār al-'Ilm". This was the first boarding Islamic seminary school in the history of Islam, and it had excellent facilities for the students, including a big library.[1]

The Books Written by al-Sayyid al-Raḍī

Al-'Allāmah al-Amīnī has listed 19 books written by al-Sayyid al-Raḍī, the most notable of which is the Nahj al-Balāghah, which is a collection of the speeches, letters, and aphorisms of Imam Ali ('a). He then presented a list of 81 books written as commentaries on the Nahj al-Balāghah up until his time.

Among the other important books written by al-Raḍī are the following:

1. Al-Khaṣā'iṣ al-A'immah; al-Sayyid al-Raḍī has mentioned this book in the introduction has written to the Nahj al-Balāghah.
2. Majāzāt al-Āthār al-Nabawīyah.
3. Al-Raḍī's scientific letters, compiled and edited into a book of three volumes.
4. Ma'ānī al-Quran
5. Ḥaqā'iq al-Ta'wīl fī Mutashābih al-Tanzīl, a book referred to as Ḥaqā'iq al-Tanzīl by the eminent Shi'a scholar, "Kashshī"

The late Shaykh 'Abbās al-Qummī has quoted his master, al-Muḥaddith al-Nūrī as saying the following regarding this book:

1. Cited from the introduction of the booklet published in commemoration of al-'Allāmah al-Sharīf al-Raḍī, p. 29.

Just as Abū al-Ḥasan ‘Omarī has stated, the book Ḥaqā’iq al-Tanzīl is a much greater and more valuable exegesis of the Quran than even the great Quranic exegesis by al-Shaykh al-Ṭūsī, i.e. Al-Tibyān. Unfortunately, the only part of this book which we could find was the fifth section of the book, which included the exegesis of the beginning of Surah Āl-i-‘Imrān up to the middle of Surah al-Nisā’.

The approach adopted by al-Sayyid al-Raḍī in this book had been to choose the ambiguous verses of the Quran, point out the ambiguity in them, and then provide comprehensive answers and interpretations of those verses. But when discussing the interpretation of these ambiguous verses, he would discuss other related verses of the Quran as well. Therefore, he did not interpret all of the verses of the Quran in this book, and he only provided interpretations for those verses which were of ambiguous and equivocal exposition.[1]

Al-Sayyid al-Raḍī and Poetry

Al-Sayyid al-Raḍī is also known as an acclaimed and important poet. Although his great fame is not particularly because of his poems, his beautiful poems show his great literary capacity and skill. Historical accounts indicate that when he was barely ten years old, al-Raḍī composed a long and beautiful poem in which he explained his noble ancestry.

Many renowned scholars and literary figures consider him to be the most gifted and skilled poet who has ever been born to the Quraysh clan. For instance, al-Khaṭīb al-Baghdadi, the famous historian, has written the following in his chronicle in this regard:

I heard that Muḥammad ibn ‘Abdullāh al-Kātib had once said the following in a meeting with one of the great literary figures called Abū al-Ḥusayn ibn Maḥfūẓ: “I heard a group of Arabic literary figures and experts say, ‘al-Sayyid al-Raḍī is the most gifted and skilled poet that has ever been born into the Quraysh.’ ”

Ibn Maḥfūẓ replied, “Yes, I think so too.” Then he added, “There were some poets from the Quraysh who composed good poetry but they composed very few poems. Al-Sayyid al-Raḍī was the only one among them who was both a talented and prolific poet.”

1. Safīnah al-Biḥār, vol. 3, p. 371, the entry “Riḍā”.

The Titles and Sociopolitical Position of al-Sayyid al-Raḍī

In 388 AH, Bahā' al-Dīn al-Deylamī [one of the rulers of the Buyid dynasty] gave al-Sayyid al-Raḍī the title "al-Sharīf al-Ajall" [meaning "The Greatly Honorable One"]. In 392 Ah. He was nicknamed "Dhū al-Manqabatayn" and in 398 Ah. He earned the title "Raḍī Dhū al-Ḥasabayn". In 401 AH, Bahā' al-Dīn al-Deylamī issued a directive in which he ordered that al-Sayyid al-Raḍī be referred to in all orations and correspondence as "al-Sharīf al-Ajall".

In 380 Ah., when he was only 21 years old, al-Sayyid al-Raḍī was appointed the head of the Ṭālibīyīn, the caretaker of the Ḥajj pilgrims, and the director of the judiciary system of the Muslim community by "al-Ṭā'i' Billah", the Abbasid caliph. Then on Muḥarram 16, 403 AH, he was appointed the chief of the Ṭālibīyīn [the descendants of Abū Ṭālib] in all of the regions of the Muslim world, and he was given the title "Naqīb al-Nuqabā'" [meaning the Chief of all chiefs].[1]

Due to his great competence and incredible talents, al-Sayyid al-Raḍī earned all of the social titles and positions one by one until, during the caliphate of "al-Qādir Billah", another Abbasid caliph, he was placed in charge of the affairs of the two holy cities of Mecca and Medina.

Needless to say, the reason why the Abbasid caliphs gave these posts to al-Sayyid al-Raḍī was only because he was already an enormously influential figure in the society, particularly among the Banī Hāshim

1. "Naqīb" was a social status that the most prominent scholar who was both extremely knowledgeable and pious would automatically earn in the society as the people would gather around him and refer to him as their chief and head. Since this was an automatic social phenomenon, the caliphs and kings who ruled the Muslim world would also honor it to buy themselves some reputation, and they would also endorse it as the ruler of the country. A person who enjoyed this rank and title was responsible for the following:
1. Keeping a record of the Sayyid families [i.e. the descendants of the Prophet (ṣ) and the Infallible Imams ('a)];
2. Watching over the moral and religious upbringing of people;
3. Preventing people from occupying lowly or illegitimate jobs;
4. Preventing the law and tradition of the Prophet (ṣ) from being disrespected;
5. Preventing aggression of some people against others;
6. Restoring the rights of people;
7. Giving the right share of the Muslim treasury to each of the members of community;
8. Paving the way for women and girls to get married;
9. Administering justice;
10. Supervising and monitoring the way the mortmain properties were being used. [Al-Ghadīr, vol. 4, pp. 205-207 with some excerption].

and the descendants of Imam Ali ('a). At that time, he was already the chief and the most trustworthy person among the Banī Hāshim, and therefore the Abbasid regime had, in fact, no choice but to place individuals like al-Sayyid al-Raḍī in charge of the affairs of the holy cities of Mecca and Medina.

Al-Sayyid al-Raḍī from the Viewpoint of Others 

Many scholars and scientists have spoken about al-Sayyid al-Raḍī, and we will cite some of their remarks about him below.

1. The famous Muslim scholar al-Tha'ālibī, who was a contemporary of al-Raḍī, has stated the following about him: "Presently, he is the most knowledgeable man of our time and the most honorable al-Sayyid in Iraq. In addition to his noble lineage and ancestry, he is an extremely virtuous, courteous and righteous man ..."[1]

2. In his book entitled Al-Muntaẓam, Ibn al-Jawzī has likewise made the following remarks about him: "al-Sayyid al-Raḍī was the chief of the Ṭālibīyīn in Baghdad; he had memorized the Quran completely when he was just over thirty years of age and he had learnt Fiqh deeply and was a knowledgeable expert in the field."

He was a knowledgeable scholar, a gifted and skilled poet, and a truly devout and magnanimous man. According to some historical narratives, once he bought a clump of wool from a woman for five Dirhams. When he took it home and opened it, he found a piece of paper in it which turned out to be a manuscript of Abī 'Alī ibn Muqallah. He then sent for the middleman and asked him to bring that woman to him. When she arrived, al-Sayyid al-Raḍī told her, "I found a piece of Ibn Muqallah's manuscript in the clump of wool I bought from you. Now the choice is yours; you can take this piece of paper back if your wish, or you can put a price on it and I will pay you any price you ask."

So the woman agreed to sell it to him and after getting her money she thanked al-Raḍī, prayed for his well-being, and left. Due to acts like these, al-Sayyid al-Raḍī was also known for his great generosity and munificence.[2]

3. One of the contemporary researchers, Dr. Zakī Mubārak, the famous

1. For more information in this regard, refer to Al-Ghadīr, vol. 4, p. 202.

2. Ibid, p. 203; Al-Muntaẓam, vol. 15, p. 115, No. 3065.

Egyptian scholar who is himself a skilled writer, has made the following remarks about him: "Undoubtedly, al-Sayyid al-Raḍī was a great writer, but his style was more scientific than technical, though some of his writings are also technical.

When we set aside his poems and decide to examine his prose, we find a totally different aspect of his character. In prose, he is a great scientist whose scientific writings are the best proof that he is one of the leading literary figures of the world. He was a scientist who has authored various works in the field of Arabic lexicology as well as Islamic sciences using a beautiful literary style."

In yet another part of his book he writes, "If we had access to all of the works of al-Sayyid al-Raḍī today, we could then claim that he is an unparalleled and unique writer and the greatest of all of the literary figures and writers of the world."[1]

The Demise of al-Sayyid al-Raḍī

Al-Sayyid al-Raḍī passed away on Muḥarram 6, 406 when he was only 47 years old; when people heard the news of his passing, great social and government figures, including viziers, judges, and other notables from all social classes rushed to his house in the Karkh neighborhood barefoot, all mourning his demise in a majestic and great ceremony.

According to some historical accounts, his pure body was taken to Karbala and buried next to the tomb of his father. What appears from historical references is that his sacred tomb has always been believed to be in the holy shrine of Imam al-Ḥusayn ('a).

His brother, al-Sayyid al-Murtaḍā, could not even come and visit his brother's body out of his severe grief, nor could he bring himself to attend his beloved brother's funeral procession or his burial prayer. The only thing he did was go and sit beside the tomb of Imam Mūsā al-Kāẓim ('a) so that the waves after waves of his enormous grief would be calmed down.

After the demise of al-Sayyid al-Raḍī, many poets, particularly his brother al-Sayyid al-Murtaḍā, composed elegies for him.[2]

1. 'Abqarīyah al-Sharīf al-Raḍī, vol. 1, pp. 204-205.

2. Most of the biographical information about al-Sayyid al-Raḍī in this book has been cited from the book Al-Ghadīr, vol. 4, pp. 181-211 as well as the books Sharḥ Nahj al-Balāghah Ibn Abī al-Ḥadīd, vol. 1m pp, 41-43, 'Abqarīyah al-Sharīf al-Raḍī, Safīnah al-Biḥār, vol. 3, pp. 370-373, and the booklet published in commemoration of al-'Allāmah al-Sharīf al-Raḍī.

A Word on the Nahj al-Balāghah and the One Whose Words it Contains

Speaking about Imam Ali ('a) and the grand book of the Nahj al-Balāghah, which is a record of his words, is both an easy and difficult task. It is undoubtedly a difficult task for those who seek to delve into the depth of the great personality and character of Imam Ali ('a) and to learn about all aspects of his great thoughts, unshakable faith in Allah, and his spiritual rank and virtues.

Needless to say, it is equally difficult to deeply understand the Nahj al-Balāghah, which is a collection of the words and sayings of such a great personality. Yet, it might be possible and even easy for everyone to catch a glimpse of these two huge oceans of knowledge and spirituality and to derive benefits from them as much as possible.

Anyone with the slightest familiarity with Imam Ali ('a) as well as his life story, words, and thoughts knows perfectly well that he was a great human being, a great Sign of Allah, and an unparalleled and unique man of spirituality. A person with such knowledge will also know that the Nahj al-Balāghah is a ray of light from that great star. The Nahj al-Balāghah is a vast ocean of knowledge, a chest of spiritual treasures, an orchard of fruitful trees, a sky full of shining stars, and a reference with solutions to all of the problems facing mankind on the path to eternal prosperity. Without a doubt, anyone who decides to embark on a journey to understand the teachings within this book more profoundly must prepare himself to write several voluminous books to contain his understanding of it.

In any case, our purpose here is just to present an introduction to this grand book and then attend to the more important task of explaining and interpreting the words of the Leader of the Believers, Imam Ali ('a).

However, before we begin discussing the contents of the Nahj al-Balāghah we need to present a few important points to the dear readers. Moreover, in order to make our point crystal clear, we will also cite the remarks of some of the other scholars and scientists who studied this book for long years.

We will particularly refer to the remarks of some Non-Muslim researchers and writers as well as some non-Shi'a Muslim scholars who were enthralled by the words and school of thought of that great teacher of humanity. All of this is done in order to prepare the dear readers for better absorbing the great teachings of this book.

A quick glance at the history of the Nahj al-Balāghah and the commentaries written on it reveals that most people, even some of the great scholars and experts, have got no more than a name from this great book. These people assume that the Nahj al-Balāghah is merely a collection of ordinary sayings or, at best, a little better than the ordinary!

Yet, when these same people try to examine it closely, they find themselves up against a huge ocean of knowledge and spirituality whose frontiers cannot be even imagined! Overwhelmed by the magnificence of the Nahj al-Balāghah and its teachings, these people will then make remarks, out of their extreme amazement, which show how deeply they have been affected by it.

These deep feelings of amazement and wonder, however, have come over these scholars and other individuals as a result of one of the many aspects of the Nahj al-Balāghah, some of which are as follows:

1. The supreme eloquence of the contents of the Nahj al-Balāghah;
2. The overwhelmingly deep contents of the Nahj al-Balāghah;
3. The compelling attraction of the Nahj al-Balāghah;

We will discuss each of these aspects separately below.

1. The Supremely Eloquent Language of the Nahj al-Balāghah

As regards the eloquence of the Nahj al-Balāghah, the literary figures and writers have always been fascinated by the kind of language used in it. The book contains so many beautiful figures of speech with a special attention paid to the minutiae of eloquence in all of its aspects. But before any other scholar, let us take a look at what the compiler of the Nahj al-Balāghah, i.e. al-Sayyid al-Raḍī had to say about its amazing contents. Let us be reminded that this man was himself a great literary figure who had been superior to most of the great Arabic literary figures in poetry and prose and had spent long years gathering, compiling, and editing the contents of the Nahj al-Balāghah into a single book.

This is the same man about whom Zakī Mubārak, the great Egyptian writer, made the following remarks in his book 'Abqarīyah al-Sharīf al-Raḍī:

When we consider his prose, we see that he is a great scholar whose scholarly writings are the best proof that he is one of the leading literary figures of the world … and when we examine his poetry, we find him a gifted and skilled poet with a beautiful and fine taste in composing poetry. Such a supreme mastery over both poetry and prose is found in very few individuals. Alas that today we do not have access to all of the works of al-Sharīf al-Raḍī, for if we did, we could confer upon him a unique and inimitable status among all the great writers and literary figures.[1]

At any rate, the great al-Sharīf al-Raḍī has written the following in his introduction to the Nahj al-Balāghah:

كَانَ أميرُ الْمُؤْمِنِينَ عليه‌السلام مَشْرَعَ الْفَصاحَةِ وَمَوْرِدَها وَمَنْشَأَ الْبلاغَةِ وَمَوْلِدَها وَمِنْهُ
ظَهَرَ مَكْنُونُها وَعَنْهُ أُخِذَتْ قوانينُها وَعلى أَمْثِلَتِهِ حَذا كُلُّ قائِلٍ خَطيبٍ وَبِكلامِهِ
اسْتَعانَ كُلُّ واعِظٍ بَليغٍ وَمَعَ ذلِكَ فَقَدْ سَبَقَ وَقَصَّرُوا وَقَدْ تَقَدَّمَ وَتَأَخَّرُوا

Indeed, Imam Amīr al-Mu'minīn ('a) was the source of eloquence and its founder; he was the first to uncover the secrets and principles of eloquence and so the rules of eloquence were learned from him. All skilled orators have tried to adopt his method of speech and they have sought help from his style; and yet he is still far ahead of all other speakers, with others being way behind him in eloquence.

He then goes on to elaborate on his previous remarks as follows:

1. 'Abqarīyah al-Sharīf al-Raḍī, vol. 1, pp. 205, 206, & 209 [with some excerption].

لِأَنَّ كَلامَهُ عليه السلام الكَلامُ الَّذي عَلَيْهِ مَسْحَةٌ مِنَ
الْعِلْمِ الإلهِيِّ وَفيهِ عَبْقَةٌ مِنَ الْكَلامِ النَبَوِيِّ

"... this is because in his words there are traces of Allah's Knowledge and the scent of the Prophet's words."

Let us now attend to the remarks of one of the most famous commentators of the Nahj al-Balāghah. He spent most of his life studying the teachings of Imam Ali ('a) recorded in the Nahj al-Balāghah and was, hence, completely aware of their eloquence and beauty. This was why whenever he spoke of Imam Ali ('a) and his teachings in the Nahj al-Balāghah, he sounded fascinated and enthralled.
The man we are talking about is 'Izziddīn 'Abd al-Ḥamīd ibn Abī al-Ḥadīd al-Mu'tazilī, a renowned Sunni scholar of the seventh century Ah.[1] In his commentary on the Nahj al-Balāghah, he frequently expresses his utter amazement at the unparalleled eloquence of the contents of the Nahj al-Balāghah. In one instance, while commenting on what Imam Ali ('a) has said about the world of Barzakh[2] in one of his sermons, recorded in the Nahj al-Balāghah sermon No. 221, Ibn Abī al-Ḥadīd writes:

وَيَنْبَغي لَوِاجْتَمَعَ فُصَحاءُ الْعَرَبِ قاطِبَةً في مَجْلِسٍ وَتُلِيَ عَلَيْهِمْ، اَنْ يَسْجُدُوا لَهُ كَمَا
سَجَدَ الشُعَراءُ لِقَوْلِ عَدِيِّ بْنِ الرُّقاعِ: قَلَمٌ أصابَ مِنَ الدَّواةِ مِدادَها... فَلَمّا قيلَ لَهُمْ في
ذلكَ قالُوا: إنّا نَعْرِفُ مَواضِعَ السُّجُودِ في الشِّعْرِ كَما تَعْرِفُونَ مَواضِعَ السُّجُودِ في الْقُرآنِ

1. He wrote his commentary on the Nahj al-Balāghah in 20 volumes and, as he himself has stated, it took him a little less than 5 years to write it, exactly as long as Imam Ali ('a) ruled the Muslim world as caliph.

2. The English equivalent for this word is "purgatory" though it is not an accurate one for this Islamic concept.

If all of the most prominent Arabic literary figures could be gathered in the same place to hear this part of the sermon, it would be befitting for them all to fall prostrate before it, just as the historical narratives indicate that a group of great Arab poets did so when they heard the famous poem of ‘Adī ibn al-Riqā‘.

As the story goes, when they were asked as to why they prostrated themselves upon hearing that magnificent piece of poetry, they replied, “We know those parts of a poem where we have to fall prostrate just as you know the verses of the Quran upon the reciting of which you also have to prostrate yourselves!”[1]

In yet another instance in his book, and amid drawing a general comparison between a part of Imam Ali’s remarks and a famous speech by Ibn Nubātah[2] [a famous Arab orator of the fourth century Ah.], Ibn Abī al-Ḥadīd writes:

فَلْيَتَأمَّلْ اَهْلُ الْمَعْرِفَةِ بِعِلْمِ الْفَصاحَةِ وَالْبيانِ هذَا الْكَلامَ بِعَيْنِ الاِنْصافِ، يَعْلَمُوا أَنَّ سَطْراً واحِداً مِنْ كَلامِ نَهْجِ الْبَلاغَةِ يُساوي أَلْفَ سَطْرٍ مِنْهُ بَل يَزيدُ وَيُرْبِي عَلى ذلِكَ

The experts of rhetoric and oratory would agree, if they considered these words of Imam Ali (‘a) impartially, that a single line in the Nahj al-Balāghah equals a thousand lines, if not more, of the famous speeches of Ibn Nubātah in worth and value! In fact a fair observer would agree that a single line in the Nahj al-Balāghah is far superior to whatever Ibn Nubātah has ever said![3]

Another interesting remark with regard to this issue has been made by Ibn Abī al-Ḥadīd amid his discussion of one of the speeches of Ibn Nubātah on the issue of Jihad, in which he had adopted the following sentence from Imam Ali (‘a) regarding the importance of Jihad:

1. Sharḥ Nahj al-Balāghah Ibn Abī al-Ḥadīd, vol. 11, p. 153.

2. His complete name was “Abū Yaḥyā ‘Abd al-Raḥīm ibn Muḥammad ibn Ismail ibn Nubātah”; he passed away in 374 Ah.

3. Sharḥ Nahj al-Balāghah Ibn Abī al-Ḥadīd, vol. 7, p. 214.

ما غُزِيَ قَوْمٌ في عُقْرِ دارِهِمْ إلّا ذَلّوا

"No nation has ever been invaded [by the enemy] inside their houses unless they were crushed and humiliated."

With regard to this issue, Ibn Abī al-Ḥadīd notes:

Just look at this sentence and how it shines brightly and stands out much more remarkably than all other things that Ibn Nubātah has said in his speech!! It calls out loud with its unequalled eloquence announcing to anyone who reads it that this specific sentence comes from a totally different source than the rest of the speech! I swear to Allah that this sentence has adorned and decorated Ibn Nubātah's speech in much the same way as a single verse of the Quran, mentioned within an ordinary oration, gives the whole oration radiance and elegance.[1]

Let us conclude our discussion of Ibn Abī al-Ḥadīd's remarks about the Nahj al-Balāghah with his following comments made in the preface to his book:

وَامّا الْفَصاحَةُ فَهُوَ عليه السلام إمامُ الْفُصَحاءِ وَسَيِّدُ الْبُلَغاءِ وَفي كَلامِهِ قيلَ: دُونَ كَلامِ الْخالِقِ وَفَوْقَ كَلامِ الْمَخْلوقينَ وَمِنْهُ تَعَلَّمَ النّاسُ الْخِطابَةَ وَالْكِتابَةَ

As for eloquence, he [meaning Imam Ali ('a)] is the chief of all eloquent speakers and the master of all rhetoricians; this is why it has been said of his words that they are second only to the words of the Creator but superior to the words of all people! In fact, the people learned the principles of rhetoric and literary writing from him![2]

1. Sharḥ Nahj al-Balāghah Ibn Abī al-Ḥadīd, vol. 2, p. 84.

2. Ibid, vol. 1, p. 23.

1. George Jordac, the famous Lebanese Christian writer, has written a valuable book about Imam Ali ('a) entitled Imam Ali ('a): the Voice of Human Justice[1]. At the end of one of the chapters which he dedicated to describing the personality, character, virtues, and merits of Imam Ali ('a), he made the following remarks about the Nahj al-Balāghah: This book is far superior to any other work in eloquence. It is like the Quran which has descended from its supreme rank to a small degree; it is a collection which has gathered all the beauties of the Arabic language in the past, present, and future within it. Its beauty and eloquence is to the extent where some have said about it: "It is second only to the words of the Creator but superior to the words of all people."'"[2]

2. Al-Jāḥiẓ was one of the outstanding Arabic literary figures and a true prodigy who lived in the early 3rd century Ah. In his notable book Al-Bayān wa al-Tabyīn, he cited some of the words of Imam Ali ('a) and lauded him [for speaking so eloquently]. For instance, in the first volume of his book, al-Jāḥiẓ has mentioned the following aphorism of Imam Ali's composition:

"The value of every person equals what they know and do perfectly."

Al-Jāḥiẓ then goes on and adds the following:
If this book contained but this single sentence, it would be enough; in fact, it would be much more than enough, because the best words are the ones that are succinct and yet they suffice you in the place of longer discourse and, at the same time, communicate their message with clarity. It is as if Allah Himself has blessed it [i.e. this sentence] with magnificence and glory and also covered it in a hue of wisdom, something that is completely in line with and befitting of the pure intentions, the supreme wisdom, and the unique righteousness of the

1. Al-Imam Ali ('a): Ṣawt al-'Adālah al-Insānīyah.

2. Al-Imam Ali: Ṣawt al-'Adālah al-Insānīyah, vol. 1, p. 282.

one who composed them.[1]

3. Amīr Yaḥyā al-ʻAlawī, the author of the book Al-Ṭarāz, has narrated the following remark from al-Jāḥiẓ: "This man [meaning al-Jāḥiẓ], who was himself a prodigious rhetorician and an eloquent writer and speaker, has stated the following: "With the words of Allah and those of His Prophet (ṣ) aside, I have never come across any words unless I have criticized and found faults with except those of Amīr al-Mu'minīn [ʻAlī (ʻa), may Allah bless his soul] as I found myself too weak to challenge or criticize them."

Words like the following are truly inimitable and unique:

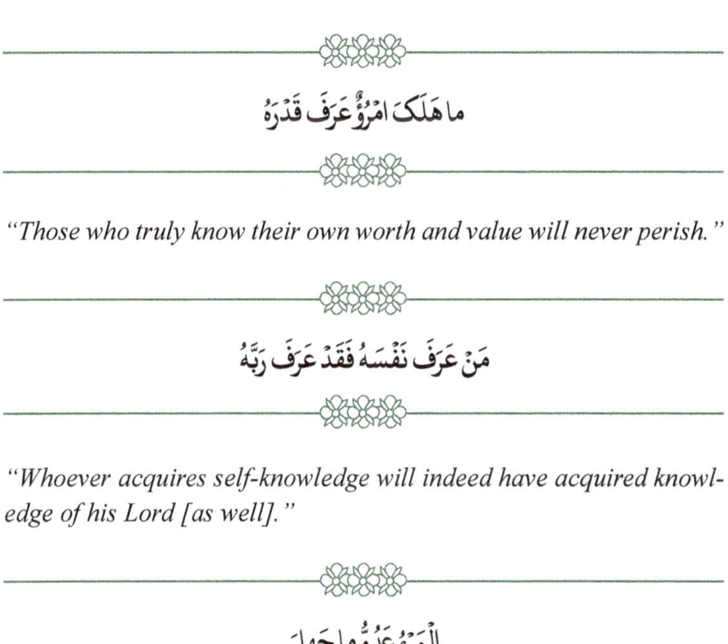

ما هَلَکَ امْرُؤٌ عَرَفَ قَدْرَهُ

"Those who truly know their own worth and value will never perish."

مَنْ عَرَفَ نَفْسَهُ فَقَدْ عَرَفَ رَبَّهُ

"Whoever acquires self-knowledge will indeed have acquired knowledge of his Lord [as well]."

الْمَرْءُ عَدُوٌّ ما جَهِلَ

"Man is enemy to whatever he does not know."

1. Al-Bayān wa al-Tabyīn, vol. 1, p. 87.

وَاسْتَغْنِ عَمَّنْ شِئْتَ تَكُنْ نَظِيرَهُ وَأَحْسِنْ إِلَى مَنْ شِئْتَ تَكُنْ أَمِيرَهُ وَاحْتَجْ إِلَى مَنْ شِئْتَ تَكُنْ أَسِيرَهُ

"If you want to be equal with someone, do not bring your needs to them, and when you want to rule over someone, treat them kindly, and if you want to be slaves to anyone, be dependent upon them!""

He then adds the following:

Just look at how fairly al-Jāḥiẓ has spoken about these sayings; he has made these remarks only because the supreme eloquence in the words of Imam Ali ('a) has shaken him and his amazing mastery over rhetoric boggled his mind. Now imagine, when al-Jāḥiẓ, who was himself a prodigious literary figure, is so bewildered and speechless [when confronted with the supreme eloquence of Imam Ali's sayings] then what can the rest of us say?![1]

This Zaidi scholar [i.e. the author of the book Al-Ṭarāz] then expresses his astonishment at the fact that the great Arabic rhetoricians and experts of oration had attended to the poems and orations of ordinary Arab poets and orators, after the Quran and the Prophetic sayings, to extract the rules of Arabic eloquence and rhetoric, but had forgotten all about the words of Imam Ali ('a).

He further states that this was particularly astonishing and disappointing at the same time, given the fact that those experts all knew well that Imam Ali's speeches and sayings were at the pinnacle of eloquence. They knew perfectly well that whatever figures of speech they thought of, including metaphor, allegory, irony, and trope, as well as the most profound notions, could all be found in his words.[2]

4. Muḥammad Ghazzālī, the famous Arab writer, has cited the following sentence in his book entitled Naẓarāt fī al-Quran from Yāzijī, who mentioned it as a sort of advice to his son:

1. Al-Ṭarāz, vol. 1, pp. 87-88.

2. Ibid.

إِذا شِئْتَ أَنْ تَفُوقَ أَقْرانَکَ فِي الْعِلْمِ وَالأَدَبِ وَ
صِناعَةِ الإِنْشاءِ فَعَلَيْکَ بِحِفْظِ الْقُرآنِ وَنَهْجِ البَلاغَةِ

"If you wish to be superior in knowledge, literature, and writing to others like you, try to memorize the Quran and the Nahj al-Balāghah."[1]

5. It was also due to the matchless elocution of the contents of the Nahj al-Balāghah that Shahāb al-Dīn al-Ālūsī, the famous Quranic exegete, made the following remarks about it:

This name [i.e. the Nahj al-Balāghah which literally translates into English as "The Path to Eloquence"] has been chosen for this book because of its contents which make one feel are second only to the words of Allah but superior to all that has ever been said by human beings. The remarks compiled in this book seem almost nearly miraculous due to the amazing poetic craft with which they have been composed and also the supreme eloquence they enjoy both in discussing hard facts directly and through tropes.[2]

6. Muḥammad Muḥyiddīn 'Abd al-Ḥamīd, another prominent Muslim scholar, has also stated the following regarding the Nahj al-Balāghah:

It is a book that is house to the vast sources of eloquence and elocution and presents the readers with a unique collection of figures of speech prepared for anyone interested in enjoying the fruits of eloquence. These amazing qualities are due to the fact that the contents of this book have been spoken by the most eloquent servant of Allah, who was only second to the Prophet of Allah (ṣ).He was a man whose mastery over logic and literature was far greater than all others, and this amazing gift allowed him to change the arrangement of words in sentences in any way that he wanted to make more beautiful sentences. He was a wise man whose wisdom is emanated from his words, an orator the magic of whose words fills the heart of anyone who hears them, and a knowledgeable scholar who acquired these brilliant skills

1. Naẓarāt fī al-Quran, p. 133.

2. Al-Kharīdah al-Ghaybīyah, p. 133 [according to Maṣādir Nahj al-Balāghah, vol. 1, p. 109].

through accompanying and learning from the Prophet (ṣ), writing the Divine Revelations, and defending the religion with his words and sword from his childhood. These virtues and merits are peculiar to him and no one else has been honored with such virtues.[1]

7. One of the most prominent scholars who has written a commentary on the Nahj al-Balāghah is the famous Sunni leader and Arab writer, al-Shaykh Muḥammad ʻAbduh. In the preface to his commentary on the Nahj al-Balāghah, he admits that he accidentally came across the Nahj al-Balāghah [which is itself a curious thing!] and that, before that, he did not know that it even existed. In any case, in that preface, he has praised the Nahj al-Balāghah greatly, stating things like the following:

When I first studied various pages of the Nahj al-Balāghah and considered its contents from different perspectives, it appeared to me that I was on a vast battlefield where a great war was going on between eloquence and rhetoric on the one hand and illusions and baseless ideas on the other, with the hosts of eloquence and rhetoric constantly attacking and crushing illusions and baseless ideas with their powerful weapons. The contents of this book crush the power of falsehood everywhere, shatter all doubt and uncertainty, and destroy the seditions of illusions. I saw in this book that the sole ruler, the commander, and the flag-bearer of the hosts which crush falsehood and came out victorious from that huge battle was Amīr al-Mu'minīn ʻAlī ibn Abī Ṭālib (ʻa).[2]

8. Sibṭ ibn al-Jawzī, the esteemed Sunni orator, historian, and Quranic exegete, has made some short, yet rather interesting remarks about Imam Ali (ʻa), in his book Tadhkirah al-Khawāṣ:

وَقَدْ جَمَعَ اللهُ لَهُ بَيْنَ الْحَلاوَةِ وَالمَلاحَةِ والطَّلاوَةِ وَالْفَصاحَةِ لَمْ يَسْقُطْ مِنْهُ كَلِمَةٌ وَلا بارَتْ لَهُ حُجَّةٌ، اَعْجَزَالنّاطِقِينَ وَحازَ قَصَبَ السَّبْقِ فِي السّابِقِينَ اَلْفاظٌ يُشْرِقُ عَلَيْها نُورُ النُّبُوَّةِ وَيُحَيِّرُ الأَفْهامَ وَالأَلْبابَ

1. The Preface to Sharḥ Nahj al-Balāghah ʻAbduh [revised by Muḥammad Muḥyiddīn], p. 2.

2. Ibid, pp. 9-10 [with some excerption].

Allah the Almighty has given 'Alī ('a) all the privileges of the sweetness, elegance, and eloquence of speech. Thus, he never missed any [important] words nor did he ever neglect a necessary argument. His unparalleled mastery over elocution outmatches all other literary figures, hence making him superior in eloquent speech to all others. He has spoken words which were informed and enlightened by the light of prophethood; hence, they bewilder all the hearts and minds of those who come to read them. [1]

Let us conclude this section with two remarks made by a famous Christian author regarding Imam Ali ('a) and his words.
9. Mikhail Naimy, the famous Arab Christian author and intellectual, has similarly written the following in this regard:
If 'Alī ('a) only belonged to Islam and Muslims, why would a Christian write a book about his life in 1956 and delve into his way of living [this is in reference to George Jordac, the Lebanese Christian writer and the author of the book Imam Ali: the Voice of Human Justice]?! Imam Ali ('a) was not merely a powerful commander on the battlefield; he was also an extremely farseeing and righteous man, a skilled orator and a master of eloquence, the possessor of lofty character qualities, one with an unshakeable faith in God, a man of steely determination, a supporter and protector of the wronged and the helpless, a follower of truth and truthfulness, and, in short, the possessor of all human virtues and sublime attributes.[2]
In yet another section of the preface to his book, he states:
That what that Arab prodigy thought and acted_ things that were between him and his Lord_ were far beyond whatever anyone has ever heard or seen and they are certainly far beyond the scope of my ability to write or relate. This is why any image of his that we try to depict is, no doubt, an awfully inadequate depiction of who he truly was.[3]

1. Tadhkirah al-Khawāṣ, chapter 6, p. 114.
2. Al-Imam Ali, Ṣawt al-'Idālah al-Insānīyah, vol. 1, p. 22.
3. Ibid, vol. 1, p. 23.

2. The Overwhelmingly Deep and Inclusive Contents of the Nahj al-Balāghah;

One of the salient features of the Nahj al-Balāghah which attracts the attention of any reader at first sight is the comprehensive and diverse nature of its contents. This diversity and comprehensiveness is to the point where one finds it extremely difficult to believe that a person could have spoken and written all of those amazingly precise and accurate things on a wide range of subjects in such an exquisite manner. Indeed, such a thing would have been impossible for anyone other than Imam Amīr al-Mu'minīn 'Alī ('a), whose great heart was a repository of the secrets of Divine Revelations and whose soul was a vast ocean of knowledge. Let us again look at some of the remarks made by different scientists regarding this aspect of the Nahj al-Balāghah.

1. It seems fitting here to begin this section with the remarks of the renowned Sunni leader and writer, al-Shaykh Muḥammad 'Abduh. He has described his first encounter with the different sermons, letters, and aphorisms in the Nahj al-Balāghah as follows:

As I went from one part of the Nahj al-Balāghah to another, I felt that the scenes around me transformed and I was transferred to a different world. Sometimes, I would find myself in a world where sublime concepts were clothed with the most beautiful figures of speech. I then found them circulating and approaching those who are pure of heart to inspire them with the knowledge of the right path and point them in the direction of the ultimate goal, guarding them against pitfalls, until they were led on to the right path of virtuousness and perfection. In yet other sections, I would see grim, angry faces, with talons and teeth at the ready to attack the enemy ... and yet in the end, the pure hearts would be conquered by them, not by force, but of their own volition. They would also penetrate the minds without the use of force; but, at the same time, they would powerfully cleanse them of falsehood and corrupt ideas.

On, yet, other occasions, I saw a luminous intellect which had no resemblance to any physical being. It was a ray of light which traveled all the way from the Divine Throne and shone on human beings' souls, saving them from the darkness of the natural world. It would then allow them to ascend up to the spiritual world to the source of all lights in the presence of Allah after it had enabled them to break free from their own baseless ideas.

In yet other moments, it was as if I was listening to a sage teacher, speaking directly to scientists and the leaders of the society, showing them the right path and keeping them from falling into doubts, uncertainties, and other pitfalls. He would then teach them the minutiae of politics and the proper methods of management, instructing them in the most advanced tactics of leadership.

Such is the book, containing the words of our master and chief, Amīr al-Mu'minīn 'Alī ibn Abī Ṭālib ('a), which al-Sayyid al-Raḍī compiled and edited and which he called the Nahj al-Balāghah. I know no worthier a title which could better represent the contents of this book, and I cannot think of any description of this book which is more accurate than what its title provides.[1]

2. Another famous commentator of the Nahj al-Balāghah, i.e. Ibn Abī al-Ḥadīd al-Mu'tazilī, has likewise made the following remarks in this regard:

I am most amazed at a man who spoke on the battlefield in a way that one would think he had a heart of a lion, but then, when on the same battlefield he decided to admonish the enemy, he spoke as if he were an ascetic and a monk living in a monastery, an extremely emotional person who had never spilled the blood of even an animal, nor had he even eaten any meat!

At times, he would appear like Basṭām ibn Qays, 'Utaybah ibn Ḥārith, and 'Āmir ibn Ṭufayl[2] and at other times he sounds like Socrates, John the Apostle, and Prophet Jesus, son of Mary. I swear by He to whom all nations swear that I have read this sermon [sermon no. 221 of the Nahj al-Balāghah] more than one thousand times in the last fifty years, and every time that I read it, I was filled with fear, awe, and a sense of awakening from my state of negligence, my heart was deeply touched, and all my body shook with the shock of the teachings in it! Every time I reflected upon the contents of this sermon, I was reminded of the dead of my family and friends, and I felt as if it

1. The preface to Sharḥ Nahj al-Balāghah 'Abduh, p. 10 [with some excerption].

2. During the pre-Islamic era, three men were the most famous warriors in the Arab community of the time and they were always referred to as examples of sheer valor and bravery; these were Basṭām ibn Qays, 'Utaybah ibn Ḥārith, and 'Āmir ibn Ṭufayl. [Zerkelī, al-A'lām. Vol. 4, p. 201].

was I myself that the Imam ('a) was describing in this sermon! How many a preacher, orator, and rhetorician has given speeches on this subject, and yet, no matter how many times I have come across their words, they have all failed to touch my heart and soul the way this sermon does![1]

3. This, however, is not the only time when Ibn Abī al-Ḥadīd has spoken of this magnificent aspect of the Nahj al-Balāghah in his commentary on it. In yet another instance, Ibn Abī al-Ḥadīd has presented a detailed discussion of the wondrous contents of the Nahj al-Balāghah, parts of which are as follows:

Glory be to God! Who has granted this exemplary man [i.e. Imam Ali ('a)] so many valuable and lofty character qualities, virtues, merits, and honors?! How is it possible for a descendant of the Arabs of Mecca, who only lived in that community and had never studied with any philosophers, be much more informed in theology and theosophy than Plato and Aristotle?! How can a person who has never had any formal education in mysticism or ethics and has never had any relations with the great masters of these fields possibly be more knowledgeable than a master such as Socrates?! How can a person who did not grow up among brave warriors [as the people of Mecca were merchants not warriors] come to be the bravest and the greatest warrior who has ever set foot on the earth?![2]

4. In his book al-Kashkūl, al-Shaykh al-Bahā'ī has related the following remarks from Abū 'Ubaydah, citing them from the book Al-Jawāhir:

'Alī ('a) has said nine sentences which [are so eloquent in exposition that they] have made the Arabic literary figures and rhetoricians lose hope in ever being able to outmatch them! Three of these sentences are prayers, three are scientific in nature, and the other three are literary sentences.[3]

He then commented on those nine sentences, some of which have been included in the Nahj al-Balāghah and the others can be found in certain other speeches and writings of the Imam ('a) which have not been related in the Nahj al-Balāghah.

5. In his book 'Abqarīyah al-Sharīf al-Raḍī, Dr. Zakī Mubārak has similarly stated the following:

1. Sharḥ Nahj al-Balāghah Ibn Abī al-Ḥadīd, vol. 11, p. 153.

2. Sharḥ Nahj al-Balāghah Ibn Abī al-Ḥadīd, vol. 16, p. 146.

3. Al-Shaykh al-Bahā'ī, al-Kashkūl, Vol. 3, p. 387.

I believe that reflecting on and contemplating the teachings of the Nahj al-Balāghah elevates one spiritually, bestowing valor, courage, and a great spiritual strength on one. This is because these teachings have emanated from a great soul that always remained steadfast and unwavering in the face of adversities and calamities.[1]

Here, we are not speaking of superior knowledge; rather, we are speaking of the brilliance of the spirit of courage and valor as well as the spiritual grandeur that one finds within the Nahj al-Balāghah following a deep contemplation of its contents.

6. The late Sayyid al-Raḍī, the compiler of the Nahj al-Balāghah, has also made some short, yet profound remarks regarding the magnificence of the contents of the Nahj al-Balāghah in the book itself. For instance, referring to sermon No. 21 in the Nahj al-Balāghah, and particularly the part that reads:

فَإِنَّ الْغَايَةَ أَمَامَكُمْ وَإِنَّ وَرَاءَكُمُ السَّاعَةَ تَحْدُوكُمْ،
تَخَفَّفُوا تَلْحَقُوا فَإِنَّمَا يُنْتَظَرُ بِأَوَّلِكُمْ آخِرُكُمْ؛

"Indeed, the Resurrection Day is ahead of you and death keeps driving you toward it. So travel light to catch up with your caravan and know that you will also be waiting for those who remain behind [in the world after you are gone from it]!"

Al-Sayyid al-Raḍī writes:

إِنَّ هٰذَا الْكَلَامَ لَوْ وُزِنَ بَعْدَ كَلَامِ اللّٰهِ سُبْحَانَهُ وَبَعْدَ كَلَامِ
رَسُولِ اللّٰهِ ﷺ بِكُلِّ كَلَامٍ لَمَالَ بِهِ رَاجِحاً وَبَرَّزَ عَلَيْهِ سَابِقاً

1. ʿAbqarīyah al-Sharīf al-Raḍī, vol. 1, p. 224.

"With the words of Allah and those of the Prophet (ṣ) being aside, this sentence is superior to any other words with which it might be compared!"

He has also made similar remarks amid his discussion of aphorism No. 81: "These remarks are truly priceless and no other words of wisdom can be found which are quite as valuable, and no other remarks can ever match them in worth!"

7. Let us now take a look at the remarks of 'Abbās Mahmoud al-'Aqqād, the famous Egyptian writer and one of the greatest contemporary Arab writers, about the Nahj al-Balāghah and embark on a journey through this book together with him. In various parts of his book 'Abqarīyah al-Imam ('a), 'Abbās Mahmoud al-'Aqqād has greatly praised the words of Imam Ali ('a), something that is indicative of his deep knowledge and understanding of the unique person of the Imam ('a) and his unparalleled teachings in the Nahj al-Balāghah. For instance, in a part of his book he notes, "The Nahj al-Balāghah is a resource of monotheistic teachings and theosophy which expands one's knowledge in theological principles, correct convictions, and the principles of monotheism."[1]

In another instance, he says, "Any example of his words is indicative of his God-given gift and his mastery over speaking about the realities of this world. Indeed, he is the descendant of Adam who was taught the Knowledge of the Names, and a referent of these phrases in the Quran: "وَعَلَّمَ آدَمَ الْأَسْمَاءَ كُلَّهَا", "أُوتُوا الْكِتَابَ" and "فَصْلَ الْخِطَابِ"."[2]

In yet another part of his book, he states the following:

The profound sayings which have been related from Imam Ali ('a) are at the pinnacle of wisdom, a level above which no other wisdom can be imagined ... the great Prophet of Islam (ṣ) once stated: "The knowledgeable scholars of my Ummah are like the prophets of the Israelites." This tradition applies, more than anyone else, to 'Alī ('a), whose wise words are much like those of the Divinely-sent prophets.[3]

8. Muḥammad Amīn al-Nawāwī, another contemporary scholar and

1. Al-'Abqarīyāt, vol. 2, p. 806.

2. Ibid, p. 813.

3. Al-'Abqarīyāt, vol. 2, p. 811.

writer, has described the Nahj al-Balāghah as follows:

The contents of this book are a manifest proof that Allah has ordained it to be the evidence as to the fact that 'Alī ('a) was the best living example of the Quran's light, wisdom, guidance, marvel, and supreme eloquence. This book is a collection of invaluable teachings by 'Alī ('a) in philosophy, principles of true politics, moral admonitions, and the realities of the world, teachings which none of the prominent theosophists, philosophers, and prodigious scholars of the world have been able to present.[1]

9. Another great Egyptian author who has spoken concerning the magnificent words of Imam Ali ('a) was Ṭāhā Ḥusayn. Once he related a part of Imam Ali's words and then stated the following regarding his response to a man who had fallen into doubts concerning their noble cause during the battle of Jamal: "Apart from the revelations of Allah, I have never heard or read a remark more magnificent and eloquent than this in my entire life!"[2]

10. In the first volume of his book al-Kāfī, the late Thiqqah al-Islam al-Kulaynī has written the following after relating one of the sermons delivered by Imam Ali ('a):

This is one of the very famous sermons [of the Imam ('a)] which most of the people know by heart. For those who seek knowledge of monotheism, it is enough just to contemplate this sermon and understand its profound teachings. If all of the eloquent men_ except for the prophets_ and the jinn were to gather around to explain the principles of monotheism, they would still be unable to explain it the way that 'Alī ('a) _ for whom may my father and mother be sacrificed_ has done. Had it not been for the extremely instructive speeches and words of that great man, the people would not have known the true path of monotheism.[3]

11. We will conclude this part with the remarks made by the great Shi'a jurist, the late Ayatollah al-Khū'ī:

Whenever Imam Ali ('a) picked up any given topic in his sermons, he would discuss it completely leaving nothing unsaid or unclear. This

1. Maṣādir Nahj al-Balāghah, vol. 1, p. 108.

2. Seyrī dar Nahj al-Balāghah, pp. 35-36.

3. Al-Kāfī, vol. 1, Bābe Jawāmi' al-Tawḥīd, p. 136.

fact has even brought some individuals, who were not completely aware of his life, to think that he dedicated his entire life to studying only this specific issue![1]

3. The Compelling Attraction of the Nahj al-Balāghah

All of the scholars and experts who have studied and contemplated the Nahj al-Balāghah, whether Shi'a, Sunni, or Christian ones, have spoken about the exceptionally powerful attraction of the Nahj al-Balāghah and their fascination with it.

In fact, it is this compelling attraction, which is abundantly evident in all of the words of Imam Ali ('a), whether the sermons, the letters, or the aphorisms, that has prompted a number of preeminent scholars to write commentaries on the Nahj al-Balāghah or write books and articles on the person of Imam Ali ('a).

We believe that this compelling attraction is due to some clear reasons, the most important of which are as follows:

1. All of the contents of the Nahj al-Balāghah address the state of the less fortunate and sympathize with the wronged; the Najh al-Balāghah constantly speaks of fighting injustice and struggling against tyrannical oppression.

The best example of this approach in the Nahj al-Balāghah can be seen in Imam Ali's directive to Mālik al-Ashtar when the Imam ('a) appointed him the ruler of Egypt. In it, the Imam ('a) laid down the principles and regulations of ruling over the people in a most eloquent yet succinct manner.

In this directive, the Imam ('a) instructs his governor concerning how to treat various classes of people, whom he categorizes into seven distinct groups. The Imam's tone is an ordinary and calm one as he discusses different classes of people, their rights, and the duty that the governor owed them.

However, as soon as the Imam ('a) begins discussing the less fortunate and the wronged, his tone suddenly changes and becomes passionate and fierce, as if the words were flames, flaring from the depth of his heart, as he commands his governor to be extremely careful

1. Al-Bayān fī Tafsīr al-Quran, p. 77.

about the rights of this oppressed class and to treat them in the best way he can. A part of this section of the directive reads:

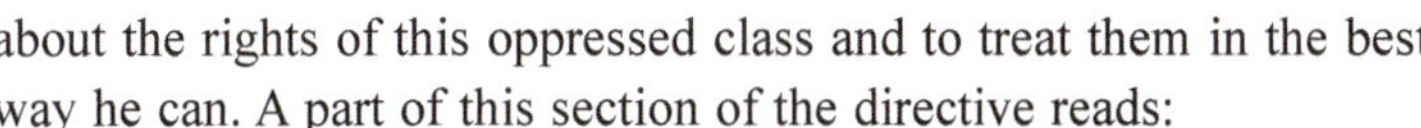

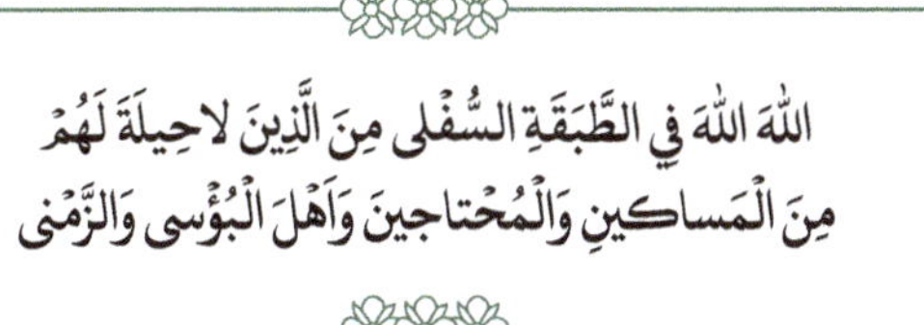

اللهَ اللهَ فِي الطَّبَقَةِ السُّفْلَى مِنَ الَّذِينَ لاحِيلَةَ لَهُمْ
مِنَ الْمَسَاكِينِ وَالْمُحْتَاجِينَ وَأَهْلِ الْبُؤْسَى وَالزَّمْنَى

"[Fear] Allah! [Fear] Allah [O' Mālik] regarding [how you treat] the less fortunate, the needy, the oppressed, and the disabled ..."

The Imam ('a) then goes on to order him to directly oversee these people's affairs all throughout the region under his rule and not to allow others to take their affairs into their hands [lest they should trample on their rights without his knowledge]. The Imam ('a) further orders him to regularly pay them visits to directly learn about their problems and to make sure that justice solves the problems of the less fortunate in the society.

But this letter and directive is not the only instance in which Imam Ali ('a) emphasizes the importance of justice and equity in the society, nor is it the sole place where he stresses the protection of the rights of the less fortunate and the oppressed. There are several different instances, in his letters and speeches, where the Imam ('a) reminds all of how important it is to safeguard the rights of the less fortunate and the oppressed.

2. The general approach of the teachings of the Nahj al-Balāghah is to help man break free from the carnal desires which can drag him toward humiliation and misery. It also seeks to help man free himself from being a slave to tyrants, oppressors, and the corrupt wealthy who only intend to exploit others and enslave them.

These two are the most important goals which have been emphasized countless times on various occasions in the Nahj al-Balāghah. Imam Ali ('a) has emphasized repeatedly that wherever wealth is accumulated in large amounts, one must be sure that it is the result of trampling on the rights of a large number of other people![1]

3. The extremely spiritual aura of the teachings of the Nahj al-Balāghah fascinates the mind and the soul such that one experiences a sort of pure rapture which fills their entire being with light.

For instance, when Imam Ali ('a) speaks of Allah and the wonders of His Divine Attributes of Glory and Beauty, his words are imbued with the highest level of pure spirituality. This gives the readers the feeling as if they were flying to the far reaches of the heavens, taken by angels to the most remote places of the world which even the human imagination would fail to reach.[2]

Then, when the Imam ('a) intends to awaken the ignorant souls from their state of negligence, he picks up the lashes of rhetoric, hitting them hard with reminders of death and the end of this mundane world, informing them of the fate of the past nations. Though they seem to be mere words, these lashes of rhetoric shake one's soul vehemently, serving as a painful yet necessary means to awaken one.[3]

4. Another reason behind the powerful appeal of the Nahj al-Balāghah, which was referred to earlier as well, is that no matter what subject it discusses, it explores it to the core, leaving not even the minutiae of the matter unclear or unexplained. This is perhaps the most peculiar characteristic of the contents of the Nahj al-Balāghah since it makes it seem to the reader that the person who discussed all of those subjects had spent an entire lifetime studying each of them to the core!

For instance, when the Imam ('a) begins giving a speech on the subject of Tawḥīd and the Oneness of Allah, elaborating on Allah's Attributes of Beauty and Glory, he appears like a Knowledgeable and skilled theosophist who has spent long years delving into the depths of this subject. It seems to the reader that he spent his entire life discussing this subject and he never attended to any other discussion.

He explains the divine attributes so precisely that he does not fall into the pitfalls pertaining to this subject. That is, he neither falls into the traps of depicting a corporeal image of Allah nor does he reject the

1. Al-Imam Ali ('a): Ṣawt al-'Idālah al-Insānīyah, vol. 1, pp. 212-213.

2. Such accounts can be found in sermon No. 1, sermon No. 91 [also known as the sermon of Ashbāḥ] as well as many other sermons in the Nahj al-Balāghah.

3. Similar accounts can be found in sermons No. 109, 111, 113 and many other sermons in the Nahj al-Balāghah.

idea that man is totally unable to fathom Allah's Divine Attributes. He describes Allah in a way that one feels as though he actually saw Him with his spiritual inner eye, finding Him present everywhere, i.e. in the heavens, on the earth, and even within his own soul. Having read the Imam's words on Allah, one feels that the light of knowledge of Allah has been shone on one's heart and soul.

At the same time, when one opens up the Nahj al-Balāghah to read the sermons on Jihad and fighting in the cause of Allah, one suddenly finds himself in the presence of a great warrior and a brave commander, standing on the battlefield giving precise instructions to his officers and soldiers based on his precisely worked-out tactics. Reading these sermons makes one feel that the person who has given them has spent his entire life on battlefields, gaining mastery over war tactics and strategies.

Moreover, when one begins reading the parts of the Nahj al-Balāghah where the Imam ('a) appears as the ruler of the Muslim Ummah, they find a just and extremely skilled and knowledgeable leader who explained the principles of politics and governance to his governors in different regions.

He explained to them the reasons behind the rise and fall of civilizations, elaborating on the ill fates of wrongdoing nations, and finally depicting the way to achieve social and political security and serenity. He does this so skillfully that one might assume that he had been busy all his life learning and practicing the art of politics, and nothing else!

As one keeps going through the contents of the Nahj al-Balāghah, suddenly one finds Imam Ali ('a) appearing as a moral trainer who sought to uplift his students morally. Based on one of the sermons in the Nahj al-Balāghah, once a righteous and pure man named Hammām asked the Imam ('a) to teach him something new in regard to the character qualities and the conduct of the pious believers. He longed so much for learning that he was not satisfied with a small amount of this knowledge and he wished to have it all.

This was why the Imam ('a) opened out to him the gates of his immense reservoir of knowledge, presenting him with an overwhelming amount of knowledge concerning the ways and the character qualities of the pious believers.

He mentioned and explained the character qualities and virtues of the pious believers one by one until he had finally presented a list of around one hundred virtues and lofty character qualities, using extremely soul-shaking phrases and an immensely influential language. The Imam ('a) put these teachings forward so skillfully and thoroughly as if he had spent several lifetimes teaching these same virtues to people in order to give them moral training.

The teachings that the Imam ('a) presented that day and the way he presented them were so soul-shaking that, when he had finally finished his sermon, the man who had asked for that information shrieked out of astonishment and fell to the ground unconscious. Undoubtedly, such influential words have never been said by any other human beings all throughout history.

These different scenes in the Nahj al-Balāghah are, without a doubt, unique and are among the most incredible features and characteristics of this unparalleled book.

The Remarks of Great Scholars about the Attraction of the Nahj al-Balāghah

The remarks made by some of the great scholars regarding the powerful attractions of the Nahj al-Balāghah are also further proof as to what was discussed above. Before mentioning any other scholar, let us first take a look at the remarks made in this regard by al-Sayyid al-Raḍī, the prodigious man who was himself one of the greatest Arabic literary figures of all time, and who compiled the Nahj al-Balāghah himself.

As he was busy compiling and editing the various sermons delivered by Imam Ali ('a) into a single book, al-Sayyid al-Raḍī explained every now and then how fascinated people had been by these sermons and how deeply they had been touched upon hearing the Imam ('a) presenting them with his teachings. He also explained how immensely he himself had been influenced and shaken by the powerful effects of these sermons. For instance, while narrating the Gharrā' sermon [sermon No. 83 of the Nahj al-Balāghah], al-Sayyid al-Raḍī writes: "According to the historical narratives, when Imam Ali ('a) was delivering this sermon, the hearts were palpitating, the eyes were tearful and the bodies were trembling [at the contents of that soul-shaking sermon]."

Moreover, when narrating the Sermon of Hammām [the man who asked the Imam ('a) to explain the virtues and sings of pious believers to him, and due to the request of whom, the Imam ('a) delivered this incredible and unique sermon], al-Sayyid al-Raḍī writes:

[When the Imam ('a) had reached the peak of his sermon] Hammām let out a loud cry and fell to the ground and passed away! The Imam ('a) [who had, at first, refused his request to say those things but had later agreed because Hammām insisted a lot] said: "Alas! I feared exactly this for him!" then he added: "Is it not that such admonition is profoundly effective on those who take admonition?!""

Furthermore, al-Sayyid al-Raḍī has made certain remarks when narrating sermon N. 28 in the Nahj al-Balāghah, which show what a great effect its contents had on his heart and soul. He writes:

If anything can lead people toward abstemiousness and toward doing good deeds to secure a felicitous life for themselves in the hereafter, it

is this same sermon! It can open man's eyes to the uselessness of enter-
taining desperate hopes in the gains of this world and awaken him from
his state of negligence and ignorance, creating a feeling of despise in him
toward evil acts.

Then, after highlighting some of the most interesting parts of this sermon
he adds the following: "I advise you to contemplate this sermon, for it
has an amazingly profound wisdom and deep teachings within it and
most of the Imam's words are like this."

Likewise, when narrating sermon No. 16, al-Sayyid al-Raḍī writes:

This sermon, which is truly at the peak of eloquence, contains subtleties
and fine details which even the most skilled poets and orators are unable
to compose into their sayings! Additionally, there are finer points and
details regarding eloquence and the art of rhetoric which have been carefully observed in this sermon which neither the mind is able to fully comprehend nor the tongue is capable of capturing completely. Moreover,
what I am explaining about the supreme eloquence in this sermon is not
understandable except to those who are skilled and learned in literature
and rhetoric, for "none will comprehend them save the erudite"[1].

Finally, while narrating the Shiqshiqīyah sermon, al-Sayyid al-Raḍī narrated the remarks of Ibn ʿAbbās, the famous hadith expert and Quranic
exegete, about it which shows how fascinated and enthralled he was by
this sermon:

فَوَاللهِ مَا أَسِفْتُ عَلَى كَلَامٍ قَطُّ كَأَسَفِي عَلَى هَذَا
الْكَلَامِ أَنْ لَا يَكُونَ أَمِيرُالْمُؤْمِنِينَ عَلَيْهِ السَّلَامُ بَلَغَ مِنْهُ حَيْثُ أَرَادَ

---

*I swear to Allah that I have never been saddened over anything like I
was over this sermon [and the fact that was left unfinished] because
Amīr al-Muʾminīn could not complete it the way he wished [all because of the untimely interference of a man who, at the middle of this
sermon, came up to him and gave him a letter to read, after which the
Imam (ʿa) did not continue his sermon].*

---

1. وَمَا يَعْقِلُهَا إِلَّا الْعَالِمُونَ [Surah al-ʿAnkabūt, v. 43]

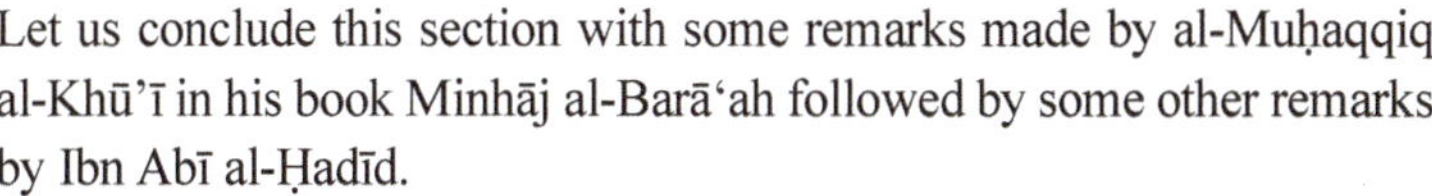

Let us conclude this section with some remarks made by al-Muḥaqqiq al-Khū'ī in his book Minhāj al-Barā'ah followed by some other remarks by Ibn Abī al-Ḥadīd.

Al-Muḥaqqiq al-Khū'ī stated:

No spoken or written work is even remotely comparable to the words of Imam Ali ('a) in terms of their organization and coherence accompanied by their lofty contents. Imam Ali ('a) is by far the most prominent orator, a rhetorician whose words cause anger and apprehension to subside. His words are a vast ocean that constantly throws its jewels on its shores in abundance; they rule the hearts of those who listen to them, prompting them to follow its instructions. The Imam's encouraging remarks lead one toward all that is good and the lashes of his warning and admonition deter one from evils. So it is only befitting for his words to be leading ones, just as he himself was and forever will be the leader and Imam of mankind.[1]

Finally, while discussing a part of sermon No. 109 in the Nahj al-Balāghah, Ibn Abī al-Ḥadīd states that if one wishes to learn the art of rhetoric, the fine techniques of eloquence, and a deep understanding of the lexical subtleties of the Arabic words, they need to deeply reflect on this sermon.

He then notes the following:

The effects of this sermon are so remarkably strong that if it were to be read to an obstinate atheist who is fiercely determined to deny the Resurrection, his resistance would soon be crushed, his heart filled with terror, his negative determination undermined, and the foundations of his atheist convictions severely shaken. May Allah recompense the speaker of these words, for this great service of his to Islam, with the best of rewards that He has ever given His most righteous servants. His aiding of Islam was rather interesting: sometimes he did it with his sword, sometimes with his words, and some other times with his heart and thoughts. Indeed, he was the chief of all those who have ever fought in the cause of Allah, the master and the most eloquent of all orators, the head of all jurists and Quranic exegetes, and the leader of all monotheists and those who seek to uphold the true justice.[2]

1. Al-Khū'ī, Minhāj al-Barā'ah, vol. 1, p. 271.

2. Sharḥ Nahj al-Balāghah Ibn Abī al-Ḥadīd, vol. 7, p. 202 [with some excerption].

The Isnād[1] of the Nahj al-Balāghah

The sermons, letters, and aphorisms collected in the Nahj al-Balāghah have all been compiled [by al-Sayyid al-Raḍī] as Mursal narratives, i.e. narratives whose chain of narrators have not been mentioned. That is to say, the chain of narrators that can be uninterruptedly traced back to any of the Infallible Imams ('a) have not been included in the book.

This issue has tempted some individuals to try to doubt the credibility and reliability of the contents of the Nahj al-Balāghah. This has particularly been done by the individuals who feared that the unique and lofty contents of the Nahj al-Balāghah could be used as evidence to eliminate any doubts concerning the legitimacy and validity of the Shi'a school of Islam as well as the superiority of Imam Ali ('a) over all other companions of the Prophet (ṣ). Thus, they used this issue as a pretext to downplay the significance of this great book and to minimize its effects on the public opinion of the Muslim Ummah.

Fortunately, these attempts have largely been futile in affecting the ideas of the Muslim intellectuals, as the Muslim scholars, whether Sunni or Shi'a, have greatly praised it and even written commentaries on it to unravel its secrets. We included some of the ideas of the prominent Muslim scholars about the Nahj al-Balāghah in the previous sections.

Nevertheless, it seems necessary to present a discussion on the chain of narrators of the contents of the Nahj al-Balāghah in order to eliminate the miniscule amount of doubt that might still remain concerning the credibility and reliability of this shining book. But before presenting that discussion, two essential points need to be made:

1. The majority of the sermons, letters, and aphorisms compiled in the Nahj al-Balāghah contain discussions which are either sound logical discussions themselves or the validity of their contents can be easily proven through logical arguments. In other words, they contain issues whose validity is self-evident. Therefore, there is no need to ascertain their Isnād the way that the Isnād of the Islamic traditions on jurisprudential and devotional issues needs to be ascertained.

Most of these sermons contain discussions on Islamic theology, the Origin and the End, Divine Attributes of Allah, and the reasons for the great-

1. The chain of testimony by which a hadith is transmitted.

ness of the Quran and the Prophet of Islam (ṣ), etc.

Furthermore, another part of the contents of the Nahj al-Balāghah concern advice and admonition which revolve mostly around being edified by the fate of the past nations, teachings on politics and how to run a country, principles of social life, principles and rules of Jihad and the like. These discussions are mostly logical ones whose validity and reliability are likewise self-evident or they can be easily proven to be valid through simple logical arguments.

It is a customary practice to accept the books ascribed to great philosophers and great poets to be credible and reliable writings of those same authors. Interestingly, this is easily done today without having access to their chain of narrators, and it is justified by arguing that they contain logical and sound contents. The same argument can also be advanced about the Nahj al-Balāghah, because its unparalleled and stunning contents are undeniable evidence concerning its credibility and reliability.

There is only a small portion of the contents of the Nahj al-Balāghah which contain discussions of secondary jurisprudential and devotional rules. Therefore, the issue of checking the chain of narrators is only applicable to these sections which do not make up even one tenth of this book. Therefore, the ruckus created by some about the chain of narrators of the contents of the Nahj al-Balāghah is basically rather unimportant and baseless.

2. Another noteworthy point is that if the issue here were establishing the reliability of the Isnād of the Nahj al-Balāghah, then it could easily be established as well.

This is because, according to the science of the Principles of Islamic Jurisprudence, the most important point about any Islamic tradition and narrative is to prove that it has indeed been spoken by the person to whom it has been ascribed and this can be ascertained in different ways. Sometimes this is established through studying the Isnād of the narrative in question, and some other times it is ascertained owing to the fact that the narrative in question has been transmitted through a large number of different chains of narrators and related in many famous and reliable references. Finally, sometimes the contents of a tradition or a narrative are so sublime and lofty that their credibility is self-evident, meaning that it is crystal clear that it could not have been stated by anyone other than the Prophet (ṣ) or the Infallible Imams (ʻa).

This latter argument has been made about the contents of the book al-Ṣaḥīfah al-Sajjādīyah [albeit in addition to the countless valid Isnāds that have also been mentioned for them]. This book contains a collection of supplications composed by Imam al-Sajjād ('a) which enjoy such a sublime discourse and such lofty teachings that leave no doubt as to the fact that they have indeed been related from Imam al-Sajjād ('a).

Undoubtedly, anyone who studies the contents of the Nahj al-Balāghah carefully, contemplating its teachings deeply and learning some of the secret within it, will quickly agree that no ordinary human being could have ever composed them. The extraordinary contents and language of the teachings of the Nahj al-Balāghah leave no doubt that they must have been composed by a Divinely-sent prophet or an Infallible Imam.

This is exactly what is meant by the sentence "it is second only to the words of Allah but superior to the words of all other human beings" which has frequently been stated by countless Shi'a and Sunni scholars to describe the Nahj al-Balāghah.

Therefore, the exceptional contents of the Nahj al-Balāghah are clear proof as to its credibility and authenticity, i.e. that it contains only the words of an Infallible and not those of any ordinary human being. Moreover, the fact that Imam Ali ('a) has been the only Infallible to whom it has ever been ascribed leaves no doubt that it is indeed a collection of Imam Ali's written and spoken words.

Another point worth noting is that it is rather ridiculous for an ordinary person or even a scholar to have composed all of the contents of this magnificent book and then have ascribed it to Imam Ali ('a)! This is because even composing a tiny part of this book would have been an honor beyond compare for its author; so why would such a person ascribe it to another person and not have the honor that he truly deserved himself?!

Finally, since we know for a fact that al-Sayyid al-Raḍī was a great scientist, a reliable researcher, and a pious man, we are reassured that he would not ascribe any words to Imam Ali ('a) with certainty unless he extracted them from some extremely reliable and credible resources.

Nowhere in the Nahj al-Balāghah has al-Sayyid al-Raḍī used the term "it has been related from Imam Ali ('a) that ..." to speak about the various sermons, letters, or aphorisms. Rather, he resolutely states: "This is one of Imam Ali's sermons/letters/aphorisms", showing that he was one hundred percent sure that they were indeed Imam Ali's words.

How is it possible for a great scientist, with the kind of meticulous attention to details that is evident in his work, to ascribe some sayings to his Infallible leader without having had ascertained their authenticity in some reliable and authentic references and resources?!

In addition to all this, numerous books had been written by different scholars, before al-Sayyid al-Raḍī, in which many of the sermons, letters, and aphorisms compiled in the Nahj al-Balāghah have been recorded [as Imam Ali's words].

This fact clearly shows that even before al-Sayyid al-Raḍī these sermons, letters, and aphorisms had been well-known among Muslim scholars, narrators of hadiths, and even ordinary people as the sayings of Imam Ali ('a). This fact can also obviate the necessity for uninterrupted Isnāds in order to verify the authenticity of these sermons, letters, and aphorisms because all of those people could not have been wrong!

Some great scholars have even been of the opinion that the sermons which had been delivered by Imam Ali ('a) and which were well-known among people had been much more than what al-Sayyid al-Raḍī actually included in the Nahj al-Balāghah. This means that the Nahj al-Balāghah is only an anthology of Imam Ali's sermons and sayings.

For instance, the renowned Muslim historian, al-Mas'ūdī, who lived a century before al-Sayyid al-Raḍī, has written the following in his book Murūj al-Dhahab about Imam Ali's sermons:

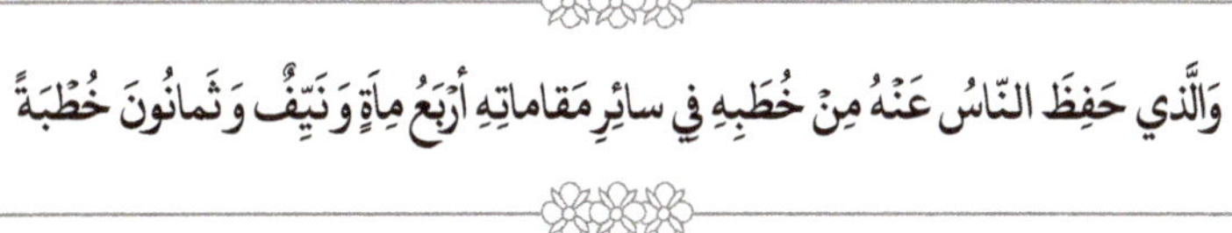

وَالَّذي حَفِظَ النّاسُ عَنْهُ مِنْ خُطَبِهِ في سائِرِ مَقاماتِهِ أَرْبَعُ مِاءَةٍ وَنَيِّفٌ وَثَمانُونَ خُطْبَةً

"The number of sermons delivered by Imam 'Alī ('a) which people now know by heart are around four hundred and eighty."[1]

This is while the Nahj al-Balāghah, as we have access to today, comprises only around two hundred and forty sermons.

Similar remarks have been made by the famous Muslim scholar, Sibṭ

1. Murūj al-Dhahab, vol. 2, p. 419.

ibn al-Jawzī, in his book entitled Tadhkirah al-Khawās. In this book, he quoted al-Sayyid al-Murtaḍā as saying: "I have been able to access four hundred of Imam Ali's sermons."[1]

Al-Jāḥiẓ, another renowned Muslim scholar, has made similar remarks in the book Al-Bayān wa al-Tabyīn: "There used to exist well-known written records of Imam Ali's sermons."[2]

In his book entitled Mushākalah al-Nās lī Zamānihim, Ibn Wāḍiḥ, who is another Muslim scholar, writes:

People have always known lots of sermons, given by Imam Ali ('a), by heart. He had delivered four hundred sermons all of which had been memorized by people. These are the same sermons that are well-known in our time period as well, from which phrases and sentences are adopted and cited in speeches.[3]

It is also noteworthy that a number of our contemporary scholars and scientists have written different books on the chain of narrators of the contents of the Nahj al-Balāghah as well as the ancient references, which had been written long before the Nahj al-Balāghah, and which transmitted the same sermons, letters, and aphorisms by Imam Ali ('a). One of the best books on the references of the Nahj al-Balāghah and its chains of narrators has been written by a leading researcher and a learned scholar named al-Sayyid 'Abd al-Zahrā' al-Ḥusaynī al-Khaṭīb. By studying this book, any fair researcher will come to admit that al-Sayyid al-Raḍī has not been the only person to relate these sermons from Imam Ali ('a) and that these same sermons had been transmitted in various other references before the Nahj al-Balāghah was written.

It is worth noting that the contents of the Nahj al-Balāghah have been related from 114 other references, 20 of which were written by scholars who lived before al-Sayyid al-Raḍī.

For more information in this regard, the dear readers can refer to this book, as the discussions and facts which it has presented cannot be contained in the introduction of this book.

A final point which needs to be made here is that amid his discussions

1. Tadhkiral al-Khawās, p. 114.

2. Al-Bayān wa al-Tabyīn, vol. 1, p. 176.

3. Mushākilah al-Nāss li Zamānihim, p. 15.

in various sections of the Nahj al-Balāghah, al-Sayyid al-Raḍī himself has mentioned some books[1] and a number of traditions[2] as references from which he collected and compiled the contents of the Nahj al-Balāghah.

Given what was discussed above, it is clear that there is no doubt in the authenticity and credibility of the Isnād of the Nahj al-Balāghah.

Commentaries Written on the Nahj al-Balāghah

The last section of our introduction concerns a short review of the translations of the Nahj al-Balāghah as well as the commentaries written on it by Muslim scholars and scientists since the time of al-Sayyid al-Raḍī up to the present time. As we move farther away from the time when this great book was compiled and edited, the number of commentaries written on it increases dramatically.

This is clearly because as years passed, this treasure of valuable teachings became more known within the Muslim world; the fact that today many different conferences are held on the Nahj al-Balāghah further corroborates this claim.

While discussing the life of al-Sayyid al-Raḍī in the fourth volume of his invaluable book Al-Ghadīr, the late 'Allāmah al-Amīnī touches upon this issue and says, "Since the time of al-Sayyid al-Raḍī up until now, more than seventy different commentaries have been written on the Nahj al-Balāghah."

He then proceeds to list all of these commentaries together with the name of their authors and the date of their death. He then mentions that during his time, a few new translations of the Nahj al-Balāghah into other languages were also published and that these would make the number of translations and commentaries of the Nahj al-Balāghah reach 81.[3]

Naturally, the commentaries written on the Nahj al-Balāghah have each looked at it from their own specific and different perspectives

1. These books and references are as follows: 1. Al-Bayān wa al-Tabyīn, by al-Jāḥiẓ; 2. The Tārīkh by al-Ṭabarī; 3. Al-Jamal, by al-Wāqidī; 4. Al-Maghāzī, by Sa'īd ibn Yaḥyā al-Umawi; 5. Al-Maqāmāt, by Abī Ja'far al-Iskāfī; Al-Muqtaḍab, by al-Mubarrid.

2. These traditions are narrated by the following narrators: Abī Ja'far Muḥammad ibn Ali al-Bāqir; Tha'lab 'an ibn al-A'rābī; Ḍirār al-Ḍibābī, Abī Juḥayfah; Kumayl ibn Ziyād al-Nakha'ī; Mas'adah ibn Ṣadaqah; Nawf al-Bikālī; Abū 'Ubayd al-Qāsim ibn Salām and Hāshim ibn al-Kalbī.

3. Al-Ghadīr, vol. 4, pp. 186-193.

[much like the different exegeses written on the Quran]. Some of these works have analyzed it from a literary perspective, shedding more light on its literary excellence, while others have interpreted it from historical, philosophical, social, or moral perspectives.

The learned author of the book Maṣādir Nahj al-Balāghah has listed 110 different commentaries written on the Nahj al-Balāghah throughout history. Moreover, a group of clerics have written a bibliography for the Nahj al-Balāghah in which they have listed 370 different commentaries on the Nahj al-Balāghah along with different translations of it.[1]

In spite of all this, we should admit that it seems that this great book still remains largely unexplored, requiring far more commentaries and interpretations to be written on it to unravel its mysteries. This is because the Nahj al-Balāghah, much like Imam Ali ('a) himself, is multidimensional with each of its dimensions being so vast that it is virtually impossible to capture all of the realities latent within them in so few commentaries. Therefore, many more commentaries need to be written on it, with different scholars delving into one of its multitude of facets, extracting the treasures within it to be used by the present and future generations of man.

It should also be noted that not all of the past commentaries are complete or comprehensive ones. While some of them have only explored and commented on some parts of the Nahj al-Balāghah, some others have presented interpretations on all of its parts and are more comprehensive in their scope. Below, we have included a list of the more comprehensive and complete commentaries on the Nahj al-Balāghah.

1. A'lām Nahj al-Balāghah. According to al-'Allāmah al-Amīnī, this is one of the first commentaries ever written on the Nahj al-Balāghah. Its writer is 'Alī ibn al-Nāṣir, who was a contemporary of the late Sayyid al-Raḍī.

2. Minhāj al-Barā'ah, which was written by Sa'īd al-Dīn Hibatullah Quṭb al-Rāwandī, a Shi'a scholar of the sixth century Ah.

3. Sharḥ Nahj al-Balāghah by Ibn Abī al-Ḥadīd al-Mu'tazilī, a Sunni scholar of the seventh century Ah. His book, written in twenty vol-

1. Ostādī, Kitābnāme-i Nahj al-Balāghah, P. 10. [It is noteworthy that according to the book "Maṣādir Nahj al-Balāghah", 101 total commentaries have been written on the Nahj al-Balāghah not 110].

umes, is one of the most famous commentaries ever written on the Nahj al-Balāghah.

4. Sharḥ Nahj al-Balāghah, written by Ibn Meytham al-Baḥrānī, a Shi'a scholar of the seventh century Ah. This is also one of the comprehensive and interesting commentaries written on the Nahj al-Balāghah.

5. Minhāj al-Barā'ah, written by the late Ḥājj Mirzā Ḥabībullah al-Khū'ī, a Shi'a scholar of the thirteenth and fourteenth centuries Ah. This book is also known as the Sharḥ-e Khū'ī.

6. Sharḥ Nahj al-Balāghah by al-Shaykh Muḥammad 'Abduh, a famous Sunni scholar of the thirteen century Ah.

There are also other interesting commentaries written on the Nahj al-Balāghah by some of the contemporary Muslim scholars, the names of which are not listed here for the sake of brevity.

In his book entitled Al-Dharī'ah, the eminent Shi'a scholar, Muḥaddith al-Tehrānī, has listed 140 commentaries on the Nahj al-Balāghah authored by Shi'a scholars and another 16 commentaries written by Sunni scholars. According to him, the earliest commentary on the Nahj al-Balāghah was written by al-Fakhr al-Rāzī [deceased, 606 Ah.].[1]

1. Al-Dharī'ah, vol. 14, pp. 111-160.

A Foreword by al-Sayyid al-Raḍī

Why I Compiled the Nahj al-Balāghah

All Praise be to Allah, who made thanksgiving [to Him] the cost of His bounties, security from calamities, the means toward earning [a felicitous life in] the eternal Paradise, and the cause of increase in His blessings [which He bestows on His servants]. And peace and blessings be upon the Prophet of compassion and kindness, the leader of all Divinely-sent leaders, and the beacon of guidance for the [Muslim] nation. He is like a blessed tree whose roots are magnanimity and whose branches are his sublime character qualities and majesty.

The origins of his existence are honor and glory and his noble lineage is fruitful and venerable. And may peace and blessings be upon his Ahl-al-Bayt ('a) who are the lanterns in the darkness of the earth, the saviors of mankind, the clear signs of the religion, and the weighty exemplars of virtues and excellence.

May peace and blessings be upon them proportionate to their great virtues and magnanimity, and which will be given to them as part of the otherworldly reward, a reward that is befitting of their pure roots and blessed branches. May peace and blessings be upon them so long as the light of dawn cleaves the veil of the night asunder, and so long as the stars keep appearing at sunset and disappearing at sunrise.

When I was young and still very energetic, I wrote a book on the virtues and sublime character qualities of the Infallible Imams ('a) which included the most interesting historical narratives about them as well as the most interesting sayings of theirs.

I wrote a preface to that book in which I explained my purpose in writing it. But then, after gathering and compiling the narratives regarding the virtues and character qualities of Amīr al-Mu'minīn ('a), I ran into certain problems in life which prevented me from completing it.

I had organized that book into several sections, and each section into different chapters, and at the end of the section on Imam Ali ('a) I had included a chapter which was basically a collection of some interesting sayings of the Imam ('a). That chapter included some short sayings, words of wisdom, short parables, and aphorisms but it did not include lengthy sermons or letters of the Imam ('a).

Later on, a number of my friends, who had found the various parts of that book rather amazing, asked me to compile a new book which would include a collection of the select sayings of Amīr al-Mu'minīn ('a). This new book was to comprise the most eloquent and beautiful sermons, letters, and aphorisms delivered, written, and said by the Imam ('a).

The reason why my friends insisted so much on compiling such a book was that they were sure it would turn out to be the most wondrous Arabic literary work as it would be a collection of the most eloquent examples of the Arabic literature. It would also be rather invaluable in that it would be a collection of the most enlightening religious teachings regarding both the material and spiritual life of mankind.

We knew that this new book would turn out to be valuable beyond compare, because it was a collection of the words of Amīr al-Mu'minīn ('a), who was the root and source of eloquence and whose heart was the birthplace of sublime rhetoric. Obviously, no book of such comprehensive nature and valuable contents had ever been written before, and for good reasons! Because it was Imam Ali ('a) who first made the secrets of eloquence manifest and it was from him that the rules and principles of eloquence were first taken! All gifted and skilled orators have followed his method of oration and all articulate preachers have been inspired by his orations.

In spite of all this, he still remains way ahead of all gifted and skilled literary figures and they still follow him; he is still far superior to all of them and they are all way below him in literary rank. The secret behind this excellence and supremacy is that Imam Ali's words bear traces of the Divine Knowledge of Allah and carry the scent of the sacred words of the Prophet (ṣ).

In the end, I accepted my friends' request and began working on this new book, knowing for certain that it would entail an abundance of spiritual benefits, would soon become widely-known, and that through compiling it, I would be granted an otherworldly reward. By compiling and editing this book, I intended to make it clear to all that, in addition to his other countless virtues and merits, Amīr al-Mu'minīn was the only one among the past people who elevated literature to its highest level and whose words reached the peak of eloquence.

His words are a vast and boundless ocean which cannot and will not be outmatched by any other eloquent discourse. So, I wanted to be the first person to compile such a book so as to have the honor of compiling the Imam's words all to myself, just as al-Farazdaq, the famous Arab poet, once composed of his ancestors, addressing a man called "Jarīr":

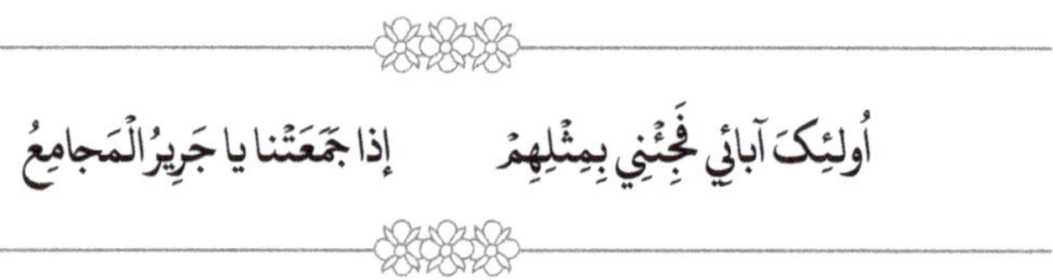

"These are my ancestors, O' Jarīr!
So do name some of yours who are [prominent] like them,
Once we gather in a gathering!"

As I conducted my research into Imam Ali's words and sayings, I realized that the Imam's words which were narrated in various references were of three kinds:

The first were his sermons and speeches, the second were his letters, treatise, and directives, and the third were his short words of wisdom and aphorisms.

Therefore, by the Grace of Allah, I decided to organize the new book into these same categories: first I included the most beautiful sermons and speeches delivered by the Imam ('a), then his most interesting and eloquent letters, and in the end, I included a collection of the most beautiful words of wisdom and aphorisms stated by him. I then organized all of these three sections into various chapters and left some empty pages within each chapter so that if I got my hand on some other beautiful words of the Imam ('a) in some other references in the future, I would be able to add them in the right section and chapter.

Furthermore, whenever I found some beautiful sayings by the Imam ('a) that did not fit in any of the above-mentioned categories [such as questions and answers, or debates], I tried to include them in a section which was closest to them in theme and subject.

The readers might find that the contents of certain chapters are not much related, organized, or coherent. This is because my intention was to collect the most beautiful and eloquent sayings of the Imam ('a), not to write a coherent and organized scientific book.

One of the exceptional and unparalleled qualities of Imam Ali's words is that, if one contemplates his teachings on abstemiousness and piety while, at the same time forgetting that they are the words of a great ruler whose commands everyone would obey, one will no doubt conclude that they must be the words of an abstemious ascetic who never busied himself with anything but worshipping Allah.

When one reads the Imam's words with such an attitude, one feels that they were spoken by an ascetic who led a pious life in solitude, away from people, worshipping Allah day and night.

Once this feeling abates, one is filled with immeasurable wonder to remember that these teachings in piety and righteousness were given by a person who would plunge into oceans of enemy soldiers at the time of war, striking down the most formidable of adversaries and the scariest enemy warriors.

When he came back from the battlefield, fighting fearlessly in the cause of Allah, blood dripped from the tip of his sword and yet, this same man was the leader of ascetics and the chief of all righteous people. This specific fact is one of the wondrous attributes and virtues of the Imam ('a), who was truly a man of many seemingly contradictory character qualities and virtues.

I frequently discussed this specific quality and attribute of the Imam ('a) with my friends, arousing a feeling of wonder and amazement in them at this rather amazing fact. Indeed, this is one of the most important issues which is worthy of research and contemplation as it is laden with grand lessons.

[Another point which is worth noting is that] it so happens that some of the sayings of the Imam ('a) that I have included in the book enjoy similar or even identical themes, wordings, or contents. My justification for including them all is that there are substantial discrepancies among the narratives in which the words of the Imam ('a) have been related. Many of these narratives have similar themes and contents with minor differences, while others differ greatly in wording but discuss the same subject as some others do.

Sometimes, I found a beautiful saying of the Imam ('a) in a reference and I included it in my book in the exact same form as I found it, but then later on, I came across another narrative from Imam Ali ('a) on the same subject which was not identical to the previous one. In such cases, I would include the second narrative as well, mostly because its contents were a little more than the first one or that its exposition and wording were more interesting and beautiful than the first one.

Moreover, since it took me a long time to finish this book, I might have forgotten that I had included a saying before and so I might have included some parts of it again in another section of the book inadvertently and due to forgetting.

This being said, I do not claim that I was able to get my hands on all of the words of Imam Ali ('a) without having missed any of them. In fact, it is not unlikely that what I could not find and compile through my research is much more than what I got my hands on and compiled in my book.

Yet, my duty is nothing but to make every effort, work hard, and attempt to the best of my ability to search for and collect as many of these glorious sayings as I can so as to prevent them from fading into oblivion, and I implore Allah for His assistance and guidance on this path.

When I had finally finished the book, I decided to give it the title "Nahj al-Balāghah" [The Peak of Eloquence], because it is a book which opens new horizons in eloquence to the readers and brings them close to what they seek. This book is beneficial both to learned scholars and students; it is a resource in which both literary figures and ascetics can find what they look for.

Amid his discussions, Imam Ali ('a) presents amazing discussions regarding Tawḥīd [i.e. the Oneness of Allah], justice, and the fact that Allah transcends this material world and that He is far above any attributes of His created beings that might be ascribed to Him. These discussions are so wonderful in nature and scope that they would satisfy any seeker of truth completely and would heal the ailments of the heart, eliminating all doubts regarding what the truth really is.

I pray to Allah the Almighty to keep me from mistakes and to give me the power to continue on this path. I seek refuge with Him against slips of the mind before those of the tongue, and against slips of the tongue before errors of deeds. I know that He will suffice me in the place of all others, for He is the best of guardians and protectors.

SERMONS

Sermon No.1

يَذْكُرُ فِيهَا ابْتِدَاءَ خَلْقِ السَّمَاءِ وَالأَرْضِ، وَخَلْقَ آدَمَ، وَفِيهَا ذِكْرُ الْحَجِّ

This is one of Imam 'Alī's sermons in which he has discussed the beginning of the creation of the heavens and the earth and the creation of Adam, and he has also made a short mention of the Ḥajj pilgrimage.[1]

1. The Isnād of this sermon:
This sermon [although not all of it in its entirety but different parts of it] has been transmitted in various different references both before and after al-Sayyid al-Raḍī. Among the great scholars who had related this sermon before al-Sayyid al-Raḍī are the following: 1. The late Shaykh al-Ṣadūq, in his book Al-Tawḥīd, p. 41, hadith No. 3; 2. The Late Ibn Shu'bah al-Ḥarrānī, in his book entitled Tuḥaf al-'Uqūl, p. 61.
As for the great scholars who lived after al-Sayyid al-Raḍī and who related this sermon in their books, the following scholars can be mentioned: 1. Al-Wāsiṭī in his book 'Uyūn al-Ḥikmah wa al-Mawā'iẓ; 2. The late 'Allāmah al-Ṭabarsī in his book Al-Iḥtijāj, vol. 1, p. 198; 3. Ibn Ṭalḥah in his book entitled Maṭālib al-Sau'ul, p. 164; 4. Al-Qāḍī al-Qaḍā'ī in Dastūr Ma'ālim al-Ḥikam, p. 153; 5. Al-Fakhr al-Rāzī in his book al-Tafsīr al-Kabīr [Mafātīḥ al-Ghayb], vol. 2, p. 164; 6. Zamakhsharī in Rabī' al-Abrār, vol. 1, p. 97; 7. Al-Quṭb al-Rāwandī in his book Minhāj al-Barā'ah, vol. 1, p. 22; 8. The late 'Allāmah al-Majlisī in volumes 4, 11, 18, 57, 77, 92, and 99 of his book Biḥār al-Anwār [according to the book Maṣādir Nahj al-Balāghah, vol. 1, p. 313].
It is noteworthy, however, that the different versions of this sermon, transmitted in these various references, are slightly different in wording from the one related in the Nahj al-Balāghah.

Sermon No. 1 at a Glance

Sermon No. 1 has some of the most important contents among the sermons of the Nahj al-Balāghah and it has been rightly placed at the beginning of the book by al-Sayyid al-Raḍī to underscore its significance.

This sermon presents a complete course in Islamic worldview; it begins with the discussion of the Divine Attributes of Perfection and Beauty and it presents some amazing details regarding them. It then describes the process of the creation of the cosmos in general and the creation of the heavens and the earth in particular.

Following this discussion, it then offers information on how the angels and Adam were created, followed by the story of the prostration of the angels [before Adam], Iblīs's refusal to obey Allah's command, and the fall of man from Paradise to the earth.

Then, Imam Ali ('a) continued this sermon, speaking of the Divine Mission of the prophets and the philosophy behind it, finally discussing the Divine Mission of the Prophet of Islam (ṣ), the greatness of the Holy Quran, and the importance of the prophetic tradition.

The Imam ('a) then focuses on the Ḥajj, among other precepts of Islam [otherwise known as the Furū' al-Dīn or "the branches of religion"]. He explained how important a ritual the Ḥajj is and then elaborated on the philosophy behind it and its secrets.

Imam Ali ('a) has discussed all of these issues so comprehensively and with such meticulous attention to details that by reflecting on his descriptions in this sermon one can gain a complete and deep understanding of the most important Islamic theological issues and eliminate many of their theological problems.

From another perspective, this sermon serves the same purpose as Surah al-Fātiḥah does in the Quran: it is a concise summary of the rest of the contents that are laid out after it. Sermon No. 1, therefore, presents a quick outline of what is explained in detail in the other sermons, the letters, and the aphorisms in the Nahj al-Balāghah.

We have divided this sermon into fifteen parts and have presented commentaries on each section differently. At the end of part fifteen, we have summed up all of the discussions on different parts of the sermon in a section called the conclusion.

Part One
Sermon No.1

اَلْحَمْدُ للهِ الَّذِي لاَيَبْلُغُ مِدْحَتَهُ الْقَائِلُونَ وَلاَ يُحْصِي نَعْمَاءَهُ الْعَادُّونَ وَلاَ
يُؤَدِّي حَقَّهُ الْمُجْتَهِدُونَ. اَلَّذِي لاَ يُدْرِكُهُ بُعْدُ الْهِمَمِ وَلاَيَنَالُهُ غَوْصُ الْفِطَنِ،
اَلَّذِي لَيْسَ لِصِفَتِهِ حَدٌّ مَحْدُودٌ، وَلاَ نَعْتٌ مَوْجُودٌ، وَلاَ وَقْتٌ مَعْدُودٌ، وَلاَ اَجَلٌ
مَمْدُودٌ، فَطَرَالْخَلَائِقَ بِقُدْرَتِهِ وَنَشَرَالرِّيَاحَ بِرَحْمَتِهِ وَوَتَّدَ بِالصُّخُورِ مَيَدَانَ أَرْضِهِ

"All praise belongs to Allah, whose true praise is far beyond the reach of those who seek to praise Him, and whose blessings the [most skilled of] reckoners are unable to reckon. Never will [even] the most avid seekers find a way to give Him thanks the way He truly deserves. [He is the Lord] whose Essence the most powerful of intellects are unable to comprehend and the keenest minds that try to delve [into the ocean of sciences] are unable to perceive. There are no boundaries to limit His Attributes, there is no description that can capture His Characteristics, and there is no beginning or end for His sacred Existence. He created all the created beings and things by His Power, He made the winds blow and spread by His Grace, and He stopped the tremor and turbulence of the earth by means of the mountains."

Commentary [Part One]

One Whose Essence is Unperceivable Even by the Most Powerful of Intellects

A quick glance at this part of sermon No. 1 shows that Imam Amīr al-Mu'minīn ('a) chose to present a discussion of twelve Attributes of Allah in a most beautiful and coherent manner in it.

He first explains how people are unable to praise and thank Allah, both in thoughts and in practice, the way that is worthy of Him [and he has also discussed three Attributes of Allah here]; then he explains the fact that even the most powerful intellects among human beings are incapable of perceiving Allah's greatness and His Divine Essence [and he has discussed two other Attributes of Allah here].

He then discusses the fact that Allah's sacred Essence is limitless in all respects and, as such, His blessings and bounties are also unbounded. This is, in fact, why we are unable to comprehend His Essence or give Him thanks for His blessings the way He truly deserves [the Imam ('a) has described four other Attributes of Allah here].

Finally, the Imam ('a) goes back to the discussion of the created world and all that has been created in it by Allah. It seems that this way he meant to imply that Allah and His sacred Essence can only be perceived through what He has created and this is the ultimate amount of understanding that we can aspire to achieve regarding Him [here, the Imam ('a) has referred to three of the Attributes of Divine Acts].

The extremely organized and coherent structure of this sermon clearly indicates that this great teacher of mankind had a special purpose in selecting these sublime teachings and that he arranged them purposefully in this way.

Given this brief introduction, let us go back to the twelve Divine Attributes discussed in this part of the sermon.

Imam Ali ('a) begins his sermon with the praise of Allah and, at the very beginning of his sermon, he expresses his inability to give Allah the praise He truly deserves:

اَلْحَمْدُ للهِ الَّذِي لاَ يَبْلُغُ مِدْحَتَهُ الْقَائِلُونَ[1]

"All praise belongs to Allah whose true praise is far beyond the reach of those who seek to praise Him..."

This is because the Divine Attributes of Perfection and Beauty are boundless in nature. However, the praises that human beings and even angels offer Allah are proportionate to their own level of knowledge and understanding of Allah and are never even remotely as great as His sacred Attributes.

According to a famous Islamic Hadith, even the Prophet of Islam (ṣ) expressed his inability to understand and comprehend Allah the way that would be truly deserving of Him:

1. One thing that needs to be kept in mind is that although we have done our best to present an accurate translation of Imam Ali's words here, we are unable to capture the amazing multi-faceted nature of his words. This is partly because of the capabilities of the Arabic language and amazing lexicological features, and partly because of Imam Ali's exceptionally eloquent employment of the Arabic language. To make this issue clearer, consider the following:
There is much controversy among the Arabic lexicologists, Quranic exegeses, and the experts of Nahj al-Balāghah regarding the meaning of the Arabic terms "حمد", "مدح", and "شكر". Yet, the most widely-held view is that "حمد" is the kind of praise and thanks that is offered in return for any good deeds that are done intentionally and willingly. According to this view, "مدح" has a wider scope of meaning and it is a kind of gratitude that is expressed in return for the good deeds that are done both intentionally and unintentionally. Finally, "شكر" is the kind of thanks offered in appreciation of a blessing and bounty by the one who has received them to the one who has given them out.
[For more information on this subject, refer to Majma' al-Baḥrayn (vol. 3, p. 353), Lisān al-'Arab (vol. 3, p. 155), al-Mufradāt (p. 256), Sharḥ Ibn Meytham (vol. 1, p. 91), and the book Minhāj al-Barā'ah by al-Khū'ī (vol. 7, p. 55)
It is also noteworthy that some of the Quranic exegetes and Nahj al-Balāghah experts like Zamakhsharī (in his Quranic exegesis entitled al-Kashshāf, vol. 1, p. 8) and Ibn Abī al-Ḥadīd (in his commentary on the Nahj al-Balāghah, vol. 1, p. 58) have put forward a different view than the one presented above. These scholars believe that the terms "مدح" and "حمد" are synonymous and there is no meaning difference between them.
We, however, believe the first view to be more accurate].

ما عَرَفْناکَ حَقَّ مَعْرِفَتِکَ[1]

"Never have we comprehended You [O' Lord], a true and perfect comprehension of You!"

When the Prophet of Islam (ṣ), who is the greatest of all the Divinely-sent prophets, states such a thing, how can anyone else claim to have a better understanding of Allah?! And how can one claim to be able to praise Allah the way that is worth his while when one is unable to gain a complete understanding of Him?

Therefore, the best kind of praise that we can offer to Allah is the one taught by Imam Amīr al-Mu'minīn ('a), i.e. to express our inability to praise Him the way that he truly deserves and also the fact that no one among His created beings can ever offer Him the kind of praise that is truly worthy of Him.

With regard to this issue, Imam al-Ṣādiq ('a) has been narrated to have said:

"Once Allah revealed to Moses ('a): "O' Moses! Thank Me the way that is Worthy of Me!"

Moses ('a) said, "O' Lord! How can I ever thank You the way that You truly deserve seeing as even my giving thanks to You is itself another bounty given to me by Yourself [as it is You who grant me the opportunity to thank You, making it yet another bounty from You, a bounty which itself needs to be appreciated and thanked]?!!"

Allah replied, "O' Moses! Now you have thanked me properly, for now you understand that even your thanking me is another blessing from Me [and that you are unable to give thanks for it].""[2]

It should be noted, however, that according to Islamic teachings when

1. The Late 'Allāmah al-Majlisī has related this Hadith from the Prophet of Allah (ṣ) without discussing its Isnād amid one of his lengthy discussions in his book Biḥār al-Anwār. He has related this Hadith while explaining some of the related Hadiths in his book and while discussing some related remarks by al-Muḥaqqiq al-Ṭūsī. According to him, the Prophet of Allah (ṣ) once prayed to Allah: "«ما عَبَدْناکَ حَقَّ عِبادَتِکَ وَما عَرَفْناکَ حَقَّ مَعْرِفَتِکَ»" [Biḥār al-Anwār, vol. 68, p. 23].

2. Al-Kāfī, vol. 2, Bāb al-Shukr, p. 98, hadith No. 27.

one offers his praises to Allah, stating "الحمد لله" [All praise be to Allah], one has offered all sorts and levels of praise to Allah as this is a comprehensive phrase which makes all the praises that exist exclusive to Allah.

This fact has been reflected in the following Islamic Hadith as well. According to this Hadith, once Imam al-Ṣādiq ('a) left the mosque, only to find that his horse was missing; the Imam ('a) said, "If Allah returns my horse to me, I shall thank Him the way that is worthy of Him!" Before long, the Imam's horse was found and brought back to him, and when the Imam ('a) had finally found his horse, he said, "الحمد لله".

One of his companions asked, "May I be sacrificed for you[1]! Did you not say that if your mount was found, you would thank Allah the way that is truly deserving of Him?! [This person thought that merely saying "الحمد لله" was not enough]".

The Imam ('a) said, "Did you not hear that I said "الحمد لله"?! [Meaning that there is no praise and thanks greater than stating "الحمد لله" as it means "All praise and thanks be to Allah"]".[2]

Imam Ali ('a) then proceeds with his sermon, describing Allah as follows:

وَلا يُحْصِي نَعْمَاءَهُ الْعَادُّونَ

"... and whose blessings the [most skilled of] reckoners are unable to reckon."

This is clearly because Allah grants so many material, spiritual, esoteric, exoteric, individual and collective blessings and bounties on each and every one of us throughout our lives that they are virtually impossible to count.

1. This phrase along with some others like it were used by the companions of the Infallible Imams ('a) to show their utmost respect and veneration for them.

2. Al-Kāfī, vol. 2, Bāb al-Shukr, p. 97, hadith No. 18.

On average, our bodies consist of approximately 37.2 trillion living cells, each of which is a living organism in its own right, each with their own complex structure and function. This makes each of these cells a blessing from Allah and giving thanks for 37.2 trillion blessings is something that cannot be accomplished in several thousand years!

Let us bear in mind that this is only one of the countless categories of the blessings bestowed upon us by Allah, and since we are unable to give thanks to Him even for this single category of His blessings, how can we ever hope to thank Him enough for His other innumerable material and spiritual bounties?!

Another problem that we have is that we are basically not aware of most of Allah's blessings at all to be able to count them and appreciate Him for them. There are some blessings which have embraced us from all directions and since we are never deprived of them, we do not even notice that they are there [because mankind usually recognizes the existence of a blessing when he is deprived of it].

Additionally, as we progress in science, we discover more of Allah's blessings on us, blessings which we were completely unaware of in the past. Considering all of these facts, we have but to admit that, as Imam Amīr al-Mu'minīn ('a) has mentioned, even if all the reckoners of the world work together, they will be unable to reckon the countless blessings of Allah.

This sentence is, in fact, explaining the reason behind what was mentioned in the preceding sentence; that is to say, since it is impossible to count Allah's blessings, how can one thank Him properly for them?!

It might be argued that Allah's blessings on us do not seem to be so many, as some ignorant and wrongdoing individuals have usurped some of His blessings, keeping them for their own exclusive use or spoiling them through extravagance and overindulgence. This might be true, but it does not mean that Allah's bounties and blessings are limited; it only means that some have wrongfully tried to cut other people's access to them.

Imam Ali ('a) then continues his sermon, presenting yet another description regarding Allah:

وَلا يُؤَدِّي حَقَّهُ الْمُجْتَهِدُونَ

"Never will [even] the most avid seekers find a way to give Him thanks the way He truly deserves."

This sentence is, in effect, a conclusion drawn based on the preceding sentences; it indicates that since we are all unable to reckon Allah's countless blessings, we are naturally unable to give Him thanks the way that is truly worthy of Him.

In other words, in order for gratitude to be worthy of Allah, it needs to be proportionate to His immense and unbounding Essence; this is while our expressions of gratitude toward Him are proportionate to our awfully limited existence! Clearly, such expressions of gratitude that are so insignificant cannot be worthy of such an immense and unlimited Being.

What is more is that, not only are we unable to practically praise and thank Allah the way that He truly deserves, we are even unable to comprehend His immense Essence in thought and even imagination! This is exactly what Imam Ali ('a) mentioned, as he presented two other descriptions of the Attributes of Allah:

اَلَّذي لا يُدْرِكُهُ بُعْدُ الْهِمَمِ وَلا يَنالُهُ غَوْصُ الْفِطَنِ[1]

"[He is the Lord] whose Essence the most powerful of intellects are unable to comprehend and the keenest minds that try to plunge [deep in the ocean of sciences] are unable to perceive."

A part of this sentence by the Imam ('a) which is extremely interesting in exposition is the phrase "بُعْدُ الْهِمَمِ وَغَوْصُ الْفِطَنِ"; it appears that by this phrase the Imam ('a) meant to say that if powerful thoughts try to go around the immense Essence of Allah in one direction while the powerful intelligences try to encircle it in another direction [hence to encompass it in knowledge], they will forever be unable to encompass it.

The Imam ('a) then continues his sermon, explaining the reason why mankind is unable to comprehend the Essence of Allah. He states the following in this regard:

1. The Arabic term "همم" used in this sentence is the plural of the word "همت", whose original meaning, according to the Arabic Dictionary Maqāyīs al-Lughah, is "melting and flowing". This is why grief is called "همّ"in Arabic as it melts away one's mind, body, and soul. This word along with its other derivatives are also used to refer to any undertaking that is of importance, or anything that preoccupies one, or stirs them into action [The same view about this word has also been put forward in the book al-Mufradāt].
Another noteworthy word in this sentence is the term "غوص", which originally means "to plunge underwater". It has also been used in the Arabic language to refer to the act of embarking on important ventures. Finally, the word "فطنه", according to the Lisān al-'Arab Dictionary, means acute intelligence and lively wit.

الَّذي لَيْسَ لِصِفَتِهِ حَدٌّ مَحْدودٌ، وَلا نَعْتٌ[1] مَوْجُودٌ، وَلا وَقْتٌ مَعْدودٌ وَلا اَجَلٌ[2] مَمْدودٌ

"Neither are there any boundaries that could limit His Attributes, nor any descriptions that could capture His Characteristics, nor a beginning or an end for His sacred Existence."

Here, the Imam ('a) has explained that the reason why we are and forever will be unable to comprehend the sacred Essence of Allah is that His Divine Essence is limitless in all respects while our entire existence, including the reach of our thoughts, is limited to certain boundaries.

So how can we, who only comprehend things within a certain time/space limit, understand the unlimited Essence and the boundless Attributes of Allah that encompass all that there is from when there was no time up to the abyss of eternity?!

How can human beings, who suffer all sorts of limitations, and who have a beginning and an end, and who only understand descriptions which fall within the scope of time and place, come to comprehend things which neither have any limitations nor can be described using means of time and space and nor do they have a beginning or an end?!

But this infiniteness is not solely a characteristic of Allah's Divine Essence; rather, His Knowledge and Power are also boundless because His Divine Knowledge and Power are not separate from His Divine Essence. In other words, Allah is pure existence and His existence is not conditional upon anything nor does it have any limitations of any kind.

This is because if there were conditions to Allah's existence or if it had any limitations, then His Existence would have been compound in nature and, as we all know, any compound thing is necessarily a created existence, not self-existent [because it is necessarily made up of two other

1. The original meaning of the Arabic word "نَعت", according to the famous Arabic lexicologist, Khalīl ibn Aḥmad, is "to describe something with positive and good descriptions" [therefore it is different from ordinary description that is used for both good and bad things and concepts].

2. The Arabic term "اجل" means the end of something's term or the time when something is due. Therefore, it can be used for man's life to refer to the end of a person's life or for when a check or some debt is due to be paid.

elements which existed before it and were later mixed to create it]. Therefore, a self-existent Being [also known as a "Necessary Being"] enjoys an Essence that is unlimited in every way, and this is why the self-existent Being is One and Unique without anyone or anything like Him. In fact, it is impossible for more than one unlimited beings to exist together because the very fact of two of such beings existing together poses limitations on their existence. This is because each of the two does not enjoy the existence of the other and, evidently, not having something is by definition an instance of limitation.

Up until this point, this sermon by Imam Ali ('a) has discussed some of the Divine Attributes of Beauty and Glory [i.e. the Affirmative Attributes and the Negating Attributes]. Following the discussion of these concepts, Imam Ali ('a) then makes reference to the Attributes of Divine Acts, stating:

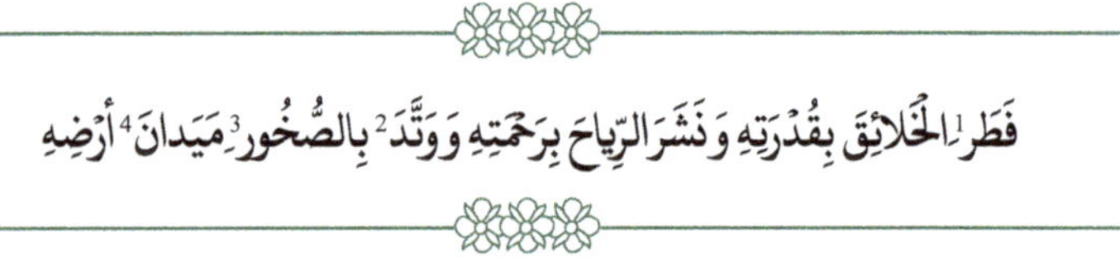

فَطَرَ[1] الْخَلَائِقَ بِقُدْرَتِهِ وَنَشَرَ الرِّيَاحَ بِرَحْمَتِهِ وَوَتَّدَ[2] بِالصُّخُورِ[3] مَيَدَانَ[4] أَرْضِهِ

"He created all the created things by His Power, He made the winds blow and spread by His Grace, and He stopped the tremor and turbulence of the earth by means of the mountains."

1. The Arabic term "فطر" [pronounced "Faṭara"] has been derived from the root word "فطر" [pronounced "Faṭr"]. According to al-Rāghib and his book al-Mufradāt, it originally means "to rend apart" and this is why breaking the fast is called "افطار" in Arabic, as if eating something after a day's fasting is like rending the state of fasting apart. This word has also been used to mean "creating", as if the act of creation rends apart the veils of nothingness, allowing something to come into existence.

2. The Arabic term "وتّد" [pronounced "Wattada"] is a derivative of the root word "وتد" [pronounced "Watd"] originally means "to fix something firmly in place". This is why the "nails" that are driven into things like chairs to fix their structure are called "وتد" [pronounced "Watad" or "Watd"] in Arabic.

3. The term "صخور" is the plural of the word "صخره" which, according to the Lisān al-'Arab Dictionary, means "huge and hard rock".

4. The Arabic word "ميدان" [pronounced "Mayadān"] has been derived from the root word "ميد" [pronounced "Mayd"] and it means "agitation and turbulence". Moreover, the term "ميدان" [pronounced "Maydān"] means a vast expanse of land and its plural is "ميادين".

Each of the phrases used in this part of the sermon is related to one or more verses of the Quran with similar contents. For instance, the phrase "فَطَرَالْخَلَائِقَ بِقُدْرَتِهِ" derives its concepts from the following Quranic phrase which has been used in various Surahs:

فَاطِرِ السَّمَاوَاتِ وَالْأَرْضِ

"... Allah, Originator of the heavens and the earth..."[1]

Moreover, the phrase "نَشَرَ الرِّياحَ بِرَحْمَتِهِ" derives its concepts and teachings from the following verse in the Quran:

وَهُوَ الَّذِى يُرْسِلُ الرِّياحَ بُشْرًا بَيْنَ يَدَىْ رَحْمَتِهِ

"And it is He who sends forth the winds as heralds of glad tidings before His Bounty [i.e. rain]..."[2]

Finally, the third sentence of this part of the sermon derives its contents from the following verse of the Quran:

وَأَلْقَى فِي الْأَرْضِ رَوَاسِىَ اَنْ تَمِيدَ بِكُمْ

"And He cast firm mountains in the earth, lest it should quack with you ..."[3]

---

1. Yūsuf, 101; Ibrāhīm, 10; Fāṭir, 1.
2. Al-A'rāf, 57.
3. Al-Naḥl, 15.

Considering the meanings of the word "فطر", Imam Ali ('a) likens the act of creation to ripping the veil of nothingness, a barrier that had been hard and firm and without any holes and cracks. Yet, the infinite Power of Allah rips it asunder, creating various creatures that did not exist out of nothing, an act which is possible only for the Omnipotent Allah.

Today, modern scientists unanimously believe that it is impossible for us to create something from nothing, or to send something that exists back into nothingness; the only thing that we can do, according to them, is to transform the various existing things into each other or other forms.

The Imam ('a) also refers to the blowing of the winds here as something caused by the Divine Grace. This is a rather charming and subtle way of referring to the various benefits of winds, including the fact that they help the ships to course toward their destinations, drive rainclouds toward dry lands, help with the pollination of plants, and soften the temperature of the various regions by moving the air there.

But as for how the mountains prevent the earth from quaking severely and destroying all that exists on it, the past scientists who believed that the earth was static had presented some ideas regarding this issue which have been refuted by modern sciences. Recently, however, more acceptable interpretations have been put forward regarding this issue which are both consistent with the hard scientific facts as well as with the Quran and the related Islamic traditions. Some of these interpretations are as follows:

1. The existence of mountains on the surface of the earth decreases the effects of the moon's gravity on the rise and fall of tides on the earth, hence, preventing the ocean and sea waters from rising too high to the lands and making the earth uninhabitable.

2. The mountains have roots which go deep into the earth's crust and their roots are all connected, forming a unified structure which holds the earth's core in place, preventing the high pressure caused by the superhot core and the gases which exist there from disturbing the earth's surface. If it had not been for this protective sphere underneath the earth's surface, the superhot lava and gases lying deep within the earth would have agitated the earth's crust to the point where it would have become virtually uninhabitable. Even with the existence of the

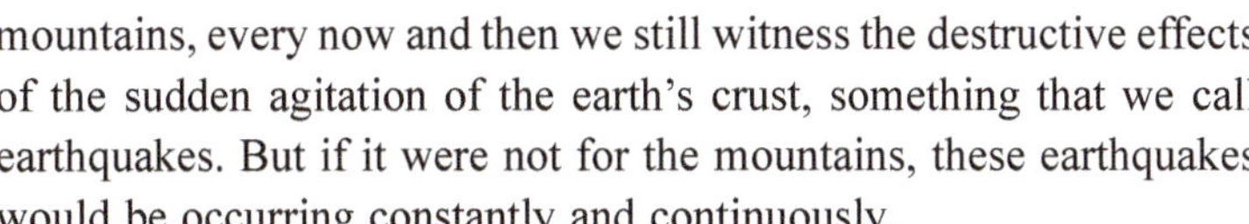

mountains, every now and then we still witness the destructive effects of the sudden agitation of the earth's crust, something that we call earthquakes. But if it were not for the mountains, these earthquakes would be occurring constantly and continuously.

3. The high mountains on the surface of the earth create the necessary friction with the air in the earth's atmosphere, allowing it to smoothly rotate together with the earth as the earth rotates fast around its axis. If the surface of the earth were completely flat and without the ups and downs of the mountains, the fast rotation of the earth around its axis would create horrendous storms. This would have been due to the absence of the necessary friction between the earth's atmosphere and its surface, causing the air in the atmosphere to move very fast over its surface creating huge storms. Such storms would, on the one hand, destroy everything on the earth's surface and, on the other, would cause the temperature on the earth's surface to rise to levels which would render it virtually uninhabitable.

This is, in fact, how the mountains [صخور] have curbed the turbulence and agitation [ميَدَان] of the earth; but this is not the only function of the mountains. They also function as great freshwater reserves for mankind and they keep supplying us with the water we need through springs and creeks which gush forth from them, allowing the underground water to emerge on the surface of the earth.

Given these vital roles of winds and mountains in supporting all sorts of life, including human life, on earth, it becomes clear why Imam Ali ('a) chose to especially focus on them and emphasize their important functions immediately after discussing the issue of the creation of the cosmos.

Part Two
Sermon No.1

اَوَّلُ الدِّينِ مَعْرِفَتُهُ وَكَمَالُ مَعْرِفَتِهِ التَّصْدِيقُ بِهِ وَكَمَالُ التَّصْدِيقِ بِهِ تَوْحِيدُهُ
وَكَمَالُ تَوْحِيدِهِ الْإِخْلَاصُ لَهُ وَكَمَالُ الْإِخْلَاصِ لَهُ نَفْيُ الصِّفَاتِ عَنْهُ لِشَهَادَةٍ كُلِّ
صِفَةٍ أَنَّها غَيْرُ الْمَوْصُوفِ وَشَهَادَةِ كُلِّ مَوْصُوفٍ أَنَّهُ غَيْرُ الصِّفَةِ فَمَنْ وَصَفَ
اللهَ سُبْحانَهُ فَقَدْ قَرَنَهُ وَمَنْ قَرَنَهُ فَقَدْ ثَنّاهُ وَمَنْ ثَنّاهُ فَقَدْ جَزَّأَهُ وَمَنْ جَزَّأَهُ فَقَدْ
جَهِلَهُ وَمَنْ جَهِلَهُ فَقَدْ اَشارَ اِلَيْهِ وَمَنْ اَشارَ اِلَيْهِ فَقَدْ حَدَّهُ وَمَنْ حَدَّهُ فَقَدْ عَدَّهُ

"The foremost in religion is [gaining] knowledge of Allah; the highest level of knowing Him is [that which brings one] to recognize Him; the greatest form of recognizing Him is having faith in His Oneness; the most unshakeable faith in His Oneness is the one that entails sincerity in devoting oneself to Him, and the sincerest devotion to Him is to negate the attributes of the created beings in regard to Him. This is because any attribute [of the created beings] is essentially distinct from what it is associated with and anything [among the created beings] that is associated with these attributes is essentially distinct from the attribute ascribed to it.

Thus, anyone who attaches the attributes [of the created beings] to Allah the Almighty has equated Him with something else, and whoever equates Allah with something else has regarded Him as two. And whoever regards Him as two has recognized parts for Him, and whoever recognizes parts for Him has, indeed, failed to know Him, and whoever fails to know Him will point at Him, and whoever points at Him has regarded Him as limited. And whoever regards Him as limited has regarded Him as numerable [and whoever considers Allah numerable has strayed far into polytheism!]"

Commentary [Part Two]

The Unity of Divine Essence and Attributes

The second part of this sermon is veritably a complete and comprehensive course in Islamic theology. Here, Imam Amīr al-Mu'minīn ('a) offers, in a few succinct yet profound sentences, such accurate knowledge of Allah that nothing more accurate than it can be imagined as far as knowing Allah is concerned. If we were to compile all of the lessons ever taught in Islamic theology in a book, they would not offer anything more than what the Imam ('a) states here.

Imam Ali ('a) has mentioned five stages of the knowledge of Allah which can be summarized as follows:

Stage one: gaining a general and incomplete knowledge of Allah;

Stage two: gaining a more detailed and comprehensive knowledge of Allah;

Stage three: having faith in the Unity of Allah's Essence and Attributes;

Stage four: attaining the sublime quality of sincerity in devoting oneself to Allah;

Stage five: negating the act of equating the attributes of the created beings with the Divine Attributes of Allah.

Imam Ali ('a) begins this part of his speech by referring to the first stage of recognizing Allah:

أَوَّلُ الدِّينِ مَعْرِفَتُهُ

"The foremost in religion is [gaining] knowledge of Allah."

Undoubtedly, what is meant here by "religion" is the whole body of monotheistic convictions, Divinely-legislated duties, acts of worship, and moral principles; clearly, then, what is of primary important among all of these is gaining knowledge of Allah, as it is the foundation for all other religious beliefs and duties.

That is to say, not only is gaining knowledge of Allah the first stage of religious belief, it forms the basis and foundation for all of the basic articles of faith and its secondary rules and laws; in fact, without this essential first step, the tree of religion would yield no fruit at all.

It is noteworthy that some have mistakenly assumed that there is another thing which is even more important than gaining knowledge of Allah, i.e. to do research about religion. This, however, is a big mistake because the necessity of doing research about religion is the first and the most essential obligatory duty of every human being, while gaining knowledge of Allah is the foundation of religion itself.

In other words, research about religion is the first step toward embracing it, and gaining knowledge of Allah is the first and most important stage of this step.[1] Needless to say, the general knowledge regarding the existence of Allah has been bestowed within man's very nature. This is an innate type of knowledge which does not need to be given to anyone as it already exists in human nature.

The mission of the Divinely-sent prophets, on the other hand, has been to complete this very general and incomplete knowledge of Allah, giving mankind a complete and comprehensive knowledge of Allah. Their other task was also to help mankind to develop their knowledge of Allah as much as they could and to eradicate the baseless and polytheistic ideas that might spring up every now and then around the concept of the Creator.

The Imam ('a) then attends to the discussion of the second stage of recognizing Allah, stating:

---

1. In his commentary on the Nahj al-Balāghah entitled Fī Ẓilāl-i Nahj al-Balāghah [vol. 1, p. 22], the renowned Muslim scholar, Mughnīyah, has defined religion as absolute obedience to Allah's orders and total submission to the laws laid down by Him, through which He has declared some things prohibited and some other things obligatory to do. Before him, al-Shāriḥ al-Khū'ī had put forward a similar definition of religion in his book Minhāj al-Barā'ah [vol. 1, p. 319].

It should be noted, however, that if this definition of theirs includes submission to Allah both in ideology and in practice, this is considered a correct definition of the religion, and if by this definition they only meant to refer to submission to Allah "in practice" [and not in conviction], then their views are also liable to the criticism mentioned above.

وَكَمالُ مَعْرِفَتِهِ التَّصديقُ بِهِ

"... the highest level of knowing Him is [that which brings one] to recognize Him..."

There are various views on what the difference between "knowing" and "recognizing" Allah is. Some believe that "knowledge of Allah" refers to the innate recognition of the existence of Allah while "recognizing Allah" is realized through scientific research and logical arguments which prove His existence. Another view holds that "knowledge of Allah" is a very general and incomplete understanding of Allah while "recognizing Allah" is the complete and detailed knowledge of Him. According to a third view, "knowledge of Allah" only includes awareness of the existence of Allah, while "recognition of Allah" is a reference made to a heartfelt faith in Him. The proponents of this view have argued that knowledge is essentially different and distinct from faith, and that it is possible for one to be certain of the existence of Allah without having heartfelt faith in Him. Therefore, faith is defined as recognition of Allah in one's heart and total submission to Him.

In order to clarify this distinction, sometimes the great theologians put forward the following simple example: there are some people who are terrified to stay by the side of a dead body alone in a dark room at night. These individuals know for certain that it is merely a corpse and that it can do them no harm; however, it seems that this knowledge has not penetrated their hearts to turn into firm faith, and it is this lack of faith that is the source of their fear.

In other words, even though "knowledge" is the certain awareness of the existence or absence of something, it can be a superficial sort of awareness which has not penetrated deep in one's heart and soul. Nevertheless, when the same "knowledge" finds its way into the human heart and soul and turns into "conviction", it is said that one has "recognized" that knowledge, and it is called "faith" from that point on.

Following the discussion of this stage, Imam Ali ('a) refers to the third state of recognizing Allah, stating:

وَكَمالُ التَّصْدِيقِ بِهِ تَوْحِيدُهُ

"... and the greatest form of recognizing Him is having faith in His Oneness."

Undoubtedly, acquiring detailed and comprehensive knowledge of Allah through research and logical reasoning and arguments does not necessarily mean that one has also acquired an unshakeable faith in Allah's Oneness, something that is referred to in Islamic theology as Tawḥīd. Perfect Tawḥīd is realized only when one rejects, from the bottom of their heart, the association of any equals with Allah.

This is because anyone who considers equals for Allah has not understood the nature of Allah at all, or what they have presumably learned about has not been Allah. Allah is an unlimited Being in every respect, which renders Him without need of anyone or anything.

Anything that has equals would naturally be limited, because two beings that are equal are necessarily distinct and separate from one another [because they are recognized as two entities and not a single one, so they must be necessarily distinct from one another in nature]. In order for any two entities to be recognized as two separate things or beings, each must necessarily have attributes which the other one lacks, and this, by definition, is limitation and deficiency.

Allah the Almighty, as we all know, is high above any limitation or deficiency, so there can logically exist no equals for Him. This is why, when one's knowledge and recognition of His Divine Essence reaches its highest point, one must necessarily recognize Him as One and Only, not in a numerical sense, but in the sense of being Unique and without any likes or equals.

The Imam ('a) then discusses the fourth stage, which is that of sincerity in devoting oneself to Allah:

وَكَمالُ تَوْحيدِهِ الْأِخْلاصُ لَهُ

"... and the most unshakeable faith in His Oneness is the one that entails sincerity in devoting oneself to Him."

The Arabic term "اخلاص" ["Ikhlāṣ" meaning "sincerity"] derives from the root word "خلوص" ["khulūṣ"], which originally means to "purify" or "refine" something from any impurities. As for whether the term "sincerity" used in this part of this sermon, there is much controversy among the commentators of the Nahj al-Balāghah as to whether it is in reference to sincerity in deeds, in convictions, or the sincerity of the heart.

What is meant by sincerity in deeds is that when one reaches the highest level of faith in the Oneness of Allah [i.e. Tawḥīd], they will exclusively worship Him and they will do everything only for the sake of Allah. This is the kind of sincerity which the Muslim jurists have particularly emphasized as an essential component of all acts of worship. This specific viewpoint has been related by "The Commentator al-Khū'ī" in his commentary on the Nahj al-Balāghah as one of the views put forward by the past scholars on the meaning of the term "sincerity" in this phrase; however, he has not made any mention of who these scholars had been.[1]

However, it seems rather unlikely for this view to be the correct one, because all of the previous sentences in this sermon are about ideological issues; therefore, it is safe to conclude that this sentence too concerns convictions and beliefs.

Another prominent scholar, "The Commentator al-Baḥrānī", believes that the term sincerity here refers to the sincerity of the heart, or what he termed as "true asceticism". This is a state where one's heart is exclusively attracted to Allah and is oblivious of all besides Him.[2]

1. Al-Khū'ī, Minhāj al-Barā'ah, vol. 1, p. 321. According to al-Shāriḥ al-Khū'ī, Ṣadr al-Dīn al-Shīrāzī has also put forward the same view in his commentary on the book al-Kāfī [vol. 4, p. 13].

2. Sharḥ Nahj al-Balāghah ibn Meytham, vol. 1, p. 122.

Although this is also a rather lofty spiritual quality, it is inconsistent with the context of this sermon, hence it is rather unlikely that what is meant here by "sincerity" be the sincerity of the heart.
Thus, the only interpretation that is consistent with the contents of this sermon is the one that holds "sincerity" to be in reference to sincerity in faith and conviction. This means that one who is sincere in his faith in Allah necessarily regards Him as One and Only, Unique and without any likes or equals, and rejects the idea of the existence of any distinct parts or components in His Pure Essence.
This fact has also been implied in the fifth stage by Imam Ali ('a):

وَكَمالُ الأخْلاصِ لَهُ نَفْيُ الصِّفاتِ عَنْهُ

"... and the sincerest devotion to Him is to negate any attributes of the created beings that are ascribed to Him."

The sort of sincerity that was discussed in the previous stage was general and incomplete in nature; this stage, however, concerns sincerity in its perfect and comprehensive form. In other words, Imam Ali ('a) explains here that in order for one's sincerity to reach its highest and most complete form, one needs to negate, from the bottom of the heart, any attributes of the created things and beings that some might presume to associate with Allah, whether these attributes ascribe components and parts to Allah or to anything else.
This is because all of the created things and beings, even non-physical things such as intellect and metaphysical beings, are compound in nature [meaning that they are made up of or consist of two or more elements or parts]. Thus, the metaphysical beings are compound [meaning that, logically speaking, they can be thought to have two or more components] and physical beings and things are made up of various physical parts which not only can be thought of, but they can actually be broken down to their constituents in the real world.
Yet, the Divine Essence of Allah neither has any physical parts nor any parts can be logically imagined for Him; in other words, neither

can his Divine Essence be broken down into other constituents in the real world, nor our intellects can imagine any parts for Him. So far as one has not correctly recognized this fact about Allah, one has not achieved true and pure Tawḥīd, i.e. the faith in the Oneness of Allah. Considering the discussion presented above, it becomes clear why the Imam (‘a) stated “the sincerest devotion to Him is to negate any attributes [of the created beings] that are ascribed to Him”. It should be noted that this is not a rejection of the Divine Attributes of Perfection, because all of the Perfect Attributes, including Knowledge, Power, and Livingness, belong to Allah.

Rather, what is rejected here is the kinds of attributes that we are used to and know in our physical world, i.e. the qualities and attributes of the created beings and things which are all, by nature, deficient and imperfect. Of course, the created beings also possess knowledge, power, etc. Yet, their knowledge and power are limited and deficient, meaning that their knowledge is always accompanied by lack of knowledge in different forms, and their power is always accompanied by weakness in some respects.

This is while the Divine Essence of Allah is far above such imperfect knowledge and power. A piece of evidence regarding this fact comes from another remark made by Imam Ali (‘a) in this same sermon regarding the Angels:

لا يَتَوَهَّمُونَ رَبَّهُمْ بِالتَّصْوِيرِ وَلا يُجْرُونَ عَلَيْهِ صِفَاتِ الْمَصْنُوعِينَ

“They never [try to] imagine an image of their Lord, and they never attach to Him the attributes of the created beings.”

Additionally, the qualities and attributes of the created beings are always detached from their essences; that is to say, they enjoy certain attributes in addition to their essences. For instance, human being is one thing but his knowledge and power are something else entirely; therefore, man’s essence is compound in nature as it is made up of these two components. This is while Allah’s Attributes and His Divine Essence are one and the same and there is no duality or multiplicity in Him.

In fact, one of the greatest pitfalls and dangers on the path toward gaining knowledge of Allah and toward a correct faith in His Oneness is "analogy", i.e. trying to compare Allah's Perfect Attributes with the qualities and attributes of the created beings which are mixed with all sorts of limitations and deficiencies. Another pitfall on this path is to believe in the existence of Divine Attributes which are distinct from the Divine Essence, a grave mistake made by the Ash'arites [a Muslim school of thought].[1]

It is due to this danger that the Imam ('a) specifically focuses on this problem and explains it in more detail in the next sentence:

لِشَهادَةِ كُلِّ صِفَةٍ أَنَّها غَيْرُ الْمَوْصُوفِ وَشَهادَةِ كُلِّ مَوْصُوفٍ أَنَّهُ غَيْرُ الصِّفَةِ

"This is because any attribute [of the created beings] is evidently distinct from what it is associated with and anything [among the created beings] that is associated with these attributes is evidently distinct from the attribute ascribed to it."

That is to say, the fact that the attributes that exist in addition to their essences are distinct from them is self-evident. The only view which is in line with Tawḥīd is the one that holds the Divine Essence and the Divine Attributes to be essentially the same thing. That is to say, the correct belief is that Allah's Essence is entirely Knowledge, Power,

1. The Ash'arites are the followers of Abū al-Ḥasan al-Ash'arī; they believe in "concepts", i.e. that concepts such as the Divine Attributes of Knowledge, Sovereignty, etc. are pre-eternal and without beginning, very much like Allah's Essence. Yet, they believe that in spite of this common point between the Divine Essence and Attributes, the Attributes are distinct from the Divine Essence. In other words, they believe in the existence of multiple pre-eternal entities, something that is undoubtedly inconsistent with pure Tawḥīd. This is why the followers of the School of the Ahl-al-Bayt ('a) have rejected the idea of "concepts" based on the teachings that they have received from the Ahl-al-Bayt ('a), including this sermon from Imam Ali ('a). This is because the theory of "concepts" holds that Divine Attributes are separate from Divine Essence, something that has been rejected by the Ahl al-Bayt ('a) through sentences such as "He is without any equals and exalted far above concepts".

Life, and an Eternal Essence that is without beginning or end; this is the only belief which is in line with Tawḥīd, though it might be difficult for us to understand. This difficulty in understanding the Divine Attributes is because we are used only to the qualities and attributes of the created things and beings around us; hence, our mindset is to regard our own essence, for example, as one thing and our knowledge and power as distinct attributes which have been added to us. Clearly, when we are born into this world, we have neither any knowledge nor any power, and we acquire them both in the course of our lives.
The Imam ('a) then proceeds to complete his discussion in this section, using some rather succinct yet profound sentences:

فَمَنْ وَصَفَ اللّهَ سُبْحانَهُ فَقَدْ قَرَنَهُ وَمَنْ قَرَنَهُ
فَقَدْ ثَنّاهُ وَمَنْ ثَنّاهُ فَقَدْ جَزَّأَهُ وَمَنْ جَزَّأَهُ فَقَدْ جَهِلَهُ

"As such, anyone who attaches the attributes [of the created beings] to Allah the Almighty has equated Him with something else, and whoever equates Allah with something else has believed in the duality of His Essence. And whoever believes in the duality of His Essence has recognized parts for Him, and whoever recognizes parts for Him has, indeed, failed to know Him;"

These remarks by the Imam ('a) indicate that the logical outcome of attaching the attributes of the created beings to Allah is the belief that Allah's Essence is compound in nature. That is to say, just as man is a compound being, made up of completely distinct components, namely his essence and his attributes and qualities, likewise Allah is made up of two distinct components, i.e. His Essence and His Attributes.
This view, however, is in direct contradiction to the concept of Allah being self-existent [i.e. a Necessary Being]; this is because any compound being or thing is in need of its components and constituents to exist, and "need" [which is a sort of weakness as it indicates a lack of ability to exist by oneself] is in contrast to being self-existent.

This sentence by Imam Ali ('a) has also been interpreted in two other ways:

The first interpretation indicates that if Allah's Attributes are considered distinct from His Divine Essence, His Essence will also have to be regarded as compound in nature. If we assume Allah's Essence and Attributes to be two distinct things, it will entail that they have some points in common with each other and also some superiority over one another in some aspects. They will necessarily have something in common with one another, which is their "existence", and, at the same time, they are distinguished from one another because they are two distinct and different entities. Based on this view of Divine Attributes, Allah will be considered a compound being, made up of two distinct entities of Essence and Attributes [something that is logically impossible for a self-existent Being].

The other interpretation is that it is an established fact that the Unity and Oneness of Allah is not a numerical concept of "oneness"; rather, the concept of Allah's Oneness means that Allah has no likes or equals. Basically, an unlimited and infinite existence cannot have any likes or equals. Therefore, by regarding Allah's Attributes as a second category of "unlimited, infinite, and pre-eternal" entities which are distinct from Allah's Essence, one will have regarded Allah as limited and also they will have considered equals for Him.

The above-mentioned remarks of Imam Ali ('a) concerning "sincerity" are also in reference to the same issue. The Imam ('a) explained that anyone who ascribes the qualities and attributes of the created beings to Allah, has equated Him with other than Him, and by doing so, they will have regarded Him as a dual existence, consisting of the Essence and the Attributes.

The Imam ('a) then explains that believing in the duality of Divine Existence will entail considering Divine Essence as a compound entity which is composed of certain components and constituents. Finally, he states that those who believe that the sacred Essence of Allah is compound in nature and made up of smaller components, have failed to know Allah as they have merely imagined an imaginary being like themselves [i.e. a compound and limited being] and have named it Allah.

Imam Ali ('a) then goes on with his sermon, completing his discussion in this section by stating the following:

وَمَنْ جَهِلَهُ فَقَدْ أَشَارَ إِلَيْهِ وَمَنْ أَشَارَ إِلَيْهِ فَقَدْ حَدَّهُ وَمَنْ حَدَّهُ فَقَدْ عَدَّهُ

"... and whoever fails to known Him will point at Him, and whoever points at Him has regarded Him as limited. And whoever regards Him as limited has regarded Him as numerable [and whoever considers Allah numerable has strayed far into polytheism!]"

A question that might arise here concerns what the Imam ('a) meant by "pointing at Allah". There are two possibilities regarding this issue: first, what is meant here by "pointing at Allah" is forming a certain mental image of Allah, and the second possibility is that it concerns both forming a mental image of Allah and also identifying Him with physical and tangible qualities.

When one fails to recognize Allah exactly as He is, an unlimited and infinite reality, one will naturally carry on to form a certain mental image of Him that will naturally be limited, hence pointing at or referring to Him based on that wrong mental image. That is to say, when one fails to understand Allah as an unlimited existence, the only remaining sort of understanding about Him would be to regard Him as a limited being much like all the beings and things that man sees around him.

The reason behind the formation of such a wrong image of Allah in man's mind is that man is a limited being himself; therefore, he can only comprehend things that he can encompass in knowledge. However, since his knowledge is limited like himself, it will only be able to encompass things that are limited as it basically lacks the capacity to encompass unlimited beings and things. Consequently, any mental image that human beings form of Allah is, due to their own limited nature, bound to be limited.

But a problem that arises here is that once Allah is imagined in a limited fashion, He will be downgraded to the level of numerable things and beings, because the necessary condition for a being to be considered limited is the possibility of imagining another being like it in another place. It is only a being that is unlimited in every respect that cannot be imagined to have any likes or equals, and that is not numerable at all.

As it is clear by now, Imam Ali ('a) explained these issues which are, in fact, the reality of the belief in the Oneness of Allah, in a few succinct yet profound sentences, emphasizing how Allah is far above and beyond imaginations, analogies, and thoughts.

This profound understanding of Allah is what has also been presented in the following remarks made by Imam al-Bāqir ('a):

كُلُّ ما مَيَّزْتُمُوهُ بِأَوْهامِكُمْ فِي أَدَقِّ مَعانِيهِ مَخْلُوقٌ مَصْنُوعٌ مِثْلُكُمْ مَرْدُودٌ إِلَيْكُمْ

"Anything that you imagine or form in your thoughts, no matter how precise and exact you think it is, will still be a creation of yours and it goes back to yourselves [as it is a fabrication of your minds and is consistent with your own existence; but Allah is exalted far above being identified with anything related to His created beings.]"[1]

As it was discussed above, another possibility regarding this phrase in Imam Ali's sermon is that it concerns both forming a mental image of Allah and also identifying Him with physical and tangible qualities. This kind of attitude and the ignorance behind it has been the root cause of the emergence of ideologies which promote the belief in the anthropomorphism of Allah, i.e. the belief that Allah has a corporeal existence. Such baseless ideas are the results of viewing the Essence of Allah as limited, considering Him numerable, and ascribing likes or equals to Him.

A Question

A question that might arise at this point is that if it is impossible to make intellectual efforts in encompassing Allah's Essence in knowledge, then there will virtually remain no way to gain knowledge of

1. Biḥār al-Anwār, vol. 66, p. 293.

Him. So, how can mankind ever come to recognize Allah's existence? Every time that man tries to reach out to the knowledge of Allah, he would end up with an image and understanding of a creation of his own mind; hence, the harder he tries to know Allah, the farther away he will be driven from recognizing Him. So, is it not better to refrain from embarking on this journey altogether, forget about gaining knowledge of Allah, and prevent ourselves from falling prey to polytheism through such efforts?

Answer:

The answer to this question lies in a subtle point which is helpful both here and also in answering the other similar questions. The point which needs to be kept in mind here is that knowledge of Allah is divided into two distinct categories: first is the general knowledge and recognition of Allah, and the second is the detailed and extensive knowledge of Him. In other words, when one speaks of gaining knowledge of Allah, one might be speaking either about understanding the nature of Divine Essence or about recognizing the origin of Divine Acts, to use theological terms.

Simply put, when we look at the cosmos and the world around us and see so many amazing creatures and things created with such precision and yet so magnificently, we come to a general understanding that all of them must have been created by a Creator [as such precision does not come about accidentally]. This is the utmost level of knowledge that man can aspire to gain regarding Allah, though as he ventures further into the secrets of the cosmos and those of the creation, his general knowledge of the Creator's Power and Knowledge becomes deeper.

However, when we begin asking the questions "what is the nature of Allah?", "How is He?" and others like them, trying to reach out to gain knowledge of His Essence, we will end up with nothing but perplexity and confusion. This is because we, as awfully limited beings, cannot encompass in knowledge an unlimited and infinite Being, hence the confusing statement "the way toward [understanding] Allah is open, and yet it is closed!"

Let us clarify this notion further through a simple example: we know well that the force of gravity exists because when we hold anything up in the air and then let go of it, it quickly drops to the earth. If it were not for the force of gravity, it would be impossible for the living beings to exist and live on the earth.

Being aware of the existence of gravity is not something that requires an extensive knowledge of physics; thus, even children can easily understand that it exists. But what is the nature of gravity? What is it composed of? Is it made up of some invisible waves, unknown particles, or some other mysterious power?

What is rather strange about gravity is that it affects everything in no time, faster than anything else that we know in our world, even faster than light which enjoys the highest speed in the world. So, what exactly is the nature of this mysterious force? What is it essentially made up of? As to this question, we do not have any clear answers. Gravity is merely one of the creations of Allah, and yet our knowledge of it remains, to a large extent, general in nature and we are miles away from a complete detailed knowledge of it.

So, when we are unable to comprehend the nature of gravity which is itself a created thing in our material world, how can we ever expect to acquire detailed and comprehensive knowledge of the nature of Allah's Essence, though He is the creator of the material world and the metaphysical world and enjoys an unbounded and infinite Essence?! Though we are unable ever to comprehend Allah's Essence, we still feel Him present and watching everywhere and with anything that exists in the world.

Another sentence that is worth more consideration in the above-mentioned remarks by Imam Ali ('a) is "وَمَنْ حَدَّهُ فَقَدْ عَدَّهُ" [And whoever regards Him as limited has regarded Him as numerable]. This is a precise indication as to the fact that anyone who regards Allah as limited has also regarded Him as numerable, meaning that they also believe that it is possible for Allah to have equals or the likes.

This is because something can be considered not to have any equals or the likes only when it is unlimited and infinite in every respect [hence leaving no room for anything like it to exist alongside it]. Therefore, anything that is limited in any way, regardless of how great or huge it might be, still leaves room for other things that are equal to it to exist besides it. Even if currently nothing like a limited thing or being exists, still, equals can be imagined for them, because there is room for them to exist.

That is to say, it is perfectly possible for two or more limited beings [no matter how huge they may be] to exist; however, it is impossible to even imagine equals or the likes for something that is unlimited in every respect, because it leaves no room for anything like it to exist as it occupies all that can be imagined to exist!

Part Three
Sermon No.1

وَمَنْ قالَ «فِيمَ»؟ فَقَدْ ضَمَّنَهُ، وَمَنْ قالَ «عَلامَ»؟ فَقَدْ أَخْلى مِنْهُ. كائِنٌ
لا عَنْ حَدَثٍ، مَوْجُودٌ لا عَنْ عَدَمٍ، مَعَ كُلِّ شَيْءٍ لا بِمُقارَنَةٍ، وَغَيْرُ
كُلِّ شَيْءٍ لا بِمُزايَلَةٍ، فاعِلٌ لا بِمَعْنَى الْحَرَكاتِ وَالآلَةِ، بَصيرٌ إِذْ لا مَنْظُورَ
إِلَيْهِ مِنْ خَلْقِهِ، مُتَوَحِّدٌ إِذْ لا سَكَنَ يَسْتَأْنِسُ بِهِ وَلا يَسْتَوْحِشُ لِفَقْدِهِ

"Anyone who asks "In what is He?" holds that He is contained [within something in the exclusion of others] and anyone who asks "On what is He?" [entertains the idea that He exists in one place and] dismisses the possibility of Him existing in another; He has forever existed and did not come about from anything else. He is an existence without any precedent of non-existence. He is with everything without accompanying them, and He is different from all else without being totally detached from them.
He is the Doer of all Acts without having any movements or instruments. He is All-Seeing, and He was so even before any of His visible creatures existed. He is the One, the Only, and He is Alone, because there exists no one besides Him who would keep Him company and whose loss would make Him afraid or grieved."

Commentary [Part Three]

There is nothing like Him

In this section of his sermon, Imam Ali ('a) touched upon some of the subtlest and precise details of the concept of Tawḥīd [i.e. the Oneness of Allah], and he outlined five important points in this regard in a few concise yet profound sentences.

These five points are as follows:

1. First, the Imam ('a) discusses how the Divine Essence of Allah is unlimited as long as the concept of place is concerned, meaning that He is high above having any place whatsoever.

The Imam ('a) has stated the following in this regard:

"Anyone who asks "In what is He?" holds that He is contained within something [in the exclusion of others]..."

The Arabic preposition "فِي" [English: in/into] implies that something is contained within the boundaries of something else, hence it is used when someone intends to convey that something encompasses something else completely. Therefore, one can say that a person is "in the house", a flower is "in the garden", or even the fragrant rose water is "in the flower petals".

Obviously, being contained in or encompassed by something else means that the essence of the thing in question is limited; this is while all of the proofs of Allah's Oneness indicate that His Divine Essence is unlimited in every respect. Imam Ali ('a) then continues his sermon, stating:

وَمَنْ قالَ عَلامَ؟ فَقَدْ أَخْلى مِنْهُ

"... anyone who asks "On what is He located?" [entertains the idea that He exists in one place and] dismisses the possibility of Him existing in another."

Such a viewpoint regarding Allah also regards Him as limited and so it is inconsistent with the self-existent nature of Allah. Therefore, all of those who believe that Allah is on a throne, in the heavens, or anywhere else are not pure monotheists. In fact, anyone who holds that Allah is in any specific place is worshipping a creation of his own mind which he has termed "Allah" and not the true Creator of all that exists [regardless of whether they are ordinary people or scholars].
Some unlearned people have argued for the anthropomorphism of Allah based on the following verse of the Quran, claiming that Allah is located on some throne in the heavens:

"The Most Gracious, established on the Throne."[1]

Let us now go back to the meaning of the above-mentioned verse; as it is clear from its contents, the literal meaning of the above-mentioned verse is that after the creation of the universe, Allah "established on the Throne". Yet, like many similar literary texts, the literal meaning is not what is meant here.
The Arabic term "استوى" has been used extensively in the Arabic literature to convey the exertion of "control or authority" on something. Therefore, while it literally means to "go up and sit on" the

1. Ṭāhā, 5.

throne, the metaphoric meaning of the phrase "he established on the Throne" is to exert control and authority on something. The opposite of this phrase is "he was toppled from the throne" which, again in a metaphoric sense, would mean to lose one's power or authority. Therefore, the verse "اَلرَّحْمٰنُ عَلَى الْعَرْشِ اسْتَوٰى" discusses the establishment of Allah's authority and control over what has been metaphorically referred to as "the Divine Throne". In any case, it would be rather childish to take such a clear metaphor in a literal sense and argue for the anthropomorphism of Allah based on it.

2. Imam Ali ('a), after speaking about the unlimited and infinite nature of Allah in terms of the concept of "space", goes on to discuss Allah's unlimited Essence in terms of the concept of "time", explaining that His Essence is pre-eternal.

The Imam ('a) has stated the following in this respect:

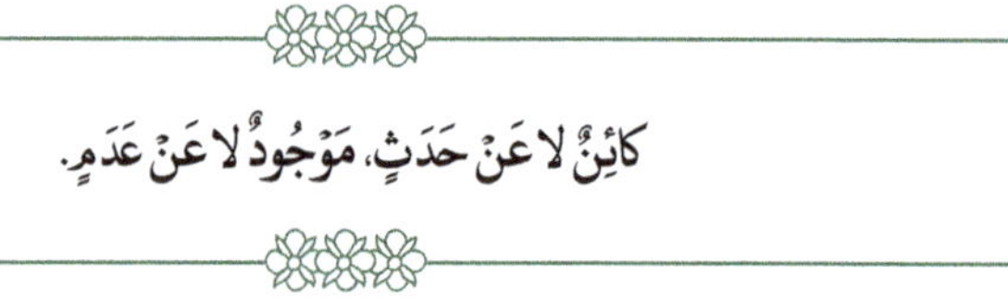

كَائِنٌ لَا عَنْ حَدَثٍ، مَوْجُودٌ لَا عَنْ عَدَمٍ.

"He has ever existed and did not come about from anything else; He is an existence without any precedent of non-existence."

This phrase points out one of the other great differences of Allah with the created beings. All of the created beings were non-existent before they come into being and, at some point in time, they sprang into existence. Yet, Allah the Almighty is different from all the created beings in that He has always existed and His Divine Essence has no history of non-existence.

It is noteworthy that the Arabic words "كائن" and "موجود" [meaning "coming into existence" and "what has sprung into existence" respectively] cannot be used to refer to Allah's Existence unless they are cleansed of the denotations and connotations that refer to the attributes of the created beings as well as their underlying implication of "having a history of non-existence".[1]

3. In the next section of his speech, Imam Ali ('a) touches upon the nature of the relationship between the created beings with their Creator, or the Necessary Being.

The Imam ('a) has stated in this regard:

"He is with everything without accompanying them, and He is different from all else without being totally detached from them."

Many people, including many of the philosophers and scholars, assume that the relationship between Allah and the created beings is the relationship of two entities that are independent and detached from one another, with the created beings merely having been created by Allah. An example in this regard is that of a huge fire and a candle which is lit using that fire and then put aside without needing

1. Some of the scholars who have written commentaries on the Nahj al-Balāghah are of the opinion that both of the above-mentioned sentences by Imam Ali ('a) refer to the same thing, while some others, including Ibn Abī al-Ḥadīd believe that they are in reference to two different notions. In his commentary on the Nahj al-Balāghah, Ibn Abī al-Ḥadīd explains that the first sentence [i.e. كائِنٌ لا عَنْ حَدَثٍ] is indicative of Allah's pre-eternal nature [in terms of time], while the second sentence [i.e. "مَوْجود لا عَنْ عَدَمٍ"] is in reference to Allah's self-existent nature as a Necessary Being [meaning that the Divine Essence is, by nature, not a created entity at all].
In other words, according to Ibn Abī al-Ḥadīd, the first sentence means that the concept of "time" is irrelevant to Allah, as He has never had a beginning nor will He have an end, while the second sentence means that regardless of the concept of time, Allah is not created but self-existent by nature [Sharḥ Nahj al-Balāghah Ibn Abī al-Ḥadīd, vol. 1, p. 79]. However, there are some scholars who believe the opposite of Ibn Abī al-Ḥadīd's view, i.e. that the first sentence rejects the idea of the createdness of Allah altogether while the second one dismisses as baseless the idea of a "time" at which point Allah might have been created [for instance: Sharḥ Nahj al-Balāghah Ibn Meytham, vol. 1, p. 127].
The fact of the matter is that none of these ideas can be proven to be the only correct ones; this is because the term "حدث", which is usually used to refer to a "time" when something came into being, is also capable of being used to refer to the "createdness" of the essence of something as well. Similarly, the term "عدم" can be used to refer to a "time" when something did not exist or to the very "inexistence" of something regardless of the concept of time. Considering this issue, it seems that these sentences mean the same thing and they have been used together for the sake of emphasis. In other words, both of these sentences reject the concept of "time" for Allah and they also reject the "createdness" of Allah's Essence.

that huge fire any longer after it was lit.

But the reality is something else entirely; the difference between the Creator and the created is not merely that of a powerful being and a weak one. Rather, it is the difference between a Being that is independent in every respect and a being that is dependent in every respect.

The entire existence, the cosmos and everything that exists in it, constantly and in every moment derive their existence from them, much like how the earth receives warmth and light from the sun. Allah is not completely detached from the world and yet He is not the "same" as what exists in this world [a wrong view which was put forward by Sufis who believed in the unity of existence and whatever exists]. The correct understanding of this concept is of prime importance because true Tawḥīd depends on the correct understanding of this reality.

This fact is further clarified through the following example [although even these examples are incapable of fully capturing this concept]:

Although the rays of light which are emitted from the sun are not the same entity as the sun itself, they are still dependent on and connected with it. In other words, although these rays are not the same entity as the sun itself, this does not mean that they are an independent entity or completely detached from it. They are connected with it but this does not mean that the rays of the sun are the same thing as the sun, meaning that they are not united in the sense that they would be considered a single entity.

Undoubtedly, the connection of all that exists in this world with the pure Essence of Allah is much closer and their dependence on the Essence of Allah much greater than this. In fact, it is such a unique connection, being characterized by simultaneous unity and plurality that no concrete or perfect example can be found for it in the world. Yet the example discussed above or the example of human's thoughts_ which are an entity that is distinct from the human being himself and yet they are dependent upon him as they mean nothing without the existence of the human being_ help to clarify this connection to some extent.

4. In the next sentence, the Imam ('a) refers to yet another Attribute of the Divine Essence, stating:

"He is the Doer of all Acts without having any movements or instruments."

In our human terms, when we speak of the "doer" or the "agent" of some act, we usually think of someone who does that act using the movements of his body limbs, his arms, legs, or his head etc.

Moreover, all living beings, including human beings, have a limited power in accomplishing different tasks with raw power. Therefore, due to their physical limitations which do not allow them to do just anything they wish to do, human beings get help from different tools and instruments in order to make up for their physical shortcomings. They, therefore, use hammers to drive nails into wood, and they cut huge logs using saws. They also use small tweezers to pick up tiny objects and also huge cranes to lift super heavy objects and loads. These shortcomings are all characteristic of the physical world and whatever exists in it.

However, considering the fact that Allah is neither a physical being nor is there any limitation to His power, His "doing" of things has nothing to do with "movement". Further, since His power is unlimited, He is in no need of any tools or instruments to do what He wishes. In fact, before even the concepts of "tool" or "instrument" were created, Allah the Almighty did whatever He wished; if He needed instruments to create things, He would have been unable to create the most primitive of things as He did not have access to any instruments. Allah can create or eliminate entire worlds just by ordering them to "be" or "not to be". It is also Him who decides whether they come into existence gradually, hence determining the time during which they are to be formed, or that they emerge abruptly.

Therefore, when we speak of Allah as the "Doer" of things, we must not downgrade His "Acts" to the level of our own existence by comparing them to our own acts. It should be noted, however, that this does not mean that Allah does not have angels through whom to direct the affairs of His creation. He gives rise to many things in the world through chains of cause and effect, but only because He wants them to occur in that way, and not because He is in need of those causes and effects for that specific thing to happen.

5. In the next sentence of this sermon, Imam Ali ('a) further describes Allah as follows:

"He is All-Seeing, and He was so even before any of His visible creatures existed."

The Arabic word "بصير", which derives from the root word "بصر" [English: eyesight], means "able to see"; however, it is never used about Allah in its literal sense. In other words, when used about Allah, this word takes on a metaphoric sense which conveys a concept much more sublime than its literal meaning.

Allah is described as "All-Seeing" because he has full knowledge of everything, including every visible thing, and this is why the Imam ('a) says that Allah was All-Seeing even before any visible thing existed.

Therefore, Allah's All-Seeing Attribute is due to His unlimited and infinite Knowledge; moreover, it is a known fact that Allah's Knowledge is pre-eternal.

Finally, in the last sentence of this part of his sermon, Imam Ali ('a) refers to the Unity of Allah's pure Essence, explaining that He is high above having any companions or any need for anyone to keep Him company:

مُتَوَحِّدٌ إِذْ لا سَكَنَ يَسْتَأْنِسُ بِهِ وَلا يَسْتَوْحِشُ لِفَقْدِهِ

"He is the One, the Only, and He is Alone, because there exists no one besides Him who would keep Him company and whose loss would make Him afraid or grieved."

One thing that needs to be kept in mind is that all created beings, including human beings, have but to get help from their own kind or even other creatures and beings to secure their interests and repel dangers because they all have limited power. Therefore, only by joining forces can the created beings feel secure in the face of the dangers that threaten them.

This is, in fact, why human beings are afraid of loneliness and also why they feel reassured and safe in company. This can particularly be seen when man is faced with dangers, sicknesses, natural disasters, and wars.

Sometimes the shortsighted man, whose existence is limited in every way, compares Allah to himself, wondering how He had been completely alone before the creation of the world, how He could bear being without company, and how He could feel secure and reassured without anyone to keep Him company!!

This is because man forgets that Allah is an unlimited Being, and that an unlimited Being is neither in need of anything so as to seek it from another being nor is He afraid of any enemies to seek another's help when facing them, nor does He have any likes or equals to befriend Him.

It is due to His unlimited and infinite Essence that Allah has always been Mutawaḥḥid [Alone and without companion] and He will forever remain so. Therefore, the term Mutawaḥḥid [Arabic "متوحّد"] is different in meaning than "Wāḥid" [Arabic "واحد"] and Aḥad [meaning "احد"].

Important Points

This part of the Imam's sermon is full of important points and valuable lessons which need to be paid special attention to. These lessons are particularly helpful in regard to unresolved ideological issues concerning "gaining knowledge of Allah and His Divine Attributes". Let us review some of these points here:

1. The Connection between the Creator and the Created Beings and the Concept of "Unity of Existence"

There is much controversy among philosophers and theologians regarding the nature of the connection between Allah and His created beings. Some of these scholars have gone to extremes, putting forward the idea of the unity of the Creator and His created beings; these individuals have assumed that the Creator and His created beings are essentially the same entity.

They explain this belief of theirs as follows: "There is only a single being, and nothing more, and the whole universe and whatever is assumed to exist besides Him are the different projections and reflections of His Essence. In other words, there exists nothing but a single reality, and the plurality that is assumed to exist in the world in the form of different creatures is nothing but a mirage and an illusion of reality which does not actually exist."

They sometimes use terms such as "incarnation" or "infusion" instead of the unity of existence, explaining their specific view as follows: "... Allah is an Essence which infuses all objects and beings, turning into different things in this world; thus, those who are unaware of this reality believe in the plurality of existence in this world, while there is only a single existence permeating the whole world."[1]

1. This is a belief which is held by most of the Sufis; in fact, the kinds of remarks which have been related from the Sufi chiefs and leaders corroborate this claim. For instance, it has been narrated that some of the Sufi chiefs would say publicly: "Indeed I am God"!! or even more offensive and blasphemous things such as: "Glorified am I! How great a God I am"!!!

Some of the Sufi chiefs have even gone so far as to clearly praise idolatry and call it the same thing as monotheism in their poems!! For instance, some of them have said in their poems: "If only Muslims knew what idol-worshipping truly is, they would know for certain that the one true religion is idol-worshipping"!!

In short, the proponents of this ideology view the entire world as a huge ocean and the creatures as the drops of water in that ocean. They also believe that any duality or plurality that is seen in this world is nothing but an illusion and a mirage.

They further believe that as long as a person does not truly believe in the concept of the unity of existence, he is not a true Sufi because the belief in the unity of existence forms the basis and the core belief of Sufism!

This is, however, not to say that everything that the Sufis believe in is false; in fact, some of what they believe in can be justified as true beliefs. For instance, it is true that there is only a single true self-subsistent being in the world and that everything else that exists is dependent on that single being. It is also true that compared to the unlimited and infinite Essence of Allah, everything else that exists is so insignificant that it is almost not considered to be anything worth mentioning; however, this does not mean that the created beings do not exist at all! But the rest of what the Sufis believe in are totally unjustifiable. An example in this regard is the fact that they believe that there is only a single existing being in the world and all else are an illusion. Another example of their baseless beliefs is that idolatry is also a legitimate creed if it is not turned into a limited form, because everything that exists in this world is God and God is everything that exists in the world!

These beliefs, regardless of who holds them, are in sharp contrast to the self-evident truth and axioms of this world and they explicitly deny the obvious relationships between the cause and effect, the Creator and created, and the worshipper and worshipped in this world. Moreover, these beliefs have some underlying corrupt principles which are all considered baseless and unacceptable according to the Islamic convictions, since if this understanding of "unity of existence" were true, then the concepts of God, servants, prophets, nations, wor-

Another piece of evidence in this regard comes from some blasphemous poems of the Persian poet Mowlawī [also known as Rumi]. In his poems, he calls Allah a "Mysterious Idol" who was once incarnated in the form of Adam, another day in the form of Noah, and later as Moses, and Jesus, and finally He was incarnated as Prophet Muḥammad (ṣ). Rumi then continues and states that Allah was later incarnated in the form of Ali ('a) and his sword, Dhulfaqār, and finally He was incarnated in the form of Manṣūr al-Hallāj [a famous Sufi] and was hanged!!! [Cited with some excerption from the book Āref wa Sufi che Mīgūyand, p. 107].

shippers, the Worshipped, the Divine legislator, and religious responsibility would be completely meaningless.

If this concept were true, then even Paradise, Hell, the residents of Paradise and the inmates of Hell would all be a single entity and the same thing as the Essence of Allah; hence, all of these concepts would be illusions which would not actually exist!

Therefore, based on this ideology, if one succeeds in breaking through these illusions, one will see that nothing exists in this world except the Essence of Allah!! Further, in order to truly believe in this concept, then one must necessarily believe in the corporeality of Allah, His incarnation, or infusion in the created beings!!!

Such beliefs are consistent neither with our intuitive knowledge of things in this world, nor are they justifiable through logical reasoning and compatible with the Islamic convictions or the teachings of the Holy Quran! It is due to this serious inconsistency of such beliefs with every religious and logical principle that the renowned Shi'a jurist, the late Muḥaqqiq al-Yazdī, has stated in his book al-'Urwah al-Wuthqā amid his discussion of disbelievers:

لا اِشْكالَ فِي نَجاسَةِ الْغُلاةِ وَالْخَوارِجِ وَالنَّواصِبِ وَأَمَّا الْمُجَسِّمَةُ وَالْمُجَبِّرَةُ
وَالْقائِلينَ بِوَحْدَةِ الْوُجُودِ مِنَ الصُّوفِيَةِ اِذا الْتَزَمُوا بِاَحْكامِ الْاِسْلامِ فَالْأَقْوى
عَدَمُ نَجاسَتِهِمْ إِلَّا مَعَ الْعِلْمِ بِالْتِزامِهِمْ بِلَوازِمِ مَذاهِبِهِمْ مِنَ الْمَفاسِدِ

Undoubtedly, the Ghulāt [i.e. the exaggerators], the Kharijites, and the Nawāṣib[1] are ritually impure and Najis. However, the people who believe in the corporeality of Allah or fatalism, as well as a group of Sufis who believe in the unity of existence are most probably not considered to be Najis on the condition that they adhere to the Islamic laws. However, they will be considered Najis if one makes sure that

1. Ghulāt are the people who exaggerate the rank of the Infallible Imams ('a), and in particular that of Imam Ali ('a), considering them to be God or united with Allah. The Kharijites are the remnants of a rebellious group that broke their allegiance to Imam Ali ('a), fought against him in the battle of Nahrawān and were defeated. Finally, Nawāṣib are the enemies of the Prophet's Ahl-al-Bayt ('a).

they firmly believe in and adhere to the corrupt convictions which form the basis of their creed.[1]

There are two points worth noting in this ruling: the first point is that the proponents of the idea of the unity of existence have been treated in the same way as fatalists and the people who believe in the corporeality of Allah. The other point is that this ruling clearly indicates that Sufi convictions are considered corrupt from a religious viewpoint and if the Sufis have only a shallow faith in them, they are regarded as Muslims, but if they firmly believe in them and closely adhere to them, they are not considered Muslims.

It is obvious, then, that Sufism is based on such corrupt ideas and that if a person fully adheres to them, he will no longer be considered a Muslim. What is even more interesting is that, to the best of our knowledge, all the other scholars who have written annotations and commentaries on the book al-'Urwah al-Wuthqā have supported this ruling as it is or have added some points to it. For instance, some of these scholars have added the condition that a Sufi will still be considered a Muslim if they do not hold beliefs that would be equal to denying the Oneness of Allah or the Divine mission of prophets].[2]

In order to better understand what evil consequences such beliefs can entail, let us take a look at some of the contents of the Mathnawī Ma'nawī, Rumi's book of poems. In chapter four of his book of poems, Rumi narrates a long story regarding how Bāyazīd, a Sufi chief, said about himself "Glorified am I! How great a God am I!" and how his disciples objected to him for saying such blasphemous things. The story goes that his disciples told him, "Why do you speak such blasphemous things as "there is no god except me, so worship me"!!"

Bāyazīd said, "If I say such things again, take up your knives and attack me with them."

The story then goes that, when he once again said, "There is none other than God in my clothes, so why do you search the heavens and the earth for Him?!" his disciples took up their knives and attacked to kill him.

1. Al-Sayyid Kāẓim al-Yazdī, al-'Urwah al-Wuthqā, Vol. 1, the section on the disbelievers being ritually impure, issue N. 2, p. 69.

2. For more information in this regard, refer to the book Miṣbāḥ al-Hudā [vol. 1, p. 410] written by the late Ayatollah al-Shaykh Muḥammad Taqi al-Āmuli [a renowned Shi'a jurist and philosopher] and also refer to Mawsū'ah al-Imam al-Khū'ī, vol. 3, p. 74 on.

However, to their surprise, they realized that every time they struck their master with their knives, they actually cut their own bodies!

This fairy tale and fake story shows how far the proponents of this ideology are prepared to go to convince others that what they claim is true!

Let us conclude this section with the remarks of a contemporary Shi'a scholar regarding this ideology:

This ideology [i.e. the belief in the unity of existence in the sense that whatever exists is a single entity] is in contradiction to all the logical principles, the intuitive knowledge, and the teachings of all of the true Divinely-sent religions. It would take up this world to the level of the self-subsistent Being [i.e. Allah] or it downgrades Allah to the level of the things which exist in this world.

It seems that this ideology has been accepted superficially and in a shallow manner by some as a kind of metaphoric way of capturing the reality or a way of evading the philosophical problems of explaining the realities of the world. However, it does not seem to have penetrated deep in their minds, i.e. that they have accepted this ideology based on logical reasoning or knowledge of the existing realities.[1]

2. The Deviation of the Unlearned from the Reality of Allah's Attributes

If one properly reflects on this part of Imam Ali's sermon, he will find that all of the deviations from the reality of Tawḥīd and the truth about Allah's Attributes will be eliminated. It will only be then that one will completely and truly understand the following remarks made by Allah Himself:

وَنَحْنُ أَقْرَبُ إِلَيْهِ مِنْ حَبْلِ الْوَرِيدِ

"... and We are closer to him [i.e. man] than his jugular vein."[2]

1. Al-'Allāmah al-Ja'fari, Tarjomeh va Tafsīr Nahj al-Balāghah, Vol. 2, p. 64.
2. Qāf, 16.

وَهُوَ مَعَكُمْ أَيْنَمَا كُنْتُمْ

"... He [i.e. Allah] is with you wheresoever you may be"[1]

مَا يَكُونُ مِنْ نَجْوَى ثَلَاثَةٍ إِلَّا هُوَ رَابِعُهُمْ

"There are no three people engaged in secret talk but He is the fourth of them..."[2]

اللَّهُ نُورُ السَّموَاتِ وَالْأَرْضِ

"Allah is the Light of the heavens and the earth."[3]

وَاعْلَمُوا أَنَّ اللَّهَ يَحُولُ بَيْنَ الْمَرْءِ وَقَلْبِهِ

"... and know that Allah [is so close to you He] intervenes between man and his heart."[4]

Doing this will not only help one complete his understanding of the concept of the Unity of Existence [in its correct sense, not the Sufi sense],

1. Al-Ḥadīd, 4.
2. Al-Mujādalah, 7.
3. Al-Nūr, 35.
4. Al-Anfāl, 24.

but it will also prevent one from falling into any pitfalls and deviations regarding the understanding of Allah's Attributes.

In addition to the deviations discussed above, there are some who have wandered far into error with regard to these issues, coming up with shameful ideas which one feels ashamed even to speak about.

One of these groups is called the "Mujassimah", whose members have ascribed the attributes and qualities of the created beings to Allah, lowering Him to the level of a corporeal being. These people believe that Allah has a face, arms, and legs, very much like a human being, and they are even of the opinion that He has curly hair!! In short, they believe that Allah is a being that is limited within the framework of time and space. Some of these people believe that Allah can be visibly seen in this world, while some others are of the idea that He will be seen only in the Hereafter. Al-Muḥaqqiq al-Davānī, a learned Shi'a philosopher, has made the following remarks about these people, basing his argument on the Islamic traditions in the book Biḥār al-Anwār:

Some of the people who believe in the corporeality of Allah really believe that Allah has a physical body that can be seen. Some of them believe that Allah's body is made up of flesh and blood, while others hold the view that His body is made up of a bright white light whose span is seven hands. They further believe that different people see Allah in different ways: some see Him as an ordinary human being, some as a very young man with very curly hair, and some others as an old man with gray hair. There are some others who believe that Allah has a physical body, but not like the ones that we know in this world. In any case, there are many people like these who hold similar baseless and childish beliefs about Allah.[1]

What is even more curious is that there are some traditions in certain tradition references that have been apparently related from the Prophet of Islam (ṣ) or his companions_ and which are undoubtedly fake and fabricated ones_ in which Allah has been described with some strange corporeal qualities and attributes.

For instance, one of such traditions, apparently narrated from Ibn 'Abbās, reads: "Once Ibn 'Abbās was asked, "Did Muḥammad (ṣ) ever see his Lord?" He replied, "Yes"; they further asked him, "And how did he see Allah?" He replied, "He saw Allah in a beautiful green garden while He

1. Biḥār al-Anwār, vol. 3, p. 289.

was sitting in a golden chair covered with a golden carpet and carried by four angels"[1]!!

There are also several traditions transmitted in the Sunni tradition sources, including Ṣaḥīḥ al-Bukhārī, Sunan Ibn Mājah, and other references like them, which explicitly indicate that Allah will be visible to people on the Resurrection Day![2] Some of these traditions even emphasize that the residents of Paradise will be able to see Allah visibly just as one can easily see the full moon at night![3]

Based on these traditions, many of the Sunni scholars have come to believe that Allah will be visible to the eye on the Resurrection Day, and therefore they have fiercely defended this notion. This is all while the holy Quran has directly rejected such ideas in the following verses:

لَا تُدْرِكُهُ الْأَبْصَارُ

"The eyes cannot perceive Him..."[4]

And Allah similarly said to Moses:

لَنْ تَرَانِي

"You shall never see Me!"[5]

---

1. Ibn Khuzymah, Al-Tawḥīd, Vol. 2, p. 483; Buḥūthun fī al-Milal wa al-Niḥal, vol. 1, p. 145.

2. Ṣaḥīḥ al-Bukhārī, vol. 5, p. 179; Tafsīr Surah al-Nisā' wa Sunan Ibn Mājah, vol. 1, p. 63, hadith No. 177.

3. For further information regarding these traditions, which are no doubt fake and fabricated ones, and also in order to read rebuttals and the evidence presented against them based on the Quran and the authentic traditions, refer to the book Payām-e Quran, vol. 4, pp. 244-285. All of these proofs from the Quran and the Islamic traditions indicate that Allah can never be seen with the eye, either in this world or in the Hereafter.

4. Al-An'ām, 103.

5. Al-A'rāf, 143.

In addition to these pieces of evidence from the Quran, similar opinions have been put forward by Imam Ali ('a) in his sermon of Ashbāḥ:

$$وَالرَّادِعُ أَنَاسِيَّ الْأَبْصَارِ عَنْ أَنْ تَنَالَهُ أَوْ تُدْرِكَهُ أَوْ تُبْصِرَهُ$$

"... He who has prevented the eyes from ever seeing or perceiving Him ..."[1]

In yet another sermon, Imam Ali ('a) states the following with the supreme eloquence that is characteristic of his words:

$$اَلْحَمْدُ لِلّٰهِ الَّذِى لاَ تُدْرِكُهُ الشَّوَاهِدُ وَلاَ تَحْوِيهِ الْمَشَاهِدُ وَلاَ تَرَاهُ النَّوَاظِرُ وَلاَ تَحْجُبُهُ السَّوَاتِرُ$$

"All praise belongs to Allah, Who cannot be perceived by the senses, encompassed by space, seen with the eyes, or concealed by any covers."[2]

In addition to all of these proofs against this idea, it should be noted that the idea of corporeality of Allah is rather illogical and against the judgments of the sound mind. This is because if Allah were visible, then it must be said that He has a physical body; being physical means being limited to a certain place and time, and any sort of limitation is characterized by weakness and change. Therefore, by believing in the corporeality of Allah, He would be downgraded from a Self-existent increate Being to the level of created beings.

It is at this point that the above-mentioned precisely-worded remarks of Imam Ali ('a) begin to shine like the sun and the moon, shedding

1. The Nahj al-Balāghah, sermon No. 91.

2. Ibid, sermon No. 185.

light on the reality and eliminating all the unfounded ideas about the Divine Essence of Allah. By employing the most precise and at the same time the most eloquent and beautiful discourse, Imam Ali ('a) has taught us the best lesson in Tawḥīd and a correct understanding of the Divine Attributes of Allah.

It should be noted that since there are always two sides to the coin of extremism, there are some who have gone to the other extreme with regard to this issue. Whereas the proponents of the corporeality of Allah have downgraded Him to the level of created beings with physical bodies, another group of extremists have gone to the other extreme, believing that it is totally impossible to gain any knowledge of Allah. They believe that it is impossible for us to gain any knowledge, whatsoever, of the nature of Allah's Essence or of His Divine Attributes, and that whatever we think we know about His Attributes are some empty words and negative concepts.

They say that, for instance, when we say that Allah is All-Knowing, the only thing that we understand from this is that He is not without knowledge; however, we have not clear perception of the nature of His knowledge or exactly how knowledgeable He is.

And so, this is how this second group of extremists deprives man of his greatest honor, i.e. the chance to gain knowledge of Allah. Therefore, instead of that blessed path, these people embarked on a path of complete darkness which is against the teachings of the Holy Quran, which has opened countless paths for us toward gaining knowledge of Allah and recognizing Him.

Let us conclude this section with another eloquent remark made by Imam Ali ('a) and recorded in the Nahj al-Balāghah:

لَمْ يُطْلِعِ الْعُقُولَ عَلَى تَحْدِيدِ صِفَتِهِ وَلَمْ يَحْجُبْهَا عَنْ وَاجِبِ
مَعْرِفَتِهِ فَهُوَ الَّذِي تَشْهَدُ لَهُ أَعْلَامُ الْوُجُودِ عَلَى إِقْرَارِ قَلْبِ ذِي الْجُحُودِ
تَعَالَى اللهُ عَمَّا يَقُولُ الْمُشَبِّهُونَ بِهِ وَالْجَاحِدُونَ لَهُ عُلُوّاً كَبِيراً

"... He has blocked the access of intellects and minds to the nature of His Attributes and [yet] He did not bar them from a necessary amount of knowledge about Himself. It is He whose existence the hearts of the deniers have been compelled to recognize and affirm by His clear Signs in the universe. He is exalted, far above what the deniers [i.e. those who disbelieve in Him or believe that gaining knowledge of Him is impossible] and those who equate Him with others [among His creation] claim about Him."[1]

Therefore, the best way toward understanding Allah, which is a middle course neither like the beliefs of those who liken Him to the created beings nor like those who reject the possibility of knowing him altogether, is the one outlined in the above-mentioned remarks by Imam Ali ('a).

As regards the nature of Allah's Attributes and the correct way of understanding them, there are rather extraordinary teachings which have captured these issues in considerable detail in other sermons in the Nahj al-Balāghah. These teachings can complement our discussion of Divine Attributes presented here; so, God-willing, we will discuss these teachings in the due course as we go through the other sermons of the Nahj al-Balāghah.

3. Negating Allah's Temporal and Essential Contingency

It can be understood from Imam Ali's remarks in this sermon that Allah is neither temporally nor essentially contingent, to use philosophical terminology. Something that is described as "temporally

1. The Nahj al-Balāghah, sermon No. 49.

contingent" is an entity which has come into being at some point in time. That is to say, such a being had been nonexistent before a certain point in time and after that point it sprang into existence.
The concept of time only came into being after the creation of the material world, and it was after that point that the concepts of temporal contingency and nonexistence came into being.
The other concept that is of concern here is "essential contingency", which is not related to time or the genesis of the material world. An entity is described as "essentially contingent" when its essence is created in nature. Put differently, this is when an entity acquires some quality or some part of its essence from a source other than its own essence, i.e. when it derives the existence of its essence from an outside source.
Obviously, then, Allah's pure Essence is pure and high above both temporal and essential contingency, because Allah is a Self-existent Necessary Being who has ever existed and will continue to exist forever. In fact, Allah's Essence is the very existence itself.

4. Is it Permissible to Use the Word "Being" for Allah?

In order to answer this question, let us take a look at Imam Ali's remarks in this sermon; the Imam ('a) describes Allah as follows:

مَوْجُودٌ لَا عَنْ عَدَمٍ

"He is a Being who exists but this does not mean that He has had a precedent nonexistence."

It can be inferred from this part of the Imam's sermon that it is permissible to refer to Allah using the term "Being". However, it should be kept in mind that, when used about Allah, this term does not mean the same thing as when it is used about the rest of beings. This is because every other being in the world has been nonexistent at some point in time; therefore, "being", when used to describe other creatures, implies that they were nonexistent and were then endowed with existence by someone else.

However, when used about Allah, "Being" means that He is the Ever-holder of existence, without any history of nonexistence and without anyone having granted Him His existence.

This viewpoint has also been endorsed and supported in some other commentaries written on the Nahj al-Balāghah. It has been explained in these commentaries that the term "being" is sometimes used to refer to the "created" beings and at other times to speak about the "existence" itself.[1] The term "Being" [Arabic: "موجود"] has been used in some of the Islamic traditions related in the book Uṣūl al-Kāfī as well.[2]

1. Miftāḥ al-Sa'ādah, vol. 1, p. 139.

2. Al-Kāfī, Bāb Adnā al-Ma'rifah, p. 86, hadith No. 1; vol. 1, Bāb al-Nahy 'an al-Ṣifah, hadith No. 1; and vol. 1, Bāb Jawāmi' al-Tawḥīd, p. 138, hadith No. 4.

Part Four
Sermon No.1

أَنْشَأَ الْخَلْقَ إِنْشَاءً وَابْتَدَأَهُ ابْتِدَاءً بِلا رَوِيَّةٍ أَجَالَها وَلا تَجْرِبَةٍ اسْتَفَادَهَا
وَلا حَرَكَةٍ أَحْدَثَهَا وَلا هَمَامَةِ نَفْسٍ اضْطَرَبَ فِيهَا أَحَالَ الأَشْياءَ
لِأَوْقَاتِهَا وَلامَ بَيْنَ مُخْتَلِفَاتِها وَغَرَّزَ غَرائِزَها وَأَلْزَمَها أَشْبَاحَهَا عَالِماً
بِهَا قَبْلَ ابْتِدائِها مُحِيطاً بِحُدُودِها وَانْتِهائِها عارِفاً بِقَرائِنِها وَأَحْنَائِها.

"He brought forth the creation originally and commenced it abruptly without needing to think [about it] beforehand, use any prior experience, weigh different options [before acting], or meditate on any decisions [before implementing them]. He originated everything at its due time, and harmonized all the created things with one another, giving each of them their own peculiar qualities and binding them to their own specific conditions. He was fully aware of them all before originating them; He had all-encompassing power over their limits and confines, and He had full knowledge of all their inclinations and intricacies."

Commentary [Part Four]

The Genesis of Creation

The previous parts of this important sermon dealt with the issue of knowledge of Allah and understanding His Divine Attributes in a rather precise and profound manner. The reason why Imam Ali ('a) focuses first on the recognition of Allah and the knowledge of His Divine Attributes is that this knowledge forms the basis for man's knowledge of everything else that exists.

From this section on, however, the Imam ('a) presents a discussion of the creation of the universe, how the process of creation began, as well as some of the wonders of the heavens and the earth. Although this section of the sermon might seem to concern a different topic than the previous sections, it is in some respects a complement to the previous discussions on the Attributes of Allah.

Imam Ali ('a) begins this section of his sermon, stating the following:

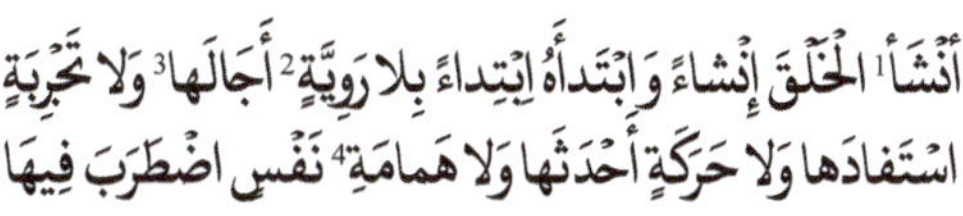

"He brought forth the creation originally and commenced it abruptly without needing to think [about it] beforehand, use any prior experience, weigh different options [before acting], or meditate on any decisions [before implementing them]."

At the beginning of this section, the Imam ('a) stresses the fact that Allah's creation is a completely different matter than any act of creation done by the created beings. This is because when human beings, for instance, intend to do something or make something which has never been done or made before, they first need to think about it and use their innovative minds to accomplish what they have in mind. Moreover, if the thing that they intend to do is not unprecedented, they will try to use the past experience of others or those of themselves to do what they wish to do.

Thus, when making plans to achieve what they have in mind, human beings would contemplate the matter, weighing different options, thinking

1. The Arabic term "أَنْشَأَ" derives from the root word "أنْشاء" [pronounced "Inshā'"], which can mean many things in different contexts. However, it is completely clear from the context of this sentence that it has been used here to mean "bring forth" or "create".

2. The original meaning of the Arabic word "رويّة", according to the Maqāyīs al-Lughah Arabic dictionary, is "to drink to satiety"; however, it has been used to convey the idea of "careful reflection" on something as well. When one reflects deeply and carefully on some important matter, it is as if one satiates oneself by giving that matter enough thought.

3. The Arabic word "أجال" derives from the root word "جولان" [pronounced "Jawalān"] which means to move in a circular way.

4. The scholars who have written commentaries and interpretations on the Nahj al-Balāghah have mentioned different meanings for the word "هَمامة": some have defined it as a sort of mental inclination toward something whose absence would upset one [for instance, refer to Sharḥ Nahj al-Balāghah Ibn Meytham, vol. 1, p. 132]. Some others are of the opinion that it means uncertainty in doing something [for instance, refer to Minhāj al-Barā'ah, al-Khū'ī, p. 352]. There is also a third group of scholars who believe that it means "to pay special attention" to something [for instance, refer to Fī Ẓilāl-i Nahj al-Balāghah, vol. 1, p. 27].

about the preparations they need to do prior to commencing their actions. They would then try to anticipate any setbacks and try to prevent them and also to predict the consequences of their actions.

Sometimes, it so happens that they even remain in a state of uncertainty and doubt in this stage for a long time, until they finally make up their minds and choose one of the options that they have in mind to start with their plan.

All of these stages before the execution of a plan or the making of something are characteristic of the created beings, and none of them applies to the kind of creation that is done by Allah the Almighty. That is to say, when creating things, Allah does not have any need either for contemplating beforehand, making plans, using prior experience, or considering the prerequisites and the consequences of His creation.

Moreover, He is never uncertain or doubtful about His decisions; consequently, no sooner does He will anything than it will come into existence; this is a fact that has been corroborated by the Quran as well:

"His command, once He wills something, is that He says to it "Be" and it immediately comes into existence."[1]

In other words, these four stages of planning and thinking before acting are characteristic of the beings that have limited knowledge and power. Thus, their limitations force them to think carefully prior to acting and also to use others' past experience to increase their knowledge and decrease the possibility of their failure. It is also such limited creatures that will have doubts and uncertainty when they decide to do something that they have never done before.

On the contrary, a Being whose Knowledge is infinite and whose Power is unlimited will go through none of these states when engaged in the act of creation. It also becomes clear at this point that what is meant in

1. Yāsīn, 82.

this sentence by "movement" is the formation and rejection of different thoughts in one's mind as one weighs different options and makes plans to do something.

There is another possibility regarding what this word means as well; some scholars believe that what is meant by movement here is physical movement which is characteristic of the physical beings and their actions. Therefore, the Imam ('a) meant to say that Allah is glorified, high above any physical characteristics.

But the first possibility seems to be more acceptable, particularly given the fact that the phrases before and after this word all speak of thinking, contemplation, and decision making prior to doing something.

In short, Allah's Acts are of a completely different nature than those of the created beings because He firmly wills to do something, with complete knowledge of the weak and strong points of everything, full mastery over constructing everything in the best of ways, and unlimited power to do what He wills. It is due to His unlimited knowledge and power that He is able to bring different things and beings into existence without faltering or failing, and without needing to think or use any prior experience. He has been like this at the beginning of creation and He will remain as such forever.

The Imam ('a) then continues his sermon, discussing how everything that Allah created came into being based on a Supreme Wisdom and a precise timing and a perfect order:

أحالَ الأشياءَ لِأوقاتِها

"He originated everything at its due time..."

Then, following the discussion of the perfect timing of the creation of different things, the Imam ('a) heeds the special order and harmony which exists in the world as well as among all created things:

وَلاَمَ[1] بَيْنَ مُخْتَلِفاتِها

"... and harmonized all the created things with one another"

This is, in fact, one of the wonders of the creation, because Allah has created the universe and everything in it in such a harmony that it seems like a single and unified entity.

He has created a perfect harmony between coldness and warmness, darkness and light, life and death, and water and fire. He has given a green tree the capability of producing fire and he has created a fantastic harmony between the parts of the body of humans and animals, and between the different sections of plants, though these various parts are all made of several substances with completely distinct qualities and characteristics. He has even harmonized the human body and soul by creating a close bond between them, though they belong to completely different worlds, with the soul belonging to the lofty non-physical realm and the body belonging to the base physical realm.

Imam Ali ('a) then goes on to add the following:

"... giving each of them their own peculiar qualities"

It is, in fact, due to the Supreme Wisdom of Allah that He invests

1. The Arabic words "لاَمَ" and "لأمَ" [pronounced as "Lāma" and "Lā'ama" respectively] mean "to gather", "to correct", to "join two things together" and to "reconcile" two things. This is why an armor is called "لامه" in Arabic because, in the past, armors were made by joining lots of iron links and pieces together.

2. The Arabic term "غَرَّزَ" [pronounced: "Gharraza"] derives from the root word "غرز" [pronounced: "Gharz"] originally means "stick a needle into something", "place something somewhere", "or stick something into another thing". It is used metaphorically to refer to the kind of genetic or intrinsic qualities that living creatures are invested with, as if these were seeds of plants cultivated within human beings and other creatures' nature.

every creature with whatever qualities that are expected of it in the form of its instincts, created within them in the form of genetic codes. This will allow each creature to begin living the kind of life they are created for as soon as they are born into this world without any external stimuli. If it were not for this innate program, inherent within the various creatures' genes, the world would sink into chaos and nothing would last in it.

The nature with which human beings and the other creatures have been created is divided into two categories: one of them is called the Fiṭrah [i.e. human original nature] and the other is called instinct. For instance, it is said that the most basic knowledge of the existence of Allah exists in human Fiṭrah, or it is said that human beings have sexual instincts, or that whatever animals do is instinctive or based on their instinct.

These two terms have been used by scientists to describe two different aspects of the nature with which different creatures have been created. They use "Fiṭrah" to refer to the intellectual aspects of this pre-programed nature and they use "instinct" to capture its non-intellectual or sensual aspect. Nevertheless, both of these terms are used to describe the basic "nature" and creation of various creatures.

Finally, in the last phrase of this sentence, the Imam ('a) states:

"... and binding them to their own specific conditions."[1]

The commentators of the Nahj al-Balāghah have offered two different interpretations for this sentence: some of these scholars, including Ibn Abī al-Ḥadīd hold the view that this sentence is indicative of the fact that Allah has bestowed these instincts as fixed and unalterable inclinations within all living creatures [therefore, the pronoun "ها"in the word "الزمها" refers to "instincts"]. They then conclude that, based

1. The term "اشباح", which is the plural of "شبح", has been defined by many lexicologists as "a person" or "something that suddenly appears".

on this interpretation, this sentence is used to emphasize the fact that the instincts are fixed and unchangeable qualities placed within the living creatures.

On the other hand, there are other scholars who believe that this sentence means that the instinct had been a general quality that Allah invested the living creatures with but then it realized in a kind of specialized way within each of them. In other words, Allah gave all the living creatures an instinct which had very general qualities within the Divine Knowledge but when it realized in the real world, it gave each creature their own specific and peculiar qualities and instincts. Based on this interpretation, these scholars conclude that the pronoun "ها"in the word "الزمها" refers to "اشياء" [created things]. There is also a third group of scholars who have mentioned both of the above-mentioned views as plausible interpretations of this sentence.

But given the fact that based on the first interpretation mentioned above the pronouns do not seem to be referring to their correct referents, and also because this would mean that this sentence is merely emphasizing the previous sentence and not presenting anything new, it seems that the second interpretation is more accurate.

It should be noted that Allah has given every creature two distinct features: the first kind are the inward features which are inherent within their nature; these are what Imam Ali ('a) has referred to as instincts. The second kind are the outward features which include the time, the place, and the other conditions in which they exist; these are, in fact, the ones that the Imam ('a) has referred to in this latter phrase.

In other words, in this phrase, Imam Ali ('a) explains that, based on His Supreme Wisdom, Allah the Almighty has ordained certain intrinsic characteristics and also extrinsic aspects for all living creatures so that they could accomplish their specific purpose in this world and be recognized from the other creatures.

The Fiṭrī [Intrinsic] and Creational Guidance Provided to All the Living Creatures in the World

The above-mentioned remarks made by Amīr al-Mu'minīn ('a) bear an important point which has been repeatedly emphasized in the Quran as well. The Quran indicates that the creation of all the creatures in the material world has been done based on a precise timing and that, despite all of their differences, they exist in harmony and complement each other.

This harmony, according to the Quran, is regulated by means of a set of intrinsic regulations which guides them to move together as parts of a single whole toward their set and final goal, and that it is this same intrinsic regulator that prevents them from swerving off their ordained course and moving away from their ordained goal.

The fact that the leaves of trees appear in spring, stay green in summer and then turn and fall down in fall, that the sun unfailingly moves in a specific orbit just as the earth does and also revolves around its orbit, causing the day and the night to follow each other regularly, are all evidence of this creational guidance which Allah has given them. This is exactly what the Holy Quran has mentioned in the following verse, quoting prophet Moses ('a) as saying:

رَبُّنَا الَّذِي أَعْطَىٰ كُلَّ شَيْءٍ خَلْقَهُ ثُمَّ هَدَىٰ

"Our Lord is He who gave everything what was necessary for its creation, and then guided it."[1]

There are also other verses in the Quran in which reference has been made to this issue, some of which are as follows:

"... the original nature of Allah based on which He has originated mankind."[2]

1. Ṭāhā, 50.
2. Al-Rūm, 30.

وَإِنْ مِنْ شَيْءٍ إِلَّا عِنْدَنَا خَزَائِنُهُ وَمَا نُنَزِّلُهُ إِلَّا بِقَدَرٍ مَعْلُومٍ

"And there is not a thing but that its sources are with Us, but We do not send it down except in a known measure."[1]

This is, in fact, one of the clear sings of Allah's omnipotence, visible in the entire world, and the more one reflects on this issue the more clearly one comes to understand it. Thus, when one contemplates the creational guidance given to all the creation by Allah, the precise order and timing of all things, and the harmony that exists between different entities in the world, one will be able to appreciate the profound wisdom and the great power that is behind them all.

In the last part of this section of his sermon, Imam Ali ('a) notes:

عَالِماً بِهَا قَبْلَ ابْتِدَائِهَا مُحِيطاً بِحُدُودِهَا وَانْتِهَائِهَا عَارِفاً بِقَرَائِنِهَا[2] وَأَحْنَائِهَا[3].[4]

"... He was fully aware of them all before originating them, He had all-encompassing power over their limits and confines, and He had full knowledge of all their inclinations and intricacies."

1. Al-Ḥijr, 21.

2. The Arabic word "قرائن" is the plural of "قرينه" and its original meaning [according to the Arabic dictionaries] is "companion", "spouse", or "friend". Some scholars, including Ibn Abī al-Ḥadīd, are of the opinion that this word is in fact the plural of "قرونة" [pronounced "Qarūnah"] meaning "self" or "soul". However, considering the context of the sentences in which it has been used, the first set of meanings seems to be more suitable for it.

3. The word "احناء" is the plural of "حنو" [pronounced either as "Ḥinw" or "Ḥanw"]. According to the Maqāyīs and Lisān al-'Arab, it is originally used to refer to anything with curvature or crook such as the chin or the ribs. It has also been used metaphorically to refer to different aspects of things.

4. Note that all of the pronouns used in these few sentences refer to "اشياء" not "غرائز", a mistake that has been made by some of the scholars who have written commentaries on the Nahj al-Balāghah. This is because taking these pronouns to refer to "غرائز" makes no sense given the specific context and contents of these sentences.

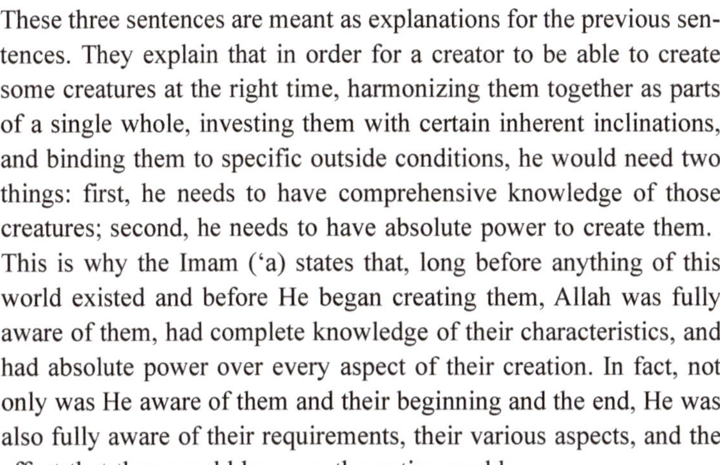

These three sentences are meant as explanations for the previous sentences. They explain that in order for a creator to be able to create some creatures at the right time, harmonizing them together as parts of a single whole, investing them with certain inherent inclinations, and binding them to specific outside conditions, he would need two things: first, he needs to have comprehensive knowledge of those creatures; second, he needs to have absolute power to create them.

This is why the Imam ('a) states that, long before anything of this world existed and before He began creating them, Allah was fully aware of them, had complete knowledge of their characteristics, and had absolute power over every aspect of their creation. In fact, not only was He aware of them and their beginning and the end, He was also fully aware of their requirements, their various aspects, and the effect that they would have on the entire world.

Without doubt, one who has such comprehensive knowledge and absolute power over creating things is also able to precisely create them in their due place and invest each of them with whatever they need, guiding them all toward the set goal of their existence.

Important Points

1. Is It Possible to Use the Word "'Ārif" to Describe Allah?

Some scholars who have written commentaries on the Nahj al-Balāghah have expressed their doubt over whether it is permissible to describe Allah using the term "عارف" ['Ārif] or not. The reason behind this doubt is twofold:

Firstly, as al-Rāghib has defined this word in his Quranic dictionary al-Mufradāt, the words "معرفت" and "عرفان" [which are paronymous with "عارف"] mean "perception" or more accurately, perceiving something through careful thought on and deep contemplation of its manifestations. This means that "معرفت" is a kind of knowledge that is limited in scope and which is acquired through reflection; hence, there is no doubt that Allah's Knowledge is not like that.

Secondly, there is an Islamic tradition according to which the Prophet of Islam (ṣ) has been quoted as saying:

اِنَّ لَهُ (تَعالى) تِسْعَةً وتِسْعينَ اِسْماً مَنْ اَحصاها دَخَلَ الْجَنَّة

"Allah [the Almighty] has ninety nine Names, and anyone who keeps count of them [i.e. has knowledge of them and faith in them] will enter Paradise".

However, Muslim scholars unanimously believe that the word "عارف" is not one of these ninety nine Names.[1] Despite these two facts, this word has been used repeatedly in different Islamic traditions to refer

1. In his commentary on the Nahj al-Balāghah, Ibn Meytham first mentions this issue and then responds to it, stating that Allah's Names are much more than this and he then presents some evidence to prove his view [Sharḥ Nahj al-Balāghah Ibn Meytham, vol. 1, p. 137]. It should be noted that this tradition has been transmitted in the book Al-Durr al-Manthūr [vol. 3, p. 147], cited from Ṣaḥīḥ al-Bukhārī [vol. 3, p. 185], Ṣaḥīḥ Muslim [vol. 8, p. 63], Musnad Aḥmad [vol. 2, p. 258], and Sunan al-Tirmidhī [vol. 5, p. 191, hadith No. 3573] as well as many other reliable resources [for more information in this regard, refer to the book Payām-e Quran, vol. 4, p. 42].

to Allah. Moreover, although it has been used in this sermon as an adjective for Allah, it has also been used in the form of a verb in other traditions to refer to Allah's knowledge. This word has also been used to refer to Allah in various traditions transmitted in the book Usūl al-Kāfī.[1]

This shows that although the Arabic word "معرفت" had originally been used to refer to limited knowledge that is acquired through reflection and contemplation, its scope of meaning was expanded later on to include any sort of knowledge, even though it is not the product of reflection and contemplation.

As for the above-mentioned tradition which indicated that Allah has 99 Names, it does not, by any means, imply that the number of Names of Allah are restricted to 99 and that there are no more Names by which Allah can be called. Rather, these 99 names are the greatest of Allah's Names, depicting His most sublime Attributes which are known as Asmā' al-Ḥusnā [Beautiful Names].

However, apart from these names, there are many other lofty names by which Allah has been called; there are some Islamic traditions some of which have listed one thousand names for Allah. But the most compelling piece of evidence which substantiates this claim is the fact that Imam Ali ('a), who is himself the most knowledgeable person regarding Allah's Names and Attributes, uses this specific name, or its other derivatives, for Allah. This is what can be clearly seen in the Imam's sermons which have been related in the Nahj al-Balāghah.

2. How does Allah Have Full Knowledge of Things before They are Even Created?

One of the most complicated philosophical and theological issues is that of Allah's knowledge about the created things before they were even created. It is a known fact that Allah is aware of all of the future events, something that has been repeatedly reiterated in various verses of the Quran. It has also been implied in the above-mentioned remarks by Imam Ali ('a).

Moreover, Allah's knowledge is not "acquired knowledge", to use a philosophical terminology. That is to say, He does not "acquire" His

1. Al-Kāfī, vol. 1, p. 91, Bāb al-Nisbah, hadith 2 and p. 113, Bāb Ḥudūth al-Asmā', hadith No. 2.

knowledge by having the depiction of the objects and creatures being reflected on His Essence because, unlike the created beings, He does not have a mind to capture the reflections of the existing things and "learn" about them.

Rather, Allah's knowledge is of a kind which is described as "immediate" or "intuitive" knowledge; this means that the existence of all that exists is present before Him. But this gives rise to another problem: immediate knowledge only works for things which already exist, not for things that have not yet come into existence. The same issue can also be argued about things or beings which existed in the past but they have died or disappeared now.

The reason why we are aware of the existence of things which have been annihilated in the past is that we keep reflections of their existence and memories of them in our mind. But how can a Being who has no mind, memory, or any record of the reflections of the existence of things, as His sacred Essence is no place for temporal origination, be aware of their existence?

Let us clarify this point with an example: although the Pharaoh and his followers have died and their corpses long decomposed, we can create a mental image of who they were through historical accounts of their time period and the remnants of their civilization. However, unlike us human beings, Allah does not acquire His knowledge; so how can He be knowledgeable about Pharaoh and his people though they are long dead and their bodies have turned into dust?

This rather sophisticated concept has stirred theologians and philosophers into constant motion in the attempts to unravel its mysterious coils, and they have come up with different explanations, some of which will be listed below:

1. Allah has always possessed full knowledge of His own Essence, which is the cause of the existence of all that exists. Put differently, Allah's Essence has always been the most present within His Essence, and this full knowledge of His own Essence has provided Him with a General knowledge of all the events and creatures of the world, both before and after their creation.

It should be noted that when we have a precise and complete knowledge of the cause of things, this will also make us knowledgeable regarding the effect or the result of that cause. This is because it is the cause of everything that invests it with its specific qualities; therefore, the cause is even more complete than the effect as it creates that certain effect.

As a result, since Allah is the Cause of everything that exists and He has complete knowledge of His own Essence, it follows that He also has knowledge of the effect of this cause, i.e. everything that exists. This, in effect, originates from a sort of in-depth and extensive knowledge of everything which is possessed by Allah.

This concept can be explained in a different way as well: the past events will never completely be obliterated as their consequences, outcomes, and effects still exist in the events of the present. Future events are, likewise, not detached from the present events as the future events stem from the present events.

Thus, the past, present, and future, are, in effect, a chain of causes and effects and knowledge of each of the links in this chain would necessitate knowledge of the links which are located immediately before and after it.

For instance, if we have detailed and precise knowledge of the weather condition on the earth as well as all of the factors that have given rise to this specific kind of condition along with all of their causes and effects, we will also know exactly how the earth's weather had been a thousand years before or what it will be like a thousand years from now. This is because the past, present, and future are linked together and having precise knowledge of one will lead to knowing the others as well.

In other words, the present is a reflection of the past, and the future is a reflection of the present; hence, being aware of all the details of a present event will mean having complete knowledge of the similar past and future events.

Now, considering the fact that Allah is the origin of all of the past, present, and future events and that He has full Knowledge of His own Essence, He naturally has knowledge of the past, present, and future events as well. Of course, whatever effects and functions different things have in this world are by Allah's Leave and Command; nevertheless, His longstanding precedent is that everything in this world has to have its own specific characteristics and effects, but He can deprive them of their characteristics and effects whenever He wills.[1]

2. The other explanation provided for this complicated concept is the following: some have argued that the concepts of past, present, and future are conventional concepts which apply only to us because we are limited beings, confined within the boundaries of time and place. However, these concepts do not apply to Allah, who enjoys an unlimited Essence; in fact, all of the things, beings, and events are present before Allah in their temporal and spacial confines and with all of their subtleties and characteristics.

Let us clarify this argument with an example: suppose that a person is held prisoner in a small room with no windows to the outside. The only connections he has to the outside world is a small hole in the wall through which he sees that several camels pass by his room every day. As each camel passes by that hole, he first sees its head and long neck, then its hump, then its legs and finally its tail.

Due to the rather limited view of his outside world, this person will create a past, present, and future for himself in order to put the things that he sees on different occasions in order. However, if a person stands on the roof of that same room, they will be able to see the entire herd of camels grazing in the vast desert all at once.

1. The individuals who have put forward this argument to solve this issue have neglected an important flaw in their argument. The flaw in this argument is that, based on this argument, Allah is considered to not have had knowledge of the multiplicity of the creatures and things in this world before they were actually created, because His Divine Essence is far above such concepts as number or multiplicity. In other words, it follows from this argument that Allah's knowledge of the creatures before creating them had been different from His knowledge of them after He created them: before creating them His knowledge of them has been of a general nature and after creating them His knowledge of them has turned into a detailed one! What is rather astonishing here is that some of the proponents of this argument have actually argued for this change in Divine Knowledge!!

Part Five

Sermon No.1

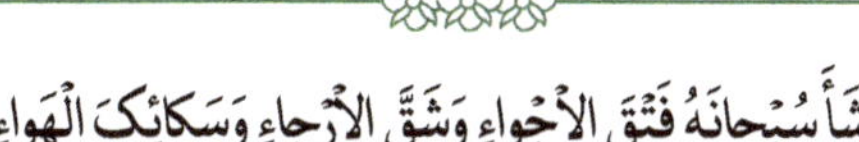

ثُمَّ أَنْشَأَ سُبْحانَهُ فَتْقَ الأَجْواءِ وَشَقَّ الأَرْجاءِ وَسَكائِكَ الْهَواءِ

"Then Allah _Glory be to Him_ caused the firmament to split [into different levels] and He ripped its ends open, creating empty spaces."

Commentary [Part Five]

The Genesis of the Creation of the Universe 

In this section of his speech, Imam Ali ('a) begins discussing the genesis of the creation of the universe, starting with how Allah created the heavens and the space:

ثُمَّ أَنْشَأَ سُبْحَانَهُ فَتْقَ[1] الْأَجْوَاءِ[2]

"Then Allah _Glory be to Him_ caused the firmament to split [into different levels]..."

And then he continues:

وَشَقَّ[3] الْأَرْجَاءِ[4]

"... and He ripped its ends open"

1. The original meaning of the Arabic term "فتق" [pronounced "Fatq"] is "creating an opening", "splitting", and dividing two things. Its antonym [according to al-Rāghib in his book al-Mufradāt], is "رتق" [pronounced "Ratq"]. In fact, the reason why "morning" is called "فتيق" in Arabic is that it splits the dark horizon of the night with its light and suddenly appears at dawn. According to the Lisān al-'Arab dictionary, eloquent individuals are also called "فتيق اللسان" because they have influential words.

2. The word "اجواء" is the plural of "جوّ"; according to al-Mufradāt and Lisān al-'Arab dictionaries, it is used to refer to the atmosphere that is around the earth or the empty space between the earth and the other planets and stars.

3. The Arabic word "شق" means an opening, tear, or schism in something. Another derivative of this word, namely "شقاق" is used to refer to the schism or divide between different groups of people.

4. According to the Maqāyīs al-Lughah dictionary, the word "أرجاء" [singular "رجا" pronounced "Rajā"] means the walls or sides of a well or anything like that; its other derivative, "رجاء" [pronounced "Rajā'"] means "hope". Some scholars, including the author of the book Al-Taḥqīq believe that the meaning of this word is a combination of the meaning of both of its derivatives, meaning that it refers to the hope that one gets from every side.

Finally, the Imam (‘a) concludes:

“... creating empty spaces.”

In this section, Imam Ali (‘a) explains how Allah expanded the space in the universe from every direction and how He created different levels of heavens in it.

This section of the Imam’s speech indicates that the creation of the material world began with the creation of a vast space which would later house the countless planets, stars, and galaxies. It is very much like a painter who prepares his canvas before beginning to paint a picture.

It should be noted that the term “ثُمَّ” [meaning “then”] used at the beginning of this sentence does not indicate the order in which Allah created different things in the world, but it is merely an indication of the specific order of the sentences said in this sermon. As we saw above, Imam Ali (‘a) discussed the creation of different creatures and beings in the previous sections of his sermon, and then in this section he begins speaking of the creation of the space and heavens. However, there is no doubt that the creation of the vast space and the celestial bodies in it preceded that of the living creatures.

So why does the Imam (‘a) mention the creation of the living creatures before that of the space and celestial bodies? The fact of the matter is

1. The Arabic term “سكائك” is the plural of the word “سُكاكه” [pronounced “Sukākah”]; according to the Lisān al-‘Arab dictionary, it is used to refer to the empty space between the earth and the other planets and stars. Ibn Abī al-Ḥadīd, however, believes that it is used to refer to deep space.

2. The word “هواء” originally means “being empty” or “falling down” and this is why any empty thing, including the space between the earth and the heaven, is called “هوا” in Arabic. Moreover, the reason why the carnal desires and lusts of human beings are also called “هوى” in Arabic is that following them will lead to fall both in this world and the hereafter [Maqāyīs al-Lughah, al-Mufradāt, and Lisān al-‘Arab dictionaries]. It seems that one of the new meanings which this word has taken on is the “atmosphere” of the earth which is actually not empty but made up of different gasses; this new meaning, however, is not completely unrelated to its original meaning as the air around us is invisible and it all seems like empty space around us [Although there are some Islamic Aḥādith which have used this word to refer to the air around us as well].

that Imam Ali ('a) first presents a general discussion of the creation of living creatures as an introduction to his discussion of Allah's Act of creation and then begins speaking about each of the stages of creation in detail from this latter section.

In any case, it appears from this part of the Imam's sermon that the vast empty space was the first or one of the first things that was created in the material world. As regards the nature of the space, a heated and complicated discussion has been going on among philosophers and theologians as to the fact that whether "space" is the existence of something or the non-existence of something.

Some are of the opinion that just as the concept of "time" came into being only after the genesis and movement of the created beings and things [because time is essentially the result of the calculation of movement], so the concept of "place" came about following the emergence of different objects and the comparison between them. This view seems to be seriously flawed, as it is almost impossible to imagine something coming into existence in the material world without first having being allocated a certain "place" to exist in. This is because any physical thing that exists in the world necessarily takes up some space. For instance, when we build a building, not only is it located at a certain place on a certain piece of land, it also takes up some space in the air, and the higher it is built, the greater space in the air it takes up.

In any case, the only thing that we know for sure about this issue is what Amīr al-Mu'minīn ('a) explains in this section of his sermon: that the space, its different sides, and its different levels were all created by Allah. As regards the nature of the space, we will leave it for now to be discussed later in its due place.

An Important Point
Is the Material World a Created Entity?

There is much controversy among philosophers and theologians regarding whether the material world is temporally created or temporally pre-eternal. Some of these scientists believe it to be pre-eternal, while a larger number of others consider it to be temporally created. This latter group of scientists argue that there is only a single pre-eternal entity, which is the Divine Essence of Allah; therefore, anything other than Allah's Essence is temporally created and dependent upon His pure Essence.

The proponents of the idea of temporal createdness of the world have sometimes offered philosophical arguments to support their views, and at other times, they have used evidence from other scientific fields to prove their idea.

One of the famous philosophical arguments which have been presented to support this view has been that of first principle [Latin: "Primum movens"]. This argument suggests that this world is constantly swinging between the two states of motion and motionlessness and that it is an established fact that motion and motionlessness are temporally created. Therefore, anything that is subject to a temporally created event is itself temporally created.

This argument can be expanded to be more inclusive in scope: this world is constantly changing and undergoing transformations and alteration, and it is an established fact that transformation and change are characteristics of created entities. This is because if something is at the same time both pre-eternal and changing, it would mean that we believe that pre-eternity and temporal createdness, whose distinguishing characteristic is constant change, are the same thing. Needless to say, this is a blatant contradiction.

This concept is more easily understood through the theory of "trans-substantial motion" which holds: "motion is inherent within the nature of things; rather, motion IS the nature of things." Based on this theory, it is rather evident that this world is temporally created because motion is a created thing and it is not a pre-eternal issue. This argument can be studied and scrutinized critically within the framework of philosophical studies and research, something which is certainly f beyond the scope of our book.

Let us now consider the scientific evidence for this issue. Modern science has proven through various pieces of evidence that this world is constantly declining and deteriorating toward a state of higher entropy: all of the planets, stars, galaxies, and even the earth and whatever exists on it are subject to this constant movement toward decline and decay.

This constant process of deterioration and decline is clear evidence that the material world has an end because declining cannot continue forever and it will logically continue indefinitely. So, when we realize that decline has an end, we must also admit that it has had a beginning too, because if something is not to last forever, it has definitely not been pre-eternal either. This is because being eternal means being limitless and infinite, and something that has no limits has no beginning; therefore, something that is not eternal will not be pre-eternal either.

Put differently, if this world had been pre-eternal and, at the same time, eroding and declining, it should not exist now as it should have been destroyed and wiped out of existence a long time ago because an eternal period of decline equals annihilation and non-existence. In other words, according to the latest scientific theories, the entire world is constantly moving toward uniformity; atoms fall apart and turn into energy and all forms of energy are also constantly transforming toward uniformity. This is very much like a campfire lit in a large room; the fuel of the fire burns and emits intense heat, but the heat gradually spreads in the room and loses its initial intensity, becoming uniform.

Based on these theories, had this world been pre-eternal and constantly declining all throughout eternity, all of the matter that exists in it should have already turned into energy and that energy should have long turned into a uniform sort of energy. This, however, does not mean that there has been a time when Allah has had no creatures or that His Bountiful Essence has withheld His bounties from living beings. In fact, the contrary is true and this can even be justified based on the above-mentioned argument. It can be argued that Allah has always had creatures to bestow His bounties and grace upon but His creatures have always been subject to transformation and change, with some of them dying out and others emerging.

However, all of those creatures in their entirety depended on Allah's Divine Essence, or put simply, they were essentially, and not temporally, created in nature; this is because when all of the creatures that have ever existed are considered as a whole, time loses its meaning regarding them and they are said to be essentially created, meaning that the very essence of their existence is a created one.

This argument will also help clarify the following Islamic hadith about Allah:

كَانَ اللّٰهُ وَلا شَيْءَ مَعَهُ

"Allah has forever existed and there existed nothing besides Him."[1]

This does not mean that the creations of Allah have always been non-existent; rather, it means that they have never enjoyed the same sort of existence as Allah's pure Essence, but that they have been created by Him.

1. Al-Shaykh al-Ṣadūq, Al-Tawḥīd, P. 67, hadith No. 20. Similar Aḥādith with similar contents can also be found on pages 145 and 226 of the same book.

Part Six

Sermon No.1

فَأَجْرَى فِيهَا مَاءً مُتَلاطِماً تَيّارُهُ مُتَراكِماً زَخّارُهُ، حَمَلَهُ عَلَى مَتْنِ
الرّيحِ الْعاصِفَةِ وَالزَّعْزَعِ الْقاصِفَةِ، فَأَمَرَهَا بِرَدِّهِ، وَسَلَّطَهَا عَلَى شَدِّهِ،
وَقَرَنَهَا إِلَى حَدِّهِ، الْهَواءُ مِنْ تَحْتِها فَتِيقٌ، وَالْماءُ مِنْ فَوْقِها دَفِيقٌ

"Then He caused to flow therein water with crushing surges and wave upon wave of tides. Then He carried the water on a fierce wind and a shattering gale, then He commanded the wind to bring its waves back, giving the wind control over its violent turbulences, and confining it within its boundaries, [while] under it there was open space and above it was the raging water."

Commentary [part Six]

The First Thing That was Created was Water 

Following his theological discussions in the previous sections, Amīr al-Mu'minīn ('a) attends to the issue of the genesis of the world in this section as well as in the next section of his sermon. A quick glance at the remarks made by the Imam ('a) in these two sections reveals that, in the beginning, Allah created a primary matter metaphorically referred to as "water"; the reason for this specific appellation might be the fact that the primary matter with which the entire universe was later created was a liquid-like matter.

Imam Ali ('a) then explains that, after creating this water, Allah carried it on a fierce wind which was charged with keeping that matter in check, preventing it from being diffused by keeping it confined within certain boundaries. Then, Allah raised up another gale whose job was to create huge waves and tides on that vast ocean of liquid, hitting waves after waves of its mountainous surges on each other, causing huge parts of that liquid to be ejected high into the empty space. It was from these huge chunks of the first matter that Allah later created the seven heavens.

Needless to say, the words which have been used here to capture the objects and events in the beginning of the creation of the world, including water, wind, and gale, are all metaphors used to make those things and events more understandable for us. Obviously, in the beginning of the process of creation, there was no water, wind, or gale as we know them today, and mankind has never been able to invent any words for the things and the events at the beginning of the creation of the world either.

Therefore, the only way that remains is to use the existing words in metaphoric ways in order to bring those things and events close to mind, and this is exactly what Imam Ali ('a) has done here.

Through a little attention, one will be able to interpret these remarks by Imam Ali ('a) based on the scientific findings of modern scientists; however, we do not claim that these are precise interpretations of what the Imam ('a) actually meant. We only present them as possible interpretations of Imam Ali's remarks made in this sermon.

According to the latest cosmological theories about the genesis of the universe, at first the cosmos had been a dense and superhot mass of gas which had been like some liquid. This might be the thing which has been referred to in the Quran as "Dukhān" [a gas-like smoke]; another possibility is that the outer parts of this huge mass had been less dense and looked like some sort of gas or smoke, while the more inner parts were more condensed and looked more like liquid.

What kept this huge mass of matter together had been the force of gravity which has always existed between all the particles of the material world; this force of gravity was what kept this great mass of liquid-like gas in check, holding it all together and preventing it from dispersing out of its boundaries into the empty space.

After some time, this huge ball of mass began rotating around itself [another possibility is that it had been rotating from the very beginning], giving rise to a centrifugal force. It was, therefore, this centrifugal force that caused huge clumps of that condensed ball of gas to eject into the empty space. This is probably what has been meant in the Nahj al-Balāghah, where it has been mentioned: "The waves of that ocean [of the First Matter] were sent in every direction and they were raised into the empty heaven and vast space". These sorts of descriptions regarding the First Matter of the universe can be seen in the subsequent sections of this same sermon as well.

It was from these ejected clumps of the First Matter that various galaxies, planets, and stars later emerged, and this is probably what the Quran and the Nahj al-Balāghah have referred to as the creation of the various levels of firmaments or "the seven heavens".

We do not intend to impose any of the current scientific theories on Imam Ali's remarks; nevertheless, we believe that the current cosmological theories regarding the formation of the cosmos, the galaxies, and the earth serve to interpret the facts mentioned by the Imam ('a) in this regard in his sermon.

Let us now take a closer look at the precise and profound remarks made by Imam Ali ('a) in this section of his sermon.

The Imam ('a) begins this section of his sermon, stating:

فَأَجْرَى فِيهَا مَاءً مُتَلاطِماً[1] تَيَّارُهُ[2]

"Then He caused to flow therein water with crushing surges..."

Is this turbulent "water" not the same thing as the condensed mass of liquid-like gasses which, according to the modern cosmological theories, formed the primary matter from which the entire universe later emerged?

Following this introduction, the Imam ('a) emphasizes further that it was an extremely turbulent mass of water:

مُتَرَاكِماً[3] زَخَّارُهُ[4]

"... and wave upon wave of tides."

1. The Arabic word "متلاطم" derives from the root word "لطم" [pronounced "Laṭm"] and it originally means to slap oneself on the face. It has also been used to refer to the instance of waves hitting each other at sea.

2. The word "تيّار" has originally been used to refer to the waves of the sea that hit the shore and throw some water offshore. However, some references indicate that it can also be used to refer to just any kind of wave [according to Maqāyīs al-Lughah and Lisān al-'Arab dictionaries].

3. The Arabic term "متراكم", which derives from the root word "ركم" [pronounced "Rakm"], means "heaped" or "place one thing on top of the other". It is used to refer to condensed clouds, water, and even crowds of people that are tightly pressed together somewhere [according to al-Mufradāt, Lisān al-'Arab, and Maqāyīs al-Lughah dictionaries].

4. The word "زخّار", which derives from the root words "زخر" [pronounced "Zakhr"] and "زخور" originally means to arise or rise up. It has also been used to refer to the flow, the phase of the tide when the water of the sea surges toward the shore and rises up.

Then he adds:

حَمَلَهُ عَلَى مَتْنِ الرِّيحِ الْعَاصِفَةِ[1] وَالزَّعْزَعِ[2] الْقَاصِفَةِ[3]

"Then He carried the water on a fierce wind and a shattering gale..."

The Arabic word "عاصف" means fierce and crushing and the term "زعزع" means "severe" or "turbulent", which has been used metaphorically here to refer to a severe gale; finally, the word "قاصف" also means "shattering". Evidently, all of these words have been used as metaphors to emphasize how horrendous, huge and fierce that gale had been. Imam Ali ('a) then continues and states the following:

فَأَمَرَهَا بِرَدِّهِ، وَسَلَّطَهَا عَلَى شَدِّهِ[4]، وَقَرَنَهَا إِلَى حَدِّهِ

"... then He commanded the wind to bring its waves back, giving the wind control over its violent turbulences, and confining it within its boundaries..."

1. The Arabic term "عاصفة" derives from the root word "عصف" [pronounced "'Aṣf"]. It has originally been used to convey lightness and speed; hence, it has been used to refer the way chaff spreads in the wind. Its other derivatives, namely "عاصف" and "معصف" [pronounced "Mu'ṣif"] are used to refer to anything that shatters or grinds something to powder. [According to al-Mufradāt, Lisān al-'Arab, and Maqāyīs al-Lughah dictionaries]

2. The original meaning of the Arabic word "زعزع" [pronounced "Za'za'"] has been motion, turbulence, and swaying. It has also been used as an adjective to mean "severe" [According to the Lisān al-'Arab and Maqāyīs al-Lughah dictionaries]

3. The Arabic term "قاصفة", which derives from the root word "قصف" [pronounced "Qaṣf"], has originally been used to refer to the breaking of something. Its other derivative, "قاصف" is used to refer to severe gales that break ships at sea and the severe thunders that break trees and houses. [According to al-Mufradāt, Lisān al-'Arab, and Maqāyīs al-Lughah dictionaries].

4. The Arabic word "شدّ" [pronounced "Shadd"] is used to emphasize the intensity or power of something or someone. This is why strong and robust individuals [particularly warriors] are described as "شديد" in Arabic. This word is also used to refer to one's preparation and steadfastness during adversities and calamities [According to al-Mufradāt, Lisān al-'Arab, and Maqāyīs al-Lughah dictionaries].

Could this “gale” be a metaphor for the force of gravity which Allah has made dominant over every physical thing that exists in this world in order to prevent them from disintegrating and dispersing, confining them all within certain limits? What better metaphor can one find to capture the purpose which the force of gravity has been created to fulfill?

The Imam (‘a) then goes on to say the following:

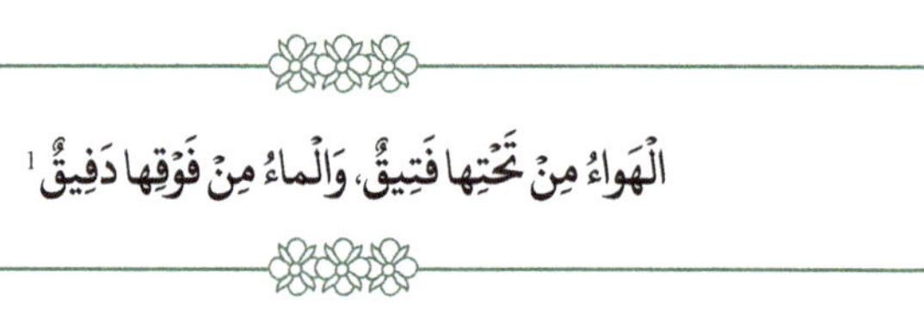

الْهَواءُ مِنْ تَحْتِها فَتِيقٌ، وَالْماءُ مِنْ فَوْقِها دَفِيقٌ [1]

“... [while] under it there was open space and above it was the raging water.”

The Arabic word “فتيق” [pronounced “Fatīq”] derives from the root word “فتق”, which means open; the word “دفيق” [pronounced “Dafīq”], which has been derived from the root word “دفق”, means move swiftly and violently.

So, the turbulence and waves of the First Matter was brought under control by that primitive gale which then confined the huge mass of that matter within certain boundaries. The question that arises here is that, since that gale kept the huge mass of the First Matter in check, why did huge waves still continue to form on its surface?

It is customary of the oceans and seas of water on the earth that waves and storms create waves on their surface; but as this sermon indicates, that primitive gale served to bring the mountainous waves of the First Matter under control, and not the other way around. So, what was creating the waves in the First Matter even before that gale was created to curb its turbulence and huge waves?

It seems that there existed an internal factor within the First Matter itself which made it unstable and agitated, creating waves on its surface. However, as to what exactly caused its instability, we have no

1. The word “دفيق”, which derives from the root word “دفق” [pronounced “Dafq”] originally means “to propel forward”; it is also used to refer to swift and violent movement. Its other derivative “ادفق” is used in Arabic to refer to a fast camel.

clear answer; nevertheless, this description of the First Matter matches the modern scientific theories regarding it.

Modern cosmological theories suggest that deep within the liquid-like gasses of the First Matter, series of nuclear explosions occurred, something like what happens deep inside our sun's surface today, and these explosions severely and constantly destabilized that huge mass of gas. It was probably due to the huge shockwaves of those nuclear explosions that the surface of the First Matter was extremely turbulent with huge waves constantly forming on its surface.

Yet, in order to get a more vivid picture of the events at the beginning of the creation of the cosmos, we need to consider the rest of Imam Ali's remarks in this regard in the next section of his sermon.

Part Seven

Sermon No.1

ثُمَّ اَنْشَأَ سُبْحانَهُ رِيحاً اعْتَقَمَ مَهَبَّها وَأَدامَ مُرَبَّها وَأَعْصَفَ مَجْراها وَأَبْعَدَ مَنْشَأَها
فَأَمَرَها بِتَصْفِيقِ الْماءِ الزَّخّارِ وَإِثارَةِ مَوْجِ الْبِحارِ فَمَخَضَتْهُ مَخْضَ السِّقاءِ
وَعَصَفَتْ بِهِ عَصْفَها بِالْفَضاءِ. تَرُدُّ أَوَّلَهُ اِلَى آخِرِهِ وَسَاجِيَهُ اِلَى مَائِرِهِ حَتَّى عَبَّ
عُبابُهُ وَرَمَى بِالزَّبَدِ رُكامُهُ فَرَفَعَهُ فِي هَواءٍ مُنْفَتِقٍ وَجَوٍّ مُنْفَهِقٍ فَسَوَّى مِنْهُ سَبْعَ
سَمواتٍ جَعَلَ سُفْلاهُنَّ مَوْجاً مَكْفُوفاً وَعُلْياهُنَّ سَقْفاً مَحْفُوظاً وَسَمْكاً مَرْفُوعاً
بِغَيْرِ عَمَدٍ يَدْعَمُها وَلا دِسارٍ يَنْظِمُها ثُمَّ زَيَّنَها بِزِينَةِ الْكَواكِبِ وَضِياءِ الثَّواقِبِ
وَأَجْرَى فِيهَا سِراجاً مُسْتَطِيراً وَقَمَراً مُنِيراً فِي فَلَكٍ دائِرٍ وَسَقْفٍ سائِرٍ وَرَقِيمٍ مائِرٍ

"Then Allah _Glory be to Him_ brought forth another wind [which was nothing like the winds and gales of the earth] with bone-dry blasts, and made it a constant companion of the water. He raised that wind from a far-off place [and increased its severity as it kept blowing in]. Then He ordered it to set that condensed water in motion, driving the mountainous waves of the oceans [of that water] in every direction, rocking them just as a water-carrier's water-skin is rocked. And it hit that water hard as it fiercely blew in the empty space, pouring its front on its rear and its calm parts on its turbulent ones until the water rose high like a mountain and its mountainous waves threw up their froth. Then He scattered that froth into an expanded atmosphere and a vast space, and He fashioned seven heavens from it. He made their lowest as a curbed wave, and their highest as a secure ceiling and an elevated canopy without any pillars to support it, or any pegs to hold it together. Then He adorned it with the ornament of stars and the shimmering of the shiners and He made to course therein a radiant lamp [i.e. the sun] and a luminous moon, [all coursing] in a moving orbit, a revolving canopy, and a moving expanse."

Commentary [Part Seven]

The Role of Fierce Winds at the Beginning of the Process of Creation

As it was discussed above, this section of Imam Ali's sermon is a complement for the previous section. In this section too, we will first try to interpret the precisely-worded and profound remarks of the Imam ('a), without trying to impose any sort of prejudgments on them, and then we will try to match the modern cosmological theories regarding the genesis of the cosmos to them afterwards.
Imam Ali ('a) begins this section of his sermon with the following remarks:

"Then Allah _Glory be to Him_ brought forth another wind [which was nothing like the winds and gales of the earth] with bone-dry blasts ..."

From what appears from these remarks, we can conclude that this was a completely dry wind as there existed no clouds there so that it could move and condense them to produce rain and help plants to grow as a result.
The Imam ('a) further describes this wind as follows:

1. The Arabic term "اعتقم" derives from the root word "عقم" [pronounced "'Uqm"]; it is used to refer to land that is so dry that nothing can penetrate it or grow from it. Its other derivative, namely "عقيم", is used to describe a woman who is infertile and unable to conceive. This word has also been used to mean "straitened" as well [According to al-Mufradāt, Lisān al-'Arab, and Maqāyīs al-Lughah dictionaries].

2. The word "مَهَبّ" derives from the root word "هبوب" [pronounced "Hubūb"] and means to wake up, circulate, or stir into motion. It is also used to refer to the way ancient warriors would swirl their swords in the air on the battlefield as they charged toward the enemy lines. In fact, this is why this word later came to be used metaphorically to refer to whirlwinds and storms.

وَأَدَامَ مُرَبَّهَا[1]

"... and made it a constant companion of the water"

This sentence indicates that, unlike usual winds that blow for a time and then stop blowing, this wind had been a relentless one.
The Imam ('a) then continues:

وَأَعْصَفَ مَجْرَاهَا وَأَبْعَدَ مَنْشَأَهَا

"He raised that wind from a far-off place and increased its severity [as it kept blowing in]."

The Imam ('a) then goes on and elaborates on the task which that fierce wind was charged with:

فَأَمَرَهَا بِتَصْفِيقِ[2] الْمَاءِ الزَّخَّارِ

"Then He ordered it to set that condensed water in motion..."

---

1. The Arabic term "مُرَبّ" derives from the root word "رَبّ", which originally means "to bring up" or "train". This is why a person's teacher, coach, and trainer are referred to in Arabic as "رَبّ"; it is also used to refer to the owner or creator of something [it is a present participle]. However, its other derivative "اربابِ" [pronounced "Irbāb"] means "to constantly accompany" someone or something [probably because training someone without constantly accompanying them is impossible]. Therefore, the word "مُرَبّ" in this sentence means "constant companionship".

2. As it was discussed previously, the Arabic term "تصفیق", which derives from the root word "صفق" [pronounced "Ṣafq"], means swift and fierce motion.

وَإِثَارَةِ مَوْجِ الْبِحَارِ

"... driving the mountainous waves of the oceans [of that water] in every direction ..."

فَمَخَضَتْهُ¹ مَخْضَ السِّقَاءِ

"... rocking them just as a water-carrier's water-skin is rocked."

وَعَصَفَتْ بِهِ عَصْفَها بِالْفَضَاءِ

"And it hit that water hard as it fiercely blew in the empty space ..."

تَرُدُّ أَوَّلَهُ إِلَى آخِرِهِ وَسَاجِيَهُ² إِلَى مَائِرِهِ³

"... pouring its front on its rear and its calm parts on its turbulent ones..."

---

1. The original meaning of the word "مَخَضَ" [pronounced "Makhaḍa"], which derives from the root word "مخض" [pronounced "Makhḍ"], is "set in motion" or "churn" and "rock" liquids in certain containers. So this word is used for when yogurt is rocked in water-skins to get its butter out.

2. The word "سَاجِي", which derives from the root word "سجو" [pronounced "Sajw"], means calm and unagitated.

3. The Arabic term "مَائِر", which derives from the root word "مور" [pronounced "Mawr"] has been originally used to refer to a fast flow of something. It later became commonly used to mean "road" because traffic flows on it.

Imam Ali ('a) then finishes this part of his remarks by stating the following:

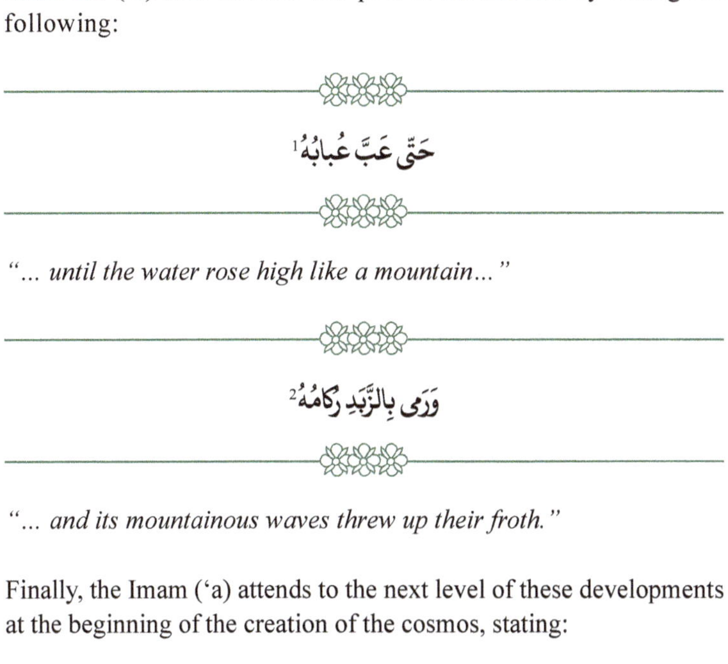

حَتّى عَبَّ عُبابُهُ[1]

"... until the water rose high like a mountain..."

وَرَمى بِالزَّبَدِ رُكامُهُ[2]

"... and its mountainous waves threw up their froth."

Finally, the Imam ('a) attends to the next level of these developments at the beginning of the creation of the cosmos, stating:

فَرَفَعَهُ في هَواءٍ مُنْفَتِقٍ وَجَوٍّ مُنْفَهِقٍ[3]

"Then He scattered that froth into an expanded atmosphere and a vast space,"

---

1. The Arabic word "عباب", which derives from the root word "عَبّ", means quickly gulping down water without pause. It is also used to refer to heavy downpours which cause floods. In this sentence, however, it is used to refer to the huge amounts of water piled up like a mountain.

2. As it has been previously mentioned, the word "رُكام" means condensed or piled up.

3. The Arabic term "منفهق" derives from the root word "فهق" [pronounced "Fahq"] and means "a vast expanse". Based on this original meaning, the widest part of a valley and the wide surface of a bowl of water are also called "منفهق" in Arabic.

فَسَوّى مِنْهُ سَبْعَ سَماواتٍ

"and He fashioned seven heavens from it."

جَعَلَ سُفْلاهُنَّ مَوْجاً مَكْفُوفاً[1] وَعُلْياهُنَّ سَقْفاً مَحْفُوظاً وَسَمْكاً[2] مَرْفُوعاً

"He made their lowest as a curbed wave, and their highest as a secure ceiling and an elevated canopy ..."

بِغَيْرِ عَمَدٍ[3] يَدْعَمُها[4] وَلا دِسارٍ[5] يَنْظِمُها

"... without any pillars to support it, or any pegs to hold it together."

Finally, in the last part of this section of his sermon, Imam Ali ('a) refers to the creation of the stars and other celestial bodies in the heaven:

1. The word "مكفوف", which derives from the root word "كف" [pronounced "Kaff"], means to clasp or constrict. The reason why the palm of the hand is called "كف" in Arabic is that it is this part of the hand that grasps different things. Moreover, the blind are called "مكفوف" in Arabic because their eyes are closed.

2. The original meaning of the Arabic term "سمک" is height or a high place; later on, the roof of building is also called "سمک" because it is usually the highest part of the building.

3. The Arabic words "عَمَد" [pronounced "'Amad"] and "عُمد" [pronounced "'Umud"] are both the plural forms of the word "عمود", which means "pillar" or "pole".

4. The Arabic word "يدعم", which derives from the root word "دعم" [pronounced "Da'ama"], means to support something in an upright position. Its other derivatives, namely, "دعام" and "دعامه" mean long pieces of wooden bars with which trellises or scaffolds are constructed in order to support the weight of something or someone.

5. The word "دسار" means peg or nail; it is also used to refer to the ropes used to fasten something firmly to something else.

ثُمَّ زَيَّنَها بِزينَةِ الْكَواكِبِ وَضِياءِ الثَّواقِبِ[1]

"Then He adorned it with the ornament of stars and the shimmering of the shiners ..."

وَأَجْرَى فِيهَا سِراجاً مُسْتَطيراً[2] وَقَمَراً مُنيراً فِي فَلَكٍ دائِرٍ وَسَقْفٍ سائِرٍ وَرَقيمٍ[3] مائِرٍ

"... and He made to course therein a radiant lamp [i.e. the sun] and a luminous moon, [all coursing] in a moving orbit, a revolving canopy, and a moving expanse."

1. The Arabic term "ثواقب" derives from the root word "ثقب" [pronounced "Thaqb"]; it means to pierce, tear, or penetrate something. It is also used to refer to luminous stars because their light seems to pierce one's eyes or their light pierces the space and arrives here on the earth for us to see.

2. The Arabic word "مستطير" derives from the root word "طير", which originally refers to something that is so light that can float in the air. It is also used to refer to something that flies fast in the sky, including birds. The term "مستطير" on the other hand means outspread and dispersed over a large area. It is also used to refer to the sunrise in the early morning when the sunlight spreads from the horizon on a vast expanse of land.

3. The Arabic word "رقيم" derives from the root word "رقم" [pronounced "Raqm"], and its original meaning is scribing and written documents; the word "رقيم" has also been used to mean "book". On the other hand, it has been used to refer to the expanse of the sky because it looks like a page of the book filled with stars and other celestial bodies and objects as its contents [According to the Maqāyīs al-Lughah, al-Mufradāt, and Lisān al-'Arab dictionaries].

Important Points

1. Making a General Match Between Imam 'Alī's Remarks and the Modern Cosmological Theories

Modern scientists have some ideas about the genesis of the cosmos which do not go beyond a number of unverified theories and hypotheses. This is because no one lived billions of years ago to personally observe the formation of the cosmos and report it precisely. However, there are certain pieces of evidence that support some of these hypotheses and theories.

A quick glance at the current scientific theories reveals that the descriptions presented by Amīr al-Mu'minīn ('a) regarding the process of the formation of the cosmos match the most well-known modern cosmological theories. However, what we present to our dear readers below is just a possible match between the Imam's remarks and the current cosmological theories, not a definite interpretation of the Imam's remarks. In other words, we do not presume to say that what the Imam ('a) meant to convey about the genesis of the cosmos is exactly what has been embodied in the current cosmological theories and hypotheses.

As it was discussed in our commentary on the previous sections of his sermon, modern cosmologists believe that our world was, in the beginning, a mass of condensed gasses which looked very much like a mass of liquid. Therefore, the fact that the Quran has referred to this First Matter both as "ماء" [water] and "دخان" [smoke-like gas] is due to the fact that the First Matter was a sort of gas, but it was so condensed and pressurized that it seemed to be liquid.

Then, after some time, the Creator of the universe allowed two very powerful forces to dominate and change the First Matter, forces which have been metaphorically referred to by Imam Ali ('a) as two powerful winds or gales. These might be: 1. The force of gravity, which holds the different constituents and particles of things together, preventing them from disintegration; and 2. The repulsive force which came about as a result of the fast rotation of that huge mass of condensed gas which, in turn, created a centrifugal effect, forcing things away from its center. This was, in fact, the second fierce wind referred to in Imam Ali's sermon.

If we accept the idea that the rotation of the First Matter had been subject to fluctuations, with its rotation slowing down at some points and then speeding up again, it will also be easy to imagine the effects of those fluctuations on the surface of the First Matter. Such fluctuations would have created huge and horrendous waves on the surface of that liquid-like gas; those waves would rise up to the air and then come down hitting on top of each other, one after another.

Finally, the substances which were lighter in weight and had a lower unit weight [things which were metaphorically referred to by Imam Ali ('a) as froth] were ejected out of that huge mass into the empty space around it. [It should be noted that the word "زَبَد" used by Imam Ali ('a) to refer to these lighter substances means both the foam that forms on water as waves hit the shore and the butter which forms on top of milk or yogurt when it is churned].

So, as the rotation of the First Matter became faster and faster, huge clumps of that mass of matter broke off of it and were thrown into deep space; those chunks that were thrown with a higher speed went up to the higher levels of the space while the ones that had a lower speed as they broke off of the First Matter found their place in the lower sections of the space.

But even the ones that were shot to the far corners of the space were not able to completely escape the gravity of the First Matter; thus, they formed a unified canopy over it. In the lower sections, however, the chunks of matter that were thrown with lower speeds formed atmospheres which Imam Ali ('a) referred to as "موج مكفوف" [a curbed wave].

It was at this point where the seven heavens, which we will discuss subsequently, emerged in the vast expanse of space and they were held high without any pillars to support their weight or any visible harnesses to keep them in place. The only thing that kept them all in place and made everything remain in their due course was a perfect balance between the force of gravity and the repulsive force which they were all subjected to.

At that time, the vast space was full of small and large chunks of matter, which have been shot into deep space by the great mass of First

Matter. But then, gradually, the smaller chunks began to be attracted to the larger ones, based on the law of gravitation, joining each other and giving rise to various celestial bodies, including planets and stars. It was at this point where the stars began shining in the dark space, adorning it with their light. It was also at around the same time when our sun also began shining on the solar system, giving the moon its luminescence to shine on the dark nights of the earth; as the celestial bodies formed in the empty space, each began moving in a specific orbit as well.

Some of the theories regarding the birth of the cosmos suggest that what made the galaxies and celestial bodies break off from the initial mass of the First Matter was a huge explosion in that huge mass [which they call Big Bang]. It is not clear why that huge explosion occurred in the First Matter, but it shot huge clumps of that primitive liquid-like gas deep into the space, giving rise to various planetary bodies and galaxies.

It is possible that Imam Ali's remarks about a fierce wind which blew on the water from a far-off place, rocking it hard and causing froth to form on it, is in reference to the same incident as the Big Bang which was triggered deep at the core of the First Matter itself.

At any rate, our goal here, as we mentioned above, is not to make definitive judgments about what exactly Imam Ali's remarks refer to, but to try to match them to the modern cosmological theories about the emergence of the cosmos, pointing out the similarities between them.

2. How the Cosmos Sprang into Existence

One of the most complex issues that the scientists and intellectuals have ever faced has been the question of how the cosmos sprang into existence. This is an issue which goes back to billions of years ago and whose process and scope might never be conceivable for the human mind. It is due to the complex nature of this issue that the scientists have been unable to find a convincing answer to it, despite forming several theories regarding it and conducting countless comprehensive studies on it.

Yet, regardless of the fact that all of these efforts have yielded rather few convincing results, man's curiosity does not allow him to stop searching for answers to his questions, particularly those regarding such a significant issue. In fact, although the scientists have been unable to arrive at a clear picture of the events at the beginning of the formation of the cosmos, they still prefer trying to form imaginations of it in their minds [through forming theories] whereby to quench their thirst for learning more about it.

As for the Quran and the Islamic traditions, they also present a rather vague picture of those events in rather brief and short remarks, probably because it is the nature of what occurred in those times that makes them unperceivable to human mind, and therefore more explanation regarding them would make no difference.

In any case, the remarks made by the Imam ('a) in this sermon are completely in line with his remarks made in sermon No. 211 of the Nahj al-Balāghah; in this latter sermon, Imam Ali ('a) makes the following remarks:

وَكانَ مِنِ اقْتِدارِ جَبَرُوتِهِ وَبَديعِ لَطائِفِ صَنْعَتِهِ اَنْ جَعَلَ مِنْ ماءِ الْبَحْرِ الزّاخِرِ
الْمُتَراكِمِ الْمُتَقاصِفِ يَبَساً جامِداً ثُمَّ فَطَرَمِنْهُ اَطْباقاً فَفَتَقَها سَبْعَ سَمواتٍ بَعْدَ ارْتِتاقِها

"It was out of the Power of His Might and His fine innovative Craftsmanship that He fashioned something solid from that ocean of turbulent and condensed water, then He fashioned it into several adjoining layers, then He peeled away those layer from one another, creating the seven heavens with them."

The Islamic traditions have also discussed this issue a lot, most of which are consistent with the contents of this sermon in the Nahj al-Balāghah. The only difference that these traditions have with this sermon in regard to the process of creation is that many of them indicate that at first some kind of froth or foam formed on the water and then, after the formation of that froth, some sort of steam or smoke rose from it and it was that steam or smoke that later transformed into the heavens.[1]

Nevertheless, just as it was stated above, these are different metaphors used to describe the same event and they do not have any essential differences with each other. This is because the First Matter had probably been some sort of condensed gas, which looked like liquid, and the terms "water", "steam", or "smoke", which have all been used to describe it in different Aḥādith, are correct descriptions considering its special form.

It is also worth noting that there is no contradiction among the various Aḥādith, which indicate that the first thing that Allah created was "water", "the light of the Prophet of Islam (ṣ)", or "intellect". The reason behind this apparent discrepancy is that some of these Aḥādith concern only the metaphysical and spiritual world, whereas the others discuss the case of the material and physical world.

Moreover, based on what was discussed above, it is clear that there is no contradiction between these Aḥādith and the verse 11 of Surah Fuṣṣilat in the Holy Quran, where it has been mentioned:

ثُمَّ اسْتَوَىٰ إِلَى السَّمَاءِ وَهِيَ دُخَانٌ

"Then He attended to the heaven, and it was smoke."

3. The Ancient Theories of the Genesis of the Cosmos Which Existed before the Advent of Islam

It is interesting to note that before the advent of Islam and the revelation of the Quran, two very famous cosmological theories already existed. The first was Ptolemaic theory of astronomy, which overshadowed the scientific communities of the world up until the late 15th century. According to Ptolemaic astronomy, the earth was located at the center of the world and nine spheres revolved around it as

1. For more information in this regard, refer to: Biḥār al-Anwār, vol. 54, p. 2, Bāb Ḥudūth al-'Ālam wa Bad'e Khalqeh.

their center.

He believed that the various heavens were transparent and adjoining layers, much like the layers of onions. He further claimed that the moving stars [i.e. planets Mercury, Venus, Jupiter, and Saturn] were each located on a different sphere and the sun and the moon were also located on their own different spheres.

Ptolemy further claimed that in addition to these seven spheres and heavens, there existed another sphere in which all of the stationary stars were located [and what he meant by stationary stars were all of the stars that appear in the night sky together and their place in the sky does not seem to change].

Finally, according to Ptolemy, there existed a ninth sphere beyond the eighth sphere which he called the sphere of the Atlas, in which there were no stars and which was responsible for moving and rotating the other spheres around the earth.

The other famous theory at that time was that of the "Ten Intellects", which was itself based on Ptolemy's theory of the natural world. This theory, which was put forward by a group of ancient Greek philosophers, suggested that, in the beginning, Allah created only one thing and that was "intellect" [and by intellect, they meant an angel or a great spiritual being, such as a spirit, that they merely called "intellect" to emphasize its non-physical nature].

The theory further suggests that following its creation, the intellect created two things, namely the second intellect and the ninth celestial sphere, i.e. the sphere of the Atlas. Then the second intellect created the third intellect along with the eighth celestial sphere, and the third intellect, in turn, gave rise to the fourth intellect, etc. In the end, ten intellects along with nine spheres were created and the tenth intellect created the living creatures in our world.

This hierarchy of intellects, much like Ptolemaic theory of astronomy, had no basis in fact and no evidence to support it, yet it ruled the minds of people for several centuries. But the Quran and the Islamic Aḥādith neither confirmed the first theory mentioned above nor the second one, as there is no trace of these theories or anything like them in the Quran or the most famous and authentic Islamic Aḥādith, particularly the ones recorded in the Nahj al-Balāghah. This is evidence as to the greatness of the Quran and the Islamic Aḥādith because although they

emerged during an area which was dominated by Ptolemaic theory of astronomy, their views and teachings were completely independent of them. This is also further proof as to the fact that the Quran and the Islamic Aḥādith stemmed from Divine revelations, not human thoughts, otherwise they would have had traces of human thinking and theories.[1]
So far, we have considered Amīr al-Mu'minīn's remarks regarding the genesis of the cosmos and we also saw how they were consistent with the contents of numerous other Islamic Aḥādith in this regard. It should be noted that as far as astronomy and cosmology are concerned, the Quran and the Islamic Aḥādith speak of seven heavens, not nine spheres or ten intellects; as for the concept of the seven heavens, we will discuss it in detail subsequently.
Although the Quran and the Nahj al-Balāghah clearly speak of the existence of "seven heavens", it is rather unfortunate that some of the scholars who have written commentaries on the Nahj al-Balāghah have tried doggedly to match the archaic Ptolemaic theory of astronomy and the theory of the ten intellects to this sermon of the Nahj al-Balāghah. This is while it was not wise to try to match the past theories to the Nahj al-Balāghah as those theories were merely hypotheses which have been long proven wrong.
Modern scientific discoveries in the field of astronomy have shown that there are no such things as "nine celestial spheres" the way that Ptolemy assumed. Modern astronomy has proven that there are billions of stars and planets in the universe, all existing in the empty space, moving in their own orbits. Additionally, modern science has

---

1. In fact, the teachings of the Quran regarding astronomical issues are so different and so ahead of their time that it can be said to have nothing at all to do with Ptolemaic system. For instance, there are certain verses in the Quran which clearly indicate that earth is a moving planet; some of these verses are as follows:
Al-Naml, 88: "And you see the mountains, reckoning them to be stagnant, while they are adrift like the drifting clouds, a handiwork of Allah, who has created everything perfectly."
Al-Mursalāt, 25: "Have We not made the earth a receptacle?" [Based on some exegeses of the Quran, this verse indicates that the earth works like a spaceship, carrying all that there is on it as it travels through the space].
There are also some verses in the Quran which indicate that the sun and the moon are suspended and floating in the empty space in the heaven; an example of these verses is the following:
Yā Sīn, 40: "Neither does it behoove the sun to overtake the moon, nor does the night get ahead of the day, and each swims in an orbit."
For the interpretation of these verses along with a more detailed explanation of this issue refer to Tafsīr-e Nemūneh.

shown that it is the sun that the solar system planets orbit around, not the earth, and that the other planets in the universe have suns and orbits of their own.

Finally, it has been proven that not only is the earth not the center of the universe, it is a small planet of the solar system, which is itself a small and insignificant part of the Milky Way galaxy which is itself only one of billions and billions of galaxies which exist in the universe.

Let us now consider the other ancient theory which was mentioned above, namely, that of Ten Intellects. The proponents of the theory of ten intellects have based their arguments, on the one hand, on the Ptolemaic system, which has been refuted by modern science, and on the other, on some principles of logic including the following principle:

اَلْواحِدُ لا يَصْدُرُ مِنْهُ اِلّا الْواحِدُ

"From the One, there proceeds nothing but One."

The discussion of this principle falls beyond the scope of our book, so we will not discuss it here. However, one point which needs to be made here is that many scholars and scientists believe that this principle lacks the proper logical basis and that it has not been proven to be an authentic principle of logic. Therefore, the second concept on which the proponents of this theory have [1]based their arguments on is also proven to be baseless.

4. The Concept of the "Seven Heavens"

The concept of the "seven heavens" is not something which has been merely mentioned in this sermon alone; it has also been mentioned in

1. In his book Tajrid al-I'tiqād, p. 155, the late Khājeh Naṣīr al-Dīn al-Ṭūsī has presented a critique of the five principles on which the theory of "Ten Intellects" is based. He has discussed those principles one by one and has proven them to be baseless through logical arguments. Then, in the end of his discussion, he makes the following brief remark: "وَأَدِلَّةُ وُجُودِهِ مَدْخُولَة" [the arguments for the existence of "ten intellects" are baseless and false]. For more information in this regard, refer to the critique of this theory by Khājeh Naṣīr al-Dīn al-Ṭūsī and the commentary of al-'Allāmah al-Ḥelli on Khājeh's critique [in the book Kashf al-Murād, p. 176].

some of the other sermons in the Nahj al-Balāghah [for instance sermon No. 211] as well as some of the verses of the Holy Quran. There are several verses in the Quran which have referred to "سبع سماوات" [seven heavens].[1]

There has been much controversy among the past and contemporary scholars as to what is exactly meant by the "seven heavens" and they have each presented their own different interpretations of this concept which cannot all be contained in this book. However, the one interpretation, among others, which seems to be more accurate and closer to reality is the one which holds that the "seven heavens" means exactly what the phrase literally means.

That is to say, "heaven", in this phrase, refers to a group of celestial bodies and objects in the space and "seven" is the exact number of these different groups of celestial bodies and objects and not merely a symbolic number indicating large numbers of things.

Moreover, from what appears from the Quran and its discussion of the seven heavens, it can be inferred that whatever we can observe in the space_ all the galaxies, celestial bodies, and celestial objects_ is located in the first heaven. Therefore, it is safe to conclude that beyond this immense world of billions of galaxies and celestial bodies, there exist six other vast worlds, or heavens, which have been inaccessible to mankind so far.

There are several verses in the Quran which have corroborated that whatever we can observe in the space around us is located within the first heaven, some of which are as follows:

1. There are seven verses in the Quran which have explicitly spoken about this concept using the term "سبع سماوات" [al-Baqarah, 29; al-Isrā', 44; al-Mu'minūn, 86; Fuṣṣilat, 12; al-Ṭalāq, 12; al-Mulk, 3, and Nūḥ, 15]. There are also other verses in the Quran which have implicitly referred to this concept.

1. The verse 6 of surah al-Ṣāffāt has confirmed this fact:

اِنَّا زَيَّنَّا السَّماءَ الدُّنْيا بِزِينَةٍ الْكَواكِبِ

"Indeed, We have adorned the closest [i.e. the lowest] heaven with the ornament of stars"

2. The same issue has also been stated in surah Fuṣṣilat, verse 12:

وَزَيَّنَّا السَّماءَ الدُّنْيا بِمَصابِيحَ

"And We adorned the closest [i.e. the lowest] heaven with lamps [i.e. stars]."

3. The fifth verse of surah al-Mulk has likewise referred to the same issue:

وَلَقَدْ زَيَّنَّا السَّماءَ الدُّنْيا بِمَصابِيحَ

"And We did indeed adorn the closest [i.e. the lowest] heaven with lamps."

Interestingly, al-'Allāmah al-Majlisī has presented this same interpretation of these verses several centuries ago in his book Biḥār al-Anwār, as a possibility that had struck him, or as we say it today, as an impression of the related Quranic verses and Islamic traditions regarding the issue of the seven heavens.[1]

Although the current scientific methods and research tools have been unable to access the other six heavens and worlds, there is no conclusive scientific evidence to reject the existence of such worlds. In fact, it is perfectly possible that, in the future, science will be able to unravel the mystery of these other six worlds. In fact, there are currently some indications and pieces of evidence in the contemporary astronomical discoveries which strengthen the possibility of the existence of such heavens beyond ours.

For instance, some astronomical journals have published reports released by the researchers at the famous Palomar Observatory which corroborate this view. These researchers have reportedly mentioned the following in their reports:

The Palomar observatory has been able to discover millions of new galaxies, some of which are one billion light years away from the earth. However, beyond the distance of one billion light years, there is a huge dark space where we could not observe any observable thing. However, there is no doubt that hundreds of millions of galaxies exist in that dark space and that our side of this huge world is being sustained in place through the gravity of the galaxies on the other side of that dark space. The huge world as we observe it today, with all of its hundreds of thousands of galaxies, seems to be an insignificant and tiny part of a much bigger world which is beyond this one. However, we are not yet sure that there is not yet another world beyond the second world which is beyond our world.[2]

Thus, whatever man has discovered in the universe, with all of its magnificence and wondrous grandeur, is just a tiny part of a greater world, and possibly of six other much greater worlds which mankind might come to discover in the future.

5. How did Imam 'Alī ('a) Know All of These Secrets and Facts about the World?

It should be noted that what Amīr al-Mu'minīn ('a) discussed regarding the creation of the cosmos is, by no means, theories or hypotheses, but

1. Biḥār al-Anwār, vol. 55, p. 78.

2. Majalleh-e Fazā, Farvardīn 1351 Sh.

hard facts. The fact that the Imam ('a) speaks of those amazing events at the beginning of the creation of the world with such certainty, much like one who had observed them in person, is proof that he derived his knowledge from the world of the Unseen and the Divine Knowledge. It is also possible that he was taught all of that by the Prophet (ṣ), who derived his knowledge from the reservoir of Divine Knowledge through Divinely-sent revelations. In any case, as Ibn Abī al-Ḥadīd has also stated, all of this clearly indicates that Imam Ali ('a) has had access to all of that immense knowledge and this is nothing surprising considering his great virtues and merits.[1]

And how can it not be so seeing as the Imam ('a) once said of himself:

"I am more knowledgeable about the paths of the heaven than those of the earth."[2]

1. Sharḥ Nahj al-Balāghah Ibn Abī al-Ḥadīd, vol. 1, p. 80.
2. Nahj al-Balāghah, sermon No. 189.

Part Eight
Sermon No.1

ثُمَّ فَتَقَ مَا بَيْنَ السَّموَاتِ الْعُلَا فَمَلَأَهُنَّ اَطْوَاراً مِنْ مَلَائِكَتِهِ، مِنْهُمْ سُجُودٌ لَايَرْكَعُونَ، وَرُكُوعٌ لَا يَنْتَصِبُونَ، وَصَافُّونَ لَا يَتَزَايَلُونَ، وَمُسَبِّحُونَ لَايَسْأَمُونَ، لَا يَغْشَاهُمْ نَوْمُ الْعُيُونِ، وَلَا سَهْوُ الْعُقُولِ، وَلَافَتْرَةُ الْاَبْدَانِ، وَلَاغَفْلَةُ النِّسْيَانِ، وَمِنْهُمْ اُمَنَاءُ عَلَى وَحْيِهِ، وَاَلْسِنَةٌ اِلَى رُسُلِهِ، وَمُخْتَلِفُونَ بِقَضَائِهِ وَاَمْرِهِ، وَمِنْهُمُ الْحَفَظَةُ لِعِبَادِهِ وَالسَّدَنَةُ لِاَبْوَابِ جِنَانِهِ، وَمِنْهُمُ الثَّابِتَةُ فِي الْاَرَضِينَ السُّفْلَى اَقْدَامُهُمْ. وَالمَارِقَةُ مِنَ السَّمَاءِ الْعُلْيَا اَعْنَاقُهُمْ، وَالْخَارِجَةُ مِنَ الْاَقْطَارِ اَرْكَانُهُمْ، وَالْمُنَاسِبَةُ لِقَوَائِمِ الْعَرْشِ اَكْتَافُهُمْ نَاكِسَةٌ دُونَهُ اَبْصَارُهُمْ مُتَلَفِّعُونَ تَحْتَهُ بِاَجْنِحَتِهِمْ، مَضْرُوبَةٌ بَيْنَهُمْ وَبَيْنَ مَنْ دُونَهُمْ حُجُبُ الْعِزَّةِ وَاَسْتَارُ الْقُدْرَةِ. لَا يَتَوَهَّمُونَ رَبَّهُمْ بِالتَّصْوِيرِ، وَلَايُجْرُونَ عَلَيْهِ صِفَاتِ الْمَصْنُوعِينَ، وَلَا يَحُدُّونَهُ بِالْاَمَاكِنِ، وَلَا يُشِيرُونَ اِلَيْهِ بِالنَّظَائِرِ

"Then He opened up spaces between the higher heavens and filled them all with various classes of His Angels. Among them are some who are constantly in prostration, but they do not bow [in worship], and there are some that constantly bow down [in their worship of Allah] but do not stand up. And [there are also] some who are in ranks and do not break rank, and they constantly glorify [Allah] and are not wearied; neither does sleep ever overcome their eyes, nor does anything slip their minds, nor do their bodies grow weary, nor do they ever fall into negligence out of forgetfulness.

Among them are some who are entrusted with [the task of delivering] His Revelations, [acting as] His messengers to His prophets, and constantly traveling to and from on His orders and instructions. There are [also] some sentinels among them assigned to His servants and [others who are] the gatekeepers of His Gardens [of Paradise]. And among them are some [others] whose feet are fixed firmly in the lower earths, their necks protruding above higher heavens, their bodies projecting from all sides of the universe, and their shoulders fit to *carry the legs of the Divine Throne; their eyes are downcast before the Divine Throne, their wings wrapped around them [as they stand] under it, and the veils of Glory and the screens of Power separate them from their inferiors. [They possess such profound and extensive knowledge of Allah that] they would never fancy images of their Lord, nor would they ever attach the attributes of the created beings to Him, nor limit Him to any specific places, nor ever refer to Him through means of any equals or likes."*

Commentary [Part Eight]

In the Realm of the Angels

Following his discussion regarding the creation of the universe and the formation of the heavens in the previous section of his sermon, Amīr al-Mu'minīn ('a) then pays attention to the creation of the various creatures in the heavens, particularly the creation of the angels in the heaven.

In this section of his sermon, the Imam ('a) discusses, rather succinctly and eloquently, the various kinds and types of angels, their qualities and attributes, and the task that each group of them is charged with. In his discussion, the Imam ('a) explains how noble and sublime their nature is and what great knowledge of Allah they possess. In fact, Imam Ali ('a) dedicates this section of his sermon to the description of the various aspects of the creation and nature of angels as well as their tasks and attributes.

The Imam ('a) begins this section, stating:

ثُمَّ فَتَقَ ما بَيْنَ السَّموات الْعُلا[1]

"Then He opened up spaces between the higher heavens..."

This sentence clearly indicates that, in the beginning, all the heavens were adjoining like a single entity and they were later separated from one another, with empty spaces emerging between them. This is the exact opposite of Ptolemy's theory, which suggested that the various heavens were like layers of onions, piled up one on the other without any space between them.

1. The Arabic term "العُلاء" is the plural of "عُليا" [feminine] and "اعلى" [masculine] and means "supreme" and "high".

Imam Ali ('a) then goes on to say:

فَمَلأَهُنَّ اَطْواراً مِنْ مَلائِكَتِهِ

"... and filled them all with various classes of His angels"[2]

Similar remarks have been made by the Imam ('a) in the Ashbāḥ sermon [sermon No. 91 in the Nahj al-Balāghah] with regard to the creation of angels:

وَمَلأَ بِهِمْ فُرُجَ فِجاجِها وَحَشا بِهِمْ فُتُوقَ اَجْوائِها

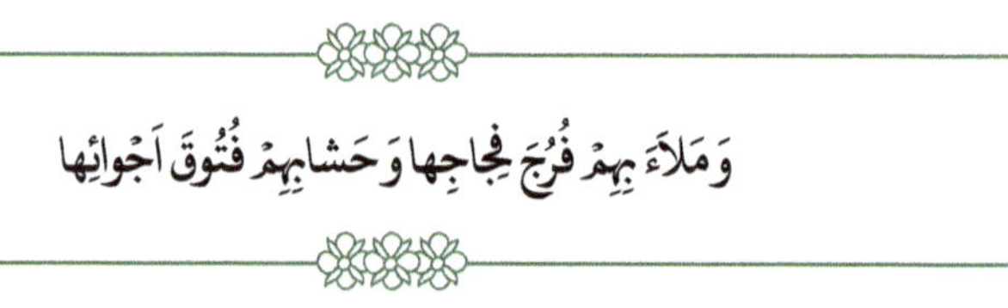

"... and He filled with them [i.e. the angels] the spaces between the
heavens, making their entire space replete with them."

In yet another part of the same sermon, the Imam ('a) mentions:

وَلَيْسَ في اَطْباقِ السَّماءِ مَوْضِعُ اِهابٍ اِلّا وَعَلَيْهِ مَلَكٌ ساجِدٌ اَوْ ساعٍ حافِدٌ

"There is no place all throughout the heavens except an angel is prostrating [before Allah] or a busy worker is striving hard [to do his tasks]."
Imam Ali ('a) then proceeds with his sermon, discussing different classes
of the angels and dividing them into four classes. He first considers the
angels whose sole occupation is worshipping; the Imam ('a) then divides

---

1. The Arabic term "اطوار", which is the plural of "طور" [pronounced "Tawr"], means "classes" or
"strata"; it has been used to refer to limits or conditions of things as well.

2. Although the pronoun "هـ" in this sentence refers to "heavens", it has actually been used to refer
to the "empty space" between the heavens.

this class of angels into two sub groups, stating the following:

"Among them are some who are constantly in prostration, but they do not bow [in worship]…"

"and there are some who constantly bow down [in their worship of Allah] but do not stand up."

"And [there are also] some who are in ranks and do not break rank …"

Some scholars believe that the term "صافون" here means "ranged in ranks for prayer", while others believe that it means these angels have stretched their wings in the sky and are in flight. The latter group of scholars have based their opinion on a similar usage of this word in the Quran, where it has been mentioned:

---

1. The Arabic term "سجود" is the plural of "ساجد" [meaning one who prostrates] just as the word "ركوع" is the plural of "راكع" [meaning one who bows down].

2. The Arabic term "صافون" is the plural of the word "صافَ" [pronounced "Ṣāff"] and it means "equal" or "parallel". It has originally been derived from the root word "صفصف", which means an even piece of land.

اَوَلَمْ يَرَوْا اِلَى الطَّيْرِ فَوْقَهُمْ صَافَّاتٍ

"Have they not regarded the birds above them spreading out their wings and closing them?"[1]

There is also a third possibility suggesting that it means the angeles are all standing in ranks prepared to execute any command that Allah gives them.

Nevertheless, it seems that the first view is more concordant with the context established by the sentences preceding and following this sentence. That is to say, just as our most prominent act of worship, i.e. Ṣalāt, has three important parts, standing up, bowing down, and prostrating, so each group of the angels is busy worshipping Allah in one of these forms.

The word "صافُّون" either describes the orderly ranks of the angels or their concerted actions when standing up. It is noteworthy that this is also the same word which the Imam ('a) has used in the sermon of Hammām to describe the pious believers:

اَمَّا اللَّيْلَ فَصَافُّونَ اَقْدَامَهُمْ تالينَ لِاجْزَاءِ الْقُرآنِ

"As for the nights, they are standing up with their feet placed beside each other, reciting the Quran."[2]

The Imam ('a) then proceeds with his description of the angels, stating:

---

1. Al-Mulk, 19.

2. Nahj al-Balāghah, sermon No. 193.

وَمُسَبِّحُونَ لَا يَسْأَمُون

"... and they constantly glorify [Allah] and are not wearied."

It appears from the wording of this sentence that it is in reference to a different group of angels than the previous three, i.e. the ones that are constantly prostrating before Allah, the ones that bow down before Him, and the ones that worship Him standing up.

However, some scholars who have written commentaries on the Nahj al-Balāghah believe that this sentence refers to the previous groups. This is quite possible, particularly because there are some Islamic Aḥādith which corroborate this view; for instance, according to one of these Islamic Aḥādith, once the Prophet (ṣ) was asked: "How do the angels perform their prayers?" the Prophet (ṣ) did not answer that question until the Archangel Gabriel was sent to him by Allah telling him the following:

أَنَّ أَهْلَ السَّمَاءِ الدُّنْيَا سُجُودٌ إِلَى يَوْمِ الْقِيَامَةِ يَقُولُونَ سُبْحَانَ ذِي الْمُلْكِ وَالْمَلَكُوتِ وَأَهْلُ السَّمَاءِ الثَّانِيَةِ رُكُوعٌ إِلَى يَوْمِ الْقِيَامَةِ يَقُولُونَ سُبْحَانَ ذِي الْعِزَّةِ وَالْجَبَرُوتِ وَأَهْلُ السَّمَاءِ الثَّالِثَةِ قِيَامٌ إِلَى يَوْمِ الْقِيَامَةِ يَقُولُونَ سُبْحَانَ الْحَيِّ الَّذِي لَا يَمُوتُ

"The dwellers of the first heaven are constantly in prostration until the Resurrection Day, and they keep chanting: "Glorified is the Owner of the material world and the spiritual realm". The dwellers of the second heaven are constantly bowing down in prayer until the Resurrection Day and they constantly chant: "Glorified is the Possessor of Might and Sovereignty". The dwellers of the third heaven are constantly standing up in prayer until the Resurrection Day and they keep chanting: "Glorified is the Living One who never dies"."[1]

---

1. Biḥār al-Anwār, vol. 56, p. 198, hadith No. 66.

Moreover, there is a great deal of controversy over whether what is meant here by "prostration, bowing down, and standing up" are the exact same thing that we do in our prayers or they serve as a metaphoric description of the various levels of the angel's devotional acts and worship before Allah based on their different spiritual ranks.

If we consider angels to possess bodies [subtle bodies] with arms, legs, and foreheads, then the first interpretation would be more sensible. However, if we regard them as non-physical beings, or beings with bodies but not bodies like ours, then the second view would be more reasonable [we will discuss this issue in more detail in the "important notes" section below].

In any case, all of these angels are constantly busy worshipping and glorifying Allah and celebrating His Name, as if they were created for nothing other than this and loved nothing but worshipping their Lord. In fact, these angels are the sings of the greatness of Allah as well as a proof of the fact that He has no need for anyone's worship.

That is to say, the philosophy behind their creation is probably to demonstrate to human beings that if they are commanded by Allah to worship Him, it is not because He needs their worship as He has worlds full of angels who are only busy worshipping Him. This makes human beings understand that whether they choose to worship Allah or not, their decision has no effect on the divinity of Allah; in fact, this is exactly what the Quran has also explicitly mentioned, reminding human beings that even if all of them become disbelievers, it will be of no consequence to Allah:

إِن تَكْفُرُوا فَإِنَّ اللَّهَ غَنِيٌّ عَنكُمْ

"If you are ungrateful, then Allah is indeed Ever Rich, beyond need of you."[1]

Imam Ali ('a) then continues his sermon, describing this latter group of angels and explaining their characteristics:

1. Al-Zumar, 7.

لايَغْشاهُمْ نَوْمُ الْعُيُونِ وَلا سَهْوُ الْعُقُولِ وَلا فَتْرَةُ الأَبْدانِ وَلا غَفْلَةُ النِّسْيانِ

"Neither does sleep ever overcome their eyes, nor does anything slip their minds, nor do their bodies grow weary, nor do they ever fall into negligence out of forgetfulness."

This section of the Imam's sermon emphasizes a fundamental difference between human beings and angels. Whereas human beings would gradually grow weary, sleepy, forgetful, and even negligent if they repeated the same act of worship over and over again, the worshipping angels would never be affected by any of these things regardless of how long they keep performing the same act of worship. They are so fascinated by the worship of Allah and they are so engrossed in spirituality that they glorify Allah and celebrate His praises that they are never overtaken by sleep or weariness. In other words, failure in carrying out duties stems from certain factors which are basically absent in the nature of the angels. One might fail to carry out their duty due to fatigue, lack of sleep, slip of mind, weakness of the body, or forgetting. Yet, since none of these things exists in the nature of the angels, they never fail in their task of worshipping Allah.
Following the discussion of the first class of angels, i.e. the worshippers, Imam Ali ('a) deals with the second class of Angels, stating:

وَمِنْهُمْ أُمَناءُ عَلى وَحْيِهِ، وَأَلْسِنَةٌ إِلى رُسُلِهِ، وَمُخْتَلِفُونَ بِقَضائِهِ وَأَمْرِهِ

"And among them are some who are entrusted with [the task of delivering] His Revelations, [acting as] His messengers to His prophets, and constantly traveling to and from on His orders and instructions."

These angels are, in effect, the intermediaries between Allah and His prophets; they are the messengers charged with delivering Divine-ly-sent revelations to the prophets.

It can be inferred from this part of the Imam's sermon that the Archangel Gabriel is not the only angel of Revelation and the messenger of Allah to His prophets; in fact, he is the head of a group of angels who work as Divinely-sent messengers to the prophets on the earth. The Quran has also made mention of this group of angels in different instances; in one instance, the Quran mentions:

$$ \text{قُلْ نَزَّلَهُ رُوحُ الْقُدُسِ مِنْ رَبِّكَ بِالْحَقِّ} $$

"Say: "The Holy Spirit has rightly brought it down from your Lord..."[1]

In yet another instance, the Quran states:

$$ \text{قُلْ مَنْ كَانَ عَدُوًّا لِجِبْرِيلَ فَإِنَّهُ نَزَّلَهُ عَلَى قَلْبِكَ بِإِذْنِ اللهِ} $$

"[They say: "we are enemies of Gabriel, who brings you the revelations from Allah"] Say: "whoever is an enemy of Gabriel [is an enemy of Allah, for] he has brought the Quran down to your heart by Allah's command."[2]

And in yet another instance, it speaks of a group of angels who carry Allah's Revelations by His command:

---

1. Al-Naḥl, 102.

2. Al-Baqarah, 97.

يُنَزِّلُ الْمَلائِكَةَ بِالرُّوحِ مِنْ اَمْرِهِ عَلى مَنْ يَشاءُ مِنْ عِبادِهِ

"He sends down the angels with the Spirit [and the Divine Revelation] by His command to whomsoever of His servants that He wills."[1]

This issue has also been discussed in some of the Islamic Aḥādith as well as some other sermons in the Nahj al-Balāghah.

It should also be noted that what is meant by Allah's "orders" and "instructions" in this section of the Imam's sermon is the religious laws and precepts, and not the creational commands of Allah as some commentators of the Nahj al-Balāghah have assumed. This is because the latter interpretation is inconsistent with the previous sentences which spoke of the trusted messengers of Allah who were entrusted with delivering His revelations to His prophets. Moreover, the term "مختلفون" in this sentence [a derivative of the root word "اختلاف"] means to travel to and from to carry out a certain task.

The Imam ('a) then goes on to make reference to the third class of angels:

وَ مِنْهُمُ الْحَفَظَةُ لِعِبادِهِ وَ السَّدَنَةُ لِأَبْوابِ جِنانِهِ

"There are [also] some sentinels among them assigned to His servants and [others who are] the gatekeepers of His Gardens [of Paradise]."

The Arabic term "حفظه" [singular: "حافظ"] means "sentinel" or "guard" and it can be interpreted in two ways here: first, it might mean that they are guards who watch people and record their every words and deeds. This specific meaning has been referenced in the

1. Al-Naḥl, 2.

verse 4 of Surah al-Ṭāriq in the Quran as well:

إِنْ كُلُّ نَفْسٍ لَمَّا عَلَيْهَا حَافِظٌ

"[By these great Signs that] there is a guard over every soul."

Similarly, in verses 10 and 11 of Surah al-Infiṭār the following has been mentioned:

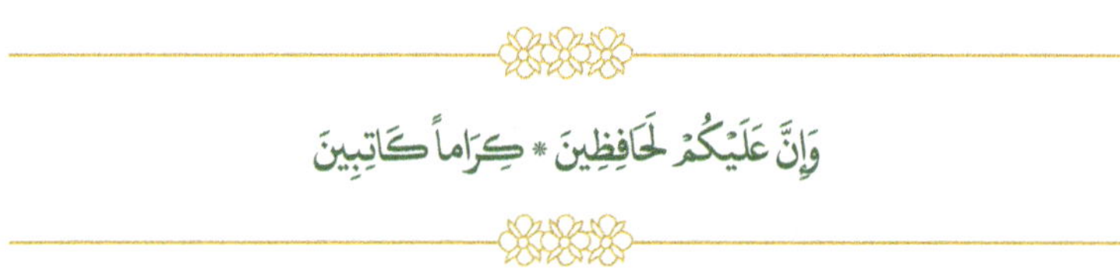

وَإِنَّ عَلَيْكُمْ لَحَافِظِينَ * كِرَاماً كَاتِبِينَ

"And indeed there are watchers appointed over you. Noble and recording [your good and bad deeds]."

The second way this word can be interpreted is that this third group of angels have been appointed as guards over people to protect them against calamities and mishaps, because if they do not do that, mankind will be in constant danger of extinction due to calamities that strike them night and day.

This second meaning has been confirmed by the Quran in verse 11 of Surah al-Ra'd:

لَهُ مُعَقِّبَاتٌ مِنْ بَيْنِ يَدَيْهِ وَمِنْ خَلْفِهِ يَحْفَظُونَهُ مِنْ أَمْرِ اللَّهِ

"For every person there are angels, to his front and his rear, who constantly guard him against Allah's command [i.e. those incidents which have not become definitive]."

However, the first interpretation of this word seems to be more concordant with the contents of the previous sentences which speak of
Divinely-revealed laws, and religious precepts and responsibilities.
It is also more consistent with its following sentence which refers
to Paradise and the recompense for man's deeds. Nevertheless, both
interpretations make sense here and it is perfectly possible that the
Imam ('a) meant both of them here.

Moreover, the word "سدنه" [singular: "سادن"] means "gatekeeper"
and the word "جنان" [pronounced "Jinān"] is the plural of "جنّت" and
means "garden" or "paradise". It can be inferred from the way this
word has been used that Allah has created several paradises. Some of
the commentators of the Nahj al-Balāghah have put forward the idea
that there exist eight paradises as the Quran has used eight different
names for Paradise: «جَنَّةُالْمَأْوَى» ، «جَنَّةُالْخُلْد» ، «جَنَّهُالْفِرْدَوْس» ، «جَنَّةُالنَّعِيمِ» ،
«جَنَّةٍ عَرْصُهَا السَّمَوَاتُ وَالْأَرْضُ ¹» ، «دَارُالْقَرَار» ، «دَارُالسَّلَام» ، «حنَّةُ عَدْن»

Imam Ali ('a) then continues his sermon, referring to the fourth class
of angels which includes the archangels who carry the Divine Throne:

وَمِنْهُمُ الثَّابِتَةُ في الْأَرَضينَ السُّفْلَى أَقْدَامُهُمْ، وَالْمَارِقَةُ مِنَ السَّماءِ الْعُلْيَا
أَعْنَاقُهُمْ، وَالْخَارِجَةُ مِنَ الْأَقْطَارِ أَرْكَانُهُمْ، وَالْمُنَاسِبَةُ لِقَوَائِمِ الْعَرْشِ أَكْتَافُهُمْ

"And among them are some [others] whose feet are fixed firmly in
the lower earths, their necks protruding above higher heavens, their
bodies projecting from all sides of the universe, and their shoulders
fit to carry the legs of the Divine Throne."

Then the Imam ('a) presents further descriptions of these magnificent
angels, stating:

---

1. Sharḥ Nahj al-Balāghah Ibn Meytham, vol. 1, p. 158; Minhāj al-Barā'ah, al-Khū'ī, vol. 2, p. 26.

نَاكِسَةٌ[1] دُونَهُ أَبْصَارُهُمْ مُتَلَفِّعُونَ[2] تَحْتَهُ بِأَجْنِحَتِهِمْ،
مَضْرُوبَةٌ بَيْنَهُمْ وَبَيْنَ مَنْ دُونَهُمْ حُجُبُ الْعِزَّةِ وَأَسْتَارُ الْقُدْرَةِ

"Their eyes are downcast before the Divine Throne, their wings wrapped around them [as they stand] under it, and the veils of Glory and the screens of Power separate them from their inferiors."

The Imam ('a) then presents yet more descriptions of these noble archangels, asserting the following:

لا يَتَوَهَّمُونَ رَبَّهُمْ بِالتَّصْوِيرِ، وَلا يُجْرُونَ عَلَيْهِ صِفَاتِ الْمَصْنُوعِينَ،
وَلا يَحُدُّونَهُ بِالأَمَاكِنِ، وَلا يُشِيرُونَ إِلَيْهِ بِالنَّظَائِرِ[3]

"[They possess such profound and extensive knowledge of Allah that] they would never fancy images of their Lord, nor would they ever attach the attributes of the created beings to Him, nor limit Him to any specific places, nor ever refer to Him through means of any equals or likes."

It should be noted that it is not a physical power that separates these lofty beings from their inferiors; rather, it is their unparalleled spiritual power that distinguishes them from all others, and it is this same spiritual grandeur which has rendered them worthy of carrying the Divine Throne.

In fact, these angels have risen up to the highest level of Tawḥīd and

1. The Arabic term "ناكسه" derives from the root word "نكس" [pronounced "Naks"] meaning "to turn something upside down or inside out". Thus, an infant who is born feet first is called "منكوس" in Arabic. Another derivative of this word, i.e. "نُكس", is used to refer to arrows whose heads are exchanged with their tails.

2. The Arabic term "متلفعون" derives from the root word "لفع" and means to "include" something or "wrap around" it. Therefore, when a woman wraps her chador around her body, she is described in Arabic as follows: "تلفّعت المرئه".

3. The word "نظائر" is the plural of "نظير", which means "like" or "equal".

monotheism, something that makes them the best role models for all servants of Allah, particularly the righteous individuals. These sublime beings do not set up any equals to Allah nor associate any likes with Him. They would not consider any limitations for the Divine Essence or attributes of Allah and regard Him as much greater than and beyond the reach of any imagination, analogy, or assumptions. This is because any entity that is imagined in the mind is a creation of the mind and Allah is glorified and high above being created.

As regards the meaning of the concepts of "Divine Throne" and the "Carriers of the Divine Throne" as well as the wondrous descriptions presented in this section of Imam Ali's sermon regarding these two concepts, we will present some explanations in the section called "important points" below.

Important Points

1. The Nature of Angels

The Holy Quran contains an extensive discussion of and references to the angels, their qualities, characteristics, acts, and responsibilities which, if gathered together, could fill a book. There is, likewise, an abundance of discussion in the Islamic Aḥādith on the angels, their responsibilities, acts, ranks, and attributes. However, there is no clear explanation, either in the Quran or the Islamic Aḥādith, regarding what the nature of the angels exactly is, and this is what has aroused considerable controversy among Muslim scholars concerning the nature of angels.

Muslim theologians, and in fact the vast majority of Muslim scholars, believe that angels are physical beings [albeit with subtle bodies]. Some of these scholars have maintained that the main constituent of the angels' bodies is light; a very famous sentence that has been used over and over again in various books regarding the nature of the angels is the following:

اَلْمَلَكُ جِسْمٌ نُورِيٌّ

"Angels are [endowed with] bodies made of light."

The late 'Allāmah al-Majlisī has even claimed the following with respect to this issue:

The Twelver Shi'a scholars, and even all Muslims [excluding a small minority of philosophers] believe that angels do indeed exist and that they possess subtle bodies made of light and that they can transform into different shapes and forms … and that the prophets and their infallible successors would see them.[1]

In other words, the Angels possess bodies which originate from light,

1. Biḥār al-Anwār, vol. 56, p. 202.

the Jinn have bodies which originate from fire, and human beings possess bodies made of condensed matter.

Another view in this regard has been put forward by a group of philosophers who hold that the angels are completely metaphysical beings and that they have qualities and attributes which are inconsistent with physical bodies.

The late al-Khū'ī, one of the commentators of the Nahj al-Balāghah, has also related a total of six other views regarding this issue in his book entitled Minhāj al-Barā'ah[1], most of which have very few proponents and supporters. Nevertheless, there is no doubt that the nature of angels, particularly the qualities, attributes, virtues, and acts which have been ascribed to them by the Quran, all pertain to the world of the Unseen and are inaccessible to us. Consequently, the only way for us to ascertain different facts about their nature and qualities is to resort to the related evidence found in the Quran and the Islamic Aḥādith.

The Holy Quran has listed a number of qualities and characteristics for them, some of which are as follows:

1. They are intelligent beings;
2. They constantly obey Allah and never disobey Him or commit transgressions;
3. They have many different important duties, given to them by Allah. Some of them are the carriers of the Divine Throne, some of them are put in charge of directing the important affairs of this world, and some of them are charged with taking the souls of people at the time of death. There are others who are charged with watching the deeds of mankind, and some others who are assigned the duty of protecting people from dangers. There are also some who are sent by Allah to aid the believers in wars, and another group of them is charged with the punishment and annihilation of transgressing and rebellious nations. Finally, there are some of them who have the duty of delivering Divinely-sent revelations and Books to Prophets.
4. Angels enjoy different ranks and they are not all at the same level.
5. They are constantly busy glorifying Allah and celebrating His praises.

1. Al-Khū'ī, Minhāj al-Barā'ah, vol. 2, p. 6.

6. When they arrive on the earth to meet with prophets or some other righteous individuals, they sometimes appear before them in the form of human beings and sometimes in other forms; an example in this regard is the angel who appeared to Mary ('a).

Although it is a rather futile attempt to try to ascertain whether angels are completely metaphysical beings or not, what appears from the verses of the Quran [without trying to interpret or justify them in any specific way] is that the angels are not made of the same base matter as the things and beings in our world are made up of.

However, they are not purely metaphysical and immaterial beings either; one indication as to this fact is that they have been described, both in the Quran and Islamic Aḥādith, as being subject to things like time and place, which are characteristic of the material and physical realm. The kind of descriptions presented by Imam Ali ('a) regarding them both in this sermon [as well as the sermon of Ashbāḥ] clearly corroborate this view.

Nonetheless, the fact that beings called "angels" actually exist and that the believers must believe in them is among the issues which have been generally mentioned and emphasized by the Holy Quran. An example in this regard is the following verse in the Quran:

"The Prophet believes in what was sent down to him from his Lord. And the believers all believe in Allah and His angels and His Books and His prophets."[1]

It is worth noting that some uninformed individuals have maintained that angels are, in fact, the natural forces and energies which exist in nature and everything that exists in it, including mankind and other living creatures. Apparently, these individuals have presented such a view of angels in order to appease or satisfy the people who disbe-

1. Al-Baqarah, 285.

lieve in the metaphysical world of the Unseen.
This is while a quick glance at the related verses in the Quran shows that this view is undoubtedly wrong. This is because the Quran has clearly and explicitly described angels as beings that possess such qualities as intelligence, intellect, faith, sincerity of devotion to Allah, and infallibility.

2. Different Classes of Angels

There are different classes and kinds of angels in the world, some of which have been referred to in the Quran and the Islamic Aḥādith. The four major classes of angels, however, are the ones which were described in this sermon by Imam Ali ('a) [i.e. the worshippers of Allah, the guardians and reckoners of the deeds of mankind, the messengers of Allah to His prophets, and the carriers of the Divine Throne].
Furthermore, as it was discussed above, a few other classes of angels can also be recognized from their descriptions in various verses of the Quran. These include the angels who are charged with the punishment and annihilation of the rebellious and transgressing nations, the ones that are sent to aid the believers, the directors of various affairs, and the ones who are tasked with taking the souls of the dead at the time of their death. Although these may seem to be quite a lot of different classes of angels, they can all be considered to be charged with directing various matters in the world.
Allah's precedent has been to direct the affairs of the universe by means of angels, who unquestioningly obey Him and who never forget anything or flag, falter, or fail in carrying out His commands. He has arranged things this way for various different purposes, one of which being to display His immense Power and His Grandeur in the entire world. These are different classes of Allah's agents who operate in the vast universe, with each class of them entrusted with specific tasks.
When man thinks about so many classes of angels, the wide variety of tasks which they are charged with, and the huge amount of work that they do, one feels how tiny he is compared to this great universe with countless agents of Allah constantly busy accomplishing different tasks in it by His command.

When we compare their sincere and constant worship of Allah with our own acts of worship, we come to realize how insignificant and infinitesimal our acts of worship are. Similarly, when we compare the angel's power with ours, we see how weak and helpless we are. So, by learning about the angels and their greatness, on the one hand, mankind comes to comprehend the immense nature of the creation and the greatness of its Creator, and on the other, the insignificance of his own self as well as whatever he does compared to the angels; this is, in effect, one of the philosophies behind the creation of angels.

3. The Divine Throne and Its Carriers

The Holy Quran has referred to the Divine Throne around twenty times in different verses; more details about the Divine Throne, however, has been presented in the Islamic Aḥādith. According to some of these traditions, the Divine Throne is so great that it is virtually unperceivable to human mind.

For instance, one such tradition indicates that all of the heavens and the planets in them along with whatever there is in them, is like a small ring in a vast desert compared to the Divine Throne. There are also other Aḥādith which suggest that if the greatest angels keep flying up until the Resurrection Day as fast as they can, they will still be unable to get any close even to the leg of the Divine Throne.

Other Aḥādith point out that Allah has created a thousand languages for the Divine Throne and that the visage and figure of all of the creatures that He has created on land and at sea are displayed there.

There are yet other Aḥādith which have mentioned the following with respect to the creation of the Divine Throne: "When Allah created the Throne, He ordered some of the angels to carry it, but they could not; so more angels kept coming to their aid, but no matter how many were added to them, they were all unable to bear its weight. So then Allah lifted it up and held it aloft with His own Might and then ordered the eight angels who were charged with carrying the Throne: "Come, carry the Throne!" They replied by asking: "How can we ever do this seeing as all of the angels together failed to carry it?!"

It was then that Allah ordered them to seek help from the Dhikr[1] "لاحول ولا قوة الا بالله العلى العظيم" [there is no strength nor might except from Allah the Almighty the Most High] and also through saluting Prophet Muḥammad and his pure progeny [i.e. Ṣalawāt]. And so when they did that, they were suddenly able to lift and carry the Divine Throne with ease."[2]

Obviously, all of these descriptions are metaphors employed to convey the unimaginably great and immense nature of the Divine Throne. However, with respect to the issue of what exactly is the Divine Throne and what its nature is, there is considerable controversy among Muslim scholars and scientists, the discussion of which will distance us far away from the course and the purpose of our book here. Therefore, we will only present a brief yet clear explanation of this issue here.

Let us first focus on the origin of the two words "عرش" [throne] and "كرسى" [seat] in order to better understand the issue at hand. In the distant past, kings and rulers usually had two kinds of chairs: they had a huge and high chair, called the throne [Arabic: عرش], which they used for special occasions and for very important and formal meetings. They also had another, less formal and much smaller chair, called the seat [Arabic: كرسى]; this was the chair that they sat on during their everyday and usual meetings to take care of the affairs of their kingdom. The term "عرش" [or throne] has been used extensively in the Arabic literature in a metaphoric sense to refer to power and complete authority; in these cases, there is no actual "throne" but only a metaphoric mention of it to convey "absolute authority" and "supreme power". For instance, the Arabic phrase "ثَلَّ عَرْشُهُ" [which literally translates into English as "His throne has collapsed!"] is a rather famous remark used frequently to refer to a person who has lost all of his power, authority, and grandeur. Clearly, this is also a metaphoric usage of "throne" as, for instance, a person who has been the head of

1. Dhikrs [literally means «remembrance, reminder» or «mention, utterance], are different Islamic devotional acts, in which phrases or prayers are repeated. These are phrases which are mentioned or recited repeatedly in the heart and by the tongue in order to remember Allah.

2. Al-Khū'ī, Minhāj al-Barā'ah, vol. 2, pp. 32-35; the late 'Allāmah al-Majlisī has also included a detailed discussion of the Islamic traditions on the Divine Throne and Seat in his book Biḥār al-Anwār, vol. 55. The above-mentioned tradition about the Divine Throne can be found on pages 5, 17, and 55 of the 55th volume of his book.

a company and has now been fired, does not actually have a throne! Let us now consider the case of Allah. Since Allah is the supreme Sovereign of the entire world and the Ruler of all in existence, He also has both of these two kinds of "Sovereign chairs"; however, since Allah does not have a physical body nor is He, in fact, a material being, both of these two "chairs" pertaining to Him are metaphoric concepts which refer to things which are entirely immaterial and non-physical. But the question remains as to what exactly Allah's "Throne" of authority is. Muslim scholars have put forward different interpretations as to the nature of the Divine "Seat" and "Throne". For example, some believe that all of the material world, including the heavens, the earth, the galaxies, and all of the celestial bodies constitute the "Seat" or the smaller chair. These scholars have referenced the following verse in the Quran to substantiate their view:

وَسِعَ كُرْسِيُّهُ السَّمَوَاتِ وَالْأَرْضَ

"His Seat [of Authority] extends over the heavens and the earth ... "[1]

The proponents of this view believe that what is meant by "Throne", on the other hand, is a much greater world which is beyond the realm of [solid] matter and encompasses it; this world is so unimaginably immense that the physical and material world is rather insignificant and trivial compared to it.

Needless to say, what is meant by the "Carriers of the Divine Throne" is not some sturdy angels with huge bodies who are carrying the legs of the Throne on which Allah is sitting on their shoulders! This is because, as it was discussed above, the terms "Seat" and "Throne" are used metaphorically when it comes to Allah, because Allah is basically not physical to need any specific place to be on.

Accordingly, it can be concluded that the "Carriers of the Divine Throne" are some lofty and high-ranking angels who are charged with

1. Al-Baqarah, 255.

directing the affairs of the metaphysical world [a world which has been metaphorically referred to as the "Divine Throne"]. These magnificent angels have the duty of executing Allah's orders all throughout the immense metaphysical world.

Thus, Imam Ali's above-mentioned descriptions of these angels as beings with long necks that "protrude above higher heavens", feet that "are fixed firmly in the lower earths", huge bodies that "project from all sides of the universe", or shoulders so vast that are "fit to carry the legs of the Divine Throne" are all metaphors, showing their vast sphere of power to direct the affairs of the entire world.

Although ordinary discourse is usually understood and interpreted literally, in cases where there is definitive rational evidence that indicates the opposite, literary discourse needs to be interpreted as metaphoric and not literal. This fact is clearly visible in the following verse of the Quran about Allah:

"The hand of Allah is above their hands."[1]

This verse clearly refers to Allah's supreme Power which outmatches that of everyone else, not an actual "hand". This is exactly like the English idiom "to have the upper hand"; when someone is said to have the "upper hand" in something, it means that they are more powerful than their opponent and that they have control over the situation in question. Likewise, there is no actual "hand" meant here.

So those angels were able to accomplish that enormous task by the power and strength that Allah granted them, not by their own power. Moreover, as they do their task, they keep glorifying Allah, praising Him and also, according to verse 7 of Surah Ghāfir, praying to Allah for His forgiveness for the believers:

1. Al-Fatḥ, 10.

الَّذِينَ يَحْمِلُونَ الْعَرْشَ وَمَنْ حَوْلَهُ يُسَبِّحُونَ بِحَمْدِ
رَبِّهِمْ وَيُؤْمِنُونَ بِهِ وَيَسْتَغْفِرُونَ لِلَّذِينَ آمَنُوا

"Those angels who bear the Throne and those [circling] around it declare the praise of their Lord and believe in Him and implore for forgiveness for those who believe"

4. The Infallibility of Angels

Angels have many special qualities and characteristics, some of which were discussed above [regarding the angels whose task was to worship Allah]: they are neither overtaken by sleep, nor do they grow weary of glorifying Allah, nor are they afflicted with problems such as error, forgetfulness, or fatigue.

Another special characteristic of angels, as explained in the following verses of the Quran, is that they are not prone to sins and transgressions at all:

بَلْ عِبَادٌ مُكْرَمُونَ * لَا يَسْبِقُونَهُ بِالْقَوْلِ وَهُمْ بِأَمْرِهِ يَعْمَلُونَ

"Rather, [the angels are] His honored servants. Never do they advance a word ahead of Him, and they [always] act by His command."[1]

As regards the angels who are agents of Divine Retribution, the Quran has mentioned the following:

1. Al-Anbiā', 26-27.

لا يَعْصُونَ اللهَ ما أَمَرَهُمْ

... angels, stern and sturdy, who never disobey Allah in what He has commanded them, and carry out what they are commanded [completely]."[1]

Some have assumed that speaking of infallibility in regard to angels is pointless because they are not invested with the same instincts and desires as human beings to be able to refuse them and become "infallible" through this refusal of lower desires. Yet, this view does not seem to be accurate; although the lowly inclinations and desires such as lust or anger do not exist in the nature of angels [or exist in extremely weak forms], it should not be forgotten that angels are endowed with freedom of will.

This means that, by nature, angels possess the power to disobey Allah but they never do that. There are certain verses in the Quran that indicate that the angels experience the extreme fear of their Lord's retribution and punishment:

"And they are awestricken by fear of Him."[2]

Considering these descriptions of angels, it is clear that they are infallible and pure of any sins and transgressions though they possess the power to disobey Allah.

A necessary point needs to be made here; there are certain Islamic Hadiths which indicate that some angels were slow in carrying out

1. Al-Taḥrīm, 6.
2. Al-Anbiyā', 28.

the commands of Allah and they were punished by Allah for their hesitation. These are the same instances as Tark al-Awlā [abandoning the better choice] that were sometimes even done by Divinely-sent prophets who were also punished for it. However, Tark al-Awlā is far from "transgression"; Tark al-Awlā is defined as doing one recommendable act instead of another one that is much better. Clearly, both of the acts in question are good deeds, and only the one that is abandoned is better than the one that is done; thus, such an act does not constitute an act of sinning at all.

5. The Throne-Carriers' Level of Knowledge Concerning Allah

It can be inferred from this section of Imam Ali's sermon that the reason why the carriers of the Divine Throne were appointed to this extremely great task has not been merely the fact that they were extremely powerful angels. Rather, they were chosen for this task because of their unparalleled high knowledge of Allah.

The angels' extensive knowledge of Allah has placed them at the peak of Tawḥīd and the belief in the Oneness of Allah; this knowledge has brought them to ward off all sorts of polytheism from themselves and to reject any equals that might be attributed to Allah. It is due to this unique qualification of theirs that they have qualified for such a great task, and this is truly a great lesson for all the servants of Allah, including astute and wise human beings.

Part Nine

Sermon No.1

ثُمَّ جَمَعَ سُبْحانَهُ مِنْ حَزْنِ الأَرْضِ وَسَهْلِها، وعَذْبِها وَسَبَخِها، تُرْبَةً سَنَّها بِالْماءِ
حَتّى خَلَصَتْ، وَلاطَها بِالْبَلَّةِ حَتّى لَزَبَتْ، فَجَبَلَ مِنْها صُورَةً ذاتَ اَحْناءٍ وَوُصُولٍ،
وَاَعْضاءٍ وَفُصُولٍ، اَجْمَدَها حَتَّى اسْتَمْسَكَتْ، وَاَصْلَدَها حَتّى صَلْصَلَتْ لِوَقْتٍ
مَعْدُودٍ، وَأَمَدٍ مَعْلُومٍ، ثُمَّ نَفَخَ فِيها مِنْ رُوحِهِ، فَمَثُلَتْ اِنْساناً ذا اَذْهانٍ يُجِيلُها، وَفِكَرٍ
يَتَصَرَّفُ بِها، وَجَوارِحَ يَخْتَدِمُها وَاَدَواتٍ يُقَلِّبُها وَمَعْرِفَةٍ يَفْرُقُ بِها بَيْنَ الْحَقِّ وَالْباطِلِ
وَالأَذْواقِ وَالْمَشامِّ وَالأَلْوانِ وَالأَجْناسِ، مَعْجُوناً بِطِينَةِ الأَلْوانِ الْمُخْتَلِفَةِ، وَالأَشْباهِ
الْمُؤْتَلِفَةِ وَالأَضْدادِ الْمُتَعادِيَةِ، وَالأَخْلاطِ الْمُتَبايِنَةِ مِنَ الْحَرِّ وَالْبَرْدِ وَالْبَلَّةِ وَالْجُمُودِ

"Then Allah- glory be to Him- collected a mixture of clay from the rough parts of the earth and its soft parts and from its sweet and salty [lands], then He splashed it with water until it was purified, and kneaded it with moisture until it became viscous.
Then He fashioned from it an image with curves, sinews, limbs and joints. Then, in order for it to retain its form, He solidified it and for it to dry up completely He kept hardening it for a limited time and a specified term.
Thereafter He breathed into him of His Spirit, so he arose as a human being with brains to stir him into action and intellect by which to exert his power and influence [on the other creatures], and limbs which he uses and tools that he turns [to accomplish his aims]. And [he was given] discernment with which to distinguish between truth and falsehood and between different flavors, fragrances, colors, and things. [in short] a mixture of different hues, analogous materials, irreconcilable opposites, and disparate humors of hot, cold, dry, and moist natures."

Commentary [Part Nine]

The Creation of Adam ('a)

Following his eloquent yet concise discussion of the creation of the cosmos, the heavens, and the earth in the previous sections of his profound sermon, Imam Ali ('a) then attends to the story of the creation of the other creatures in the world. The Imam ('a) begins this part of his speech with the discussion of the different processes of the creation of mankind, who is the veritable masterpiece of the entire creation, enumerating five stages which capture mankind's entire history of existence:

1. The creation of Adam's body and soul [in two stages];
2. The prostration of the angels before Adam and the disobedience of Iblīs to Allah;
3. Adam's settling in Paradise and then his committing of Tark al-Awlā, his subsequent remorse and repentance, and finally his expulsion from Paradise and his descent to the earth.
4. The descendants of Adam increased in number and human societies emerged: then Allah sent His prophets with Divinely-sent scriptures to them in order to guide mankind, bring order to human societies, and guide them toward spiritual development and growth.
5. The development of mankind and their societies to the point where they became competent for being given the final and most complete Divinely-sent religion. It was at this point that Allah sent His chosen prophet, Muḥammad (ṣ), together with the Quran to save mankind from error and guide them toward prosperity by means of the most complete set of instructions ever sent to mankind by Allah.

The Creation of Adam's Body and Soul

Imam Ali ('a) begins this section of his sermon with the discussion of the creation of Adam's physical body, stating:

ثُمَّ جَمَعَ سُبْحانَهُ مِنْ حَزْنِ[1] الأَرْضِ وَسَهْلِها، وَعَذْبِها[2] وَسَبَخِها[3] تُرْبَةً

"Then Allah- glory be to Him- collected a mixture of clay from the rough parts of the earth and its soft parts and from its sweet and salty [lands],"

This section of the Imam's sermon indicates that man was originally created from dust and that his body is a mixture of different elements with different qualities needed for living on different parts of the earth. This has been done so that all sorts of abilities and talents that are needed for the survival and growth of a perfect human society be invested in man's nature; and so, later on, different human beings with different talents and capabilities begin to be born on the earth to make their own contributions to the development of their societies. Imam Ali ('a) then continues and refers to another basic element that was used in the creation of man's primitive body, i.e. water that was mixed with soil:

سَنَّها[4] بِالْماءِ حَتّى خَلَصَتْ

"... then He splashed it with water until it was purified,"

1. The Arabic term "حزن" [pronounced "Ḥazn"] means the "rough parts of the earth"; its other derivative "حُزن" [pronounced "Ḥuzn" or "Ḥazan"] is used in Arabic to refer to "grief" and "heartache" because grief is tough for human soul.

2. The word "عذب" [pronounced: "'Adhb"] means "clean, fresh, and salubrious water".

3. The Arabic word "سبخ" [pronounced "Sabakh"] means "salt marsh", and its plural form is "سباخ".

4. The word "سَنَّ" derives from the root word "سنّ" [pronounced "Sann"], which means to pour or splash water on something as a verb. It has also been used in Arabic to refer to "soft" or "smooth" things.

وَلاطَهَا[1] بِالْبَلَّةِ حَتَّى لَزَبَتْ[2]

"... and kneaded it with moisture until it became viscous."

It can be inferred from these latter remarks that the role of water in the creation of man's body has been to mix all of the elements and to create bonds between them so as to create a viscous material with which man's body was later formed.

Imam Ali ('a) then goes on and refers to the formation of Adam's physical body with that viscous clay, stating:

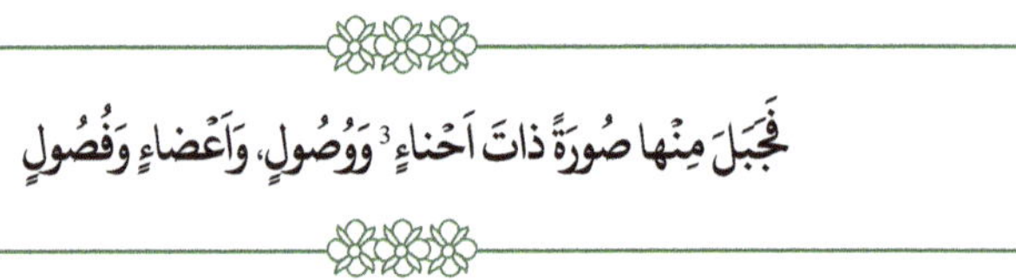

فَجَبَلَ مِنْهَا صُورَةً ذَاتَ أَحْنَاءٍ[3] وَوُصُولٍ، وَأَعْضَاءٍ وَفُصُولٍ

"Then He fashioned from it an image with curves, sinews, limbs and joints."

The term "احناء" [singular: "حنو"] refers to the curves of human body, from the rib cage to the jaw, the back of the head, and the ankles, each of which has its own functions for human body. If the human body had been created in the form of perfect geometric shapes like rectangles and squares, it would not have been able to work as perfectly as it does now, thanks to its various curved parts.

The phrase "وَأَعْضَاءٍ وَفُصُولٍ" refers to the various limbs of human body which are connected to one another by means of joints, something that has given them extraordinary capabilities and maneuverability.

1. The Arabic term "لاط", which derives from the root word "لَوط" [pronounced "Lawṭ"], means to knead something in order to mix it with something else.

2. The word "لزبت" derives from the root word "لُزُوب" [pronounced "Luzūb"] and means "sticky" or "solid".

3. The term "احناء", which is the plural of "حنو" [pronounced "Ḥinw"], means "curves" or "bends"; it has been used in Arabic to mean "sides" as well.

Take human wrist for instance; if the hand had been joined to the arm with a long bone without a joint, it would have had very limited maneuverability and very few capabilities.

However, Allah has joined the hand to the arm using a joint which is made of a few bones and some sinews to join them together but in a dynamic way to allow them to move. He has also created the fingers with their own joints, allowing them to move independently from the palm of the hand, something which is the root of various human capabilities. Undoubtedly, this is one of the great Signs of Allah's supreme Wisdom and His Greatness.

The Imam ('a) then touches upon the next stage of the creation of Adam's physical body as follows:

"Then, in order for it to retain its form, He solidified it and for it to dry up completely He kept hardening it ..."

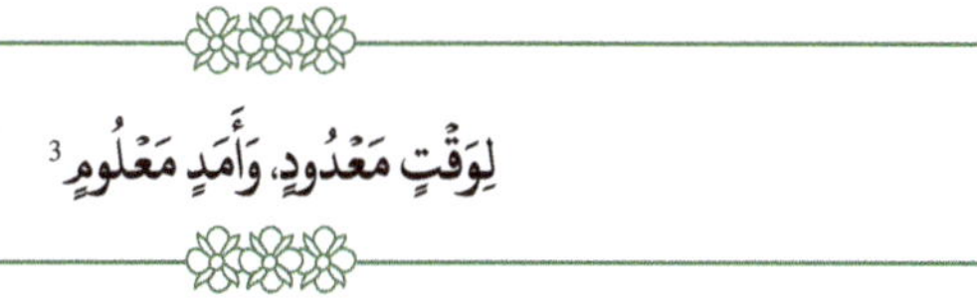

"... for a limited time and a specified term."

According to some Islamic traditions, Imam al-Bāqir ('a) has been

1. The Arabic word "اصلد", which derives from the root word "صلد" [pronounced "Ṣald"] means "solid and glassy".

2. The word "صلصل", from the root word "صلصله", means "to dry up so much so as to make a bell like sound upon impact with something else". It has also been used in Arabic to mean solid and firm.

3. The letter "ل" at the beginning of the phrase "لوقت معدود" means "until" or "for". Some have argued that it might be indicative of the "reason". Others have maintained that this phrase might mean that this state will continue until the Resurrection Day at which point man's body will start to disintegrate and decompose. However, this view seems to be quite unlikely because this sentence concerns the process of the creation of man when he did not even have a spirit.

quoted as saying that this process continued for forty years. During that time, Adam's corpse was lying on a corner and the angels would pass by it asking it: "What have you been created for?!"[1]

The reason why Adam's body was left in that state for that time might be either of the following possibilities put forward by different researchers: 1. To test the angels with respect to the Acts of Allah; 2. Teaching a lesson to mankind that, in order to do something correctly and properly, they need to stop making haste and instead spend enough time on it.

Following this stage, it was now time for Adam to be imbued with spirit; Imam Ali ('a) explains this stage of the creation of man as follows:

ثُمَّ نَفَخَ فِيها مِنْ رُوحِهِ، فَمَثُلَتْ [2] إِنْساناً ذا أَذْهانٍ يُجِيلُها [3]

"Thereafter He breathed into him of His Spirit, so he arose as a human being with brains to stir him into action ..."

The phrase "… with brains to stir him into action" in this part of the sermon is an indication made to man's various intellectual powers each of which [or a combination of which] he uses in different aspects of his life in order to make his way toward his goals. These include such intellectual faculties as perception, cognition, memorization, imagination, etc.

It should be noted that the original meaning of the word "اذهان" is "power" and it later came to be used to refer to the powers of perception, wisdom, understanding and other such intellectual faculties. This is indicative of the fact that Imam Ali ('a) means to refer to all of man's intellectual faculties and capabilities in this section of his sermon, emphasizing that they are all gifts bestowed on man by Allah.

---

1. "فَبَقِيَ أَرْبَعِينَ سَنَةً مُلْقىً تَمُرُّ بِهِ الْمَلائِكَةُ فَتَقُولُ: لِأَمْرٍ ما خُلِقْتَ؟" ['Ilal al-Sharā'i', vol. 1, p. 275, hadith No. 2].
2. The Arabic term "مثلت", from the root word "مثول" [pronounced "Muthūl"], means to arise and stand up.
3. The word "يجيل", from the root word "اجاله" [taken from the verbs "جول" and "جولان"] means to "stir" or "to revolve".

Imam Ali ('a) then continues describing Adam as follows:

وَفِكَرٍ يَتَصَرَّفُ بِها

"... and by which to exert his power and influence [on the other creatures]."

Some have assumed that this sentence has been said by the Imam ('a) as elaboration on the previous sentence, i.e. that this sentence and the sentence before it essentially mean the same thing. However, it appears from the exposition of these two sentences that they are each in reference to different issues:

The sentence "ذا اَذْهانٍ يُجيلُها" [with brains to stir him into action] refers to man's power of perception, cognition, imagination, and understanding of the truth which precedes his actions. The sentence "وَفِكَرٍ يَتَصَرَّفُ بِها", on the other hand, is indicative of man's intellectual capabilities which enable him to put what he has in mind into practice. It is these intellectual faculties that allow man to exert his power and influence [on the other creatures] [note that the original meaning of the term "فكر" (English: thought) is the development and motion of different ideas in one's mind].

In any case, the term "فكر" has been used in the plural [much like the term "اذهان" in its preceding sentence] in order to emphasize the fact that man's intellectual faculties are rather varied and manifold. This is a very important point which has also been corroborated by great philosophers and psychologists; these experts emphasize that the reason behind man's multitudinous talents is his inherent diversity of intellectual faculties.

Thus, some individuals are more powerful in some intellectual aspects than others but weaker in other aspects compared to others. There are rather amazing facts about this curious issue which, as one focuses more on them, fill one with wonder particularly as one uncovers the greatness of the Creator, who has created these mind-blowing intellectual capabilities for mankind.

The Imam ('a) then mentions two other things which man draws help from as he strives to achieve his goals:

وَجَوارِحَ يَخْتَدِمُها[1] وَأَدَواتٍ يُقَلِّبُها

"... and limbs which he uses and tools that he turns [to accomplish his aims]."

It can be said that man goes through four stages to achieve his purposes: the first stage is that of cognition, perception, imagination, and confirmation; the second stage is that of reflection and decision, and the third stage is that of using his limbs to do what he has in mind, and in case his limbs alone are unable to do what he has in mind, he will go to the fourth stage which is the employment of various tools which Allah has created in this world. It should be noted that each of these four stages are quite diverse within themselves as they might have various facets and aspects of their own.

But in order to arrive at his goals, man needs other powers as well, powers which Amīr al-Mu'minīn ('a) touches upon in the next part of his remarks. Success in arriving at different goals requires man to be able to distinguish between good and bad and between correct and incorrect; further, it requires man to be able to perceive different other things through senses as well. In this part, the Imam ('a) refers to another important gift bestowed within man's nature which, in effect, constitutes the fifth stage which he goes through in his attempts to achieve his aims, i.e. the power of discernment.

The Imam ('a) states the following in this regard:

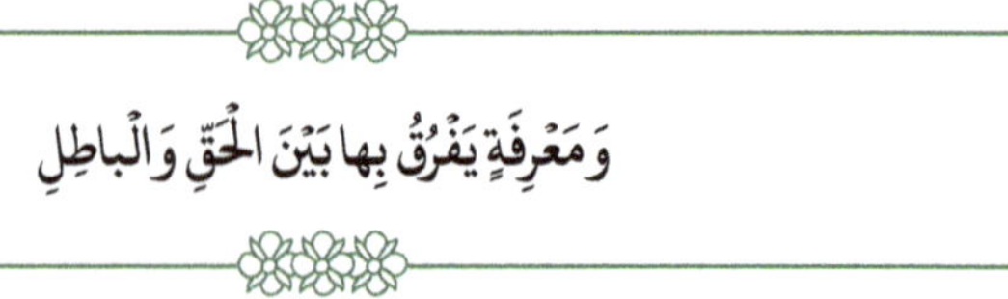
وَمَعْرِفَةٍ يَفْرُقُ بِها بَيْنَ الْحَقِّ وَالْباطِلِ

"... and discernment with which to distinguish between truth and falsehood,"

1. The Arabic term "يختدم", from the root word "اختدام", means to "wield" or "employ" something.

وَالأَذْوَاقِ وَالْمَشَامِّ وَالأَلْوَانِ وَالأَجْنَاسِ

"... and between different flavors, fragrances, colors, and things."

In fact, the power of discernment and judgment, which is one of the most important intellectual capabilities of man, enables him to make correct judgments both with regard to abstract concepts such as "good and bad" as well as concrete issues such as color, smell, and taste of things.

The question that might arise here is whether this power of "discernment" is a part of man's general intellectual power and cognition or a different power entirely. It appears from this part of the Imam's sermon that he describes it as an independent intellectual capability of mankind.

It is noteworthy that the Imam ('a) focuses particularly on three concrete issues which man needs to make judgments in his daily life through his senses, i.e. things that he needs to taste, smell, and see to make judgments about. Imam Ali ('a) finally refers to different "things" which man needs to make judgments about; "things" here is a general term that can refer to living creatures such as plants, birds, animals, and any other things in the world.[1] Moreover, the reason why the Imam ('a) makes no mention of the senses of "hearing" and "touch" is that he mentioned the other senses as an example and so any listener would automatically think of the other senses when reminded of one or two of them.

Imam Ali ('a) then goes on with his speech, referring to one of the most significant features of man which is the root cause of many phenomena in his life:

1. The Arabic term "جنس" [plural: اجناس] originally means "different" or "various" sorts of things. However, there are various pieces of evidence in different parts of the Nahj al-Balāghah [for instance in sermon No. 91] which indicate that the Imam ('a) has used this word to refer to different living creatures.

مَعْجُوناً بِطِينَةِ الأَلْوانِ الْمُخْتَلِفَةِ

"[in short] a mixture of different hues..."

This sentence might refer to different races of man with different skin colors or the different parts of man's body, each of which has its own color: some of them white [like bones, and the white part of the eyes], some of them black [like some people's hair], and others in different other colors. It is the combination of all of these colors that gives man his especially beautiful appearance. It might also be possible that this sentence is a metaphoric one with a wider scope of meaning that includes man's different talents, abilities, and instincts. Then the Imam ('a) adds:

"... analogous materials,"

These "analogous" materials might be tendons, sinews, nerves and even bones which, at first glance, might look similar in some respects, but they have different functions each.

وَالأَضْدادِ الْمُتَعادِيَةِ، وَالأَخْلاطِ الْمُتَبايِنَةِ مِنَ الْحَرِّ وَالْبَرْدِ وَالْبَلَّةِ وَالْجُمُودِ[1]

"... irreconcilable opposites, and disparate humors of hot, cold, dry, and moist natures."

1. The phrase "of hot, cold, dry, and moist natures" in this sentence might be in reference only to "desperate humors" or to both "desperate humors" and "irreconcilable opposites".

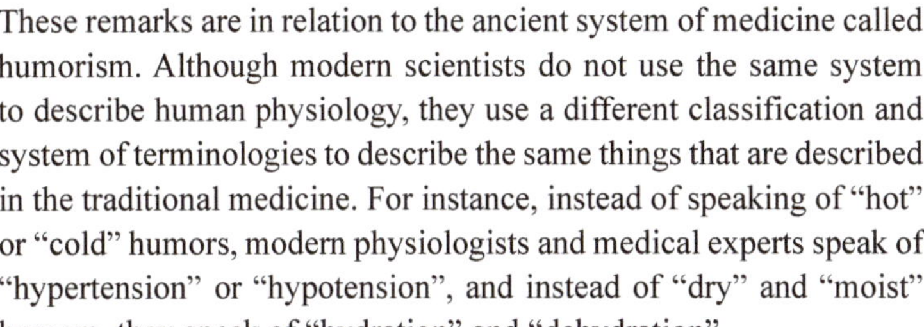

These remarks are in relation to the ancient system of medicine called humorism. Although modern scientists do not use the same system to describe human physiology, they use a different classification and system of terminologies to describe the same things that are described in the traditional medicine. For instance, instead of speaking of "hot" or "cold" humors, modern physiologists and medical experts speak of "hypertension" or "hypotension", and instead of "dry" and "moist" humors, they speak of "hydration" and "dehydration".

In any case, all of the sentences in this section of Imam Ali's sermon are indicative of a single important fact: Allah has created man's body [and possibly his soul too] in the form of a mixture of different constituents with different qualities, characteristics, capabilities and potentials.

These different components might be the reason behind people's different ideas and ways of life [as all human beings do not have similar shares of these different constituents]. The difference among people is, in fact, a blessing for human societies, as people with different qualities are always born into various communities to take charge of different occupations and positions based on their dominant talents and abilities. This way, everything seems to fall into place perfectly in human societies, creating a perfect system which could ensure the well-being and prosperity of its members. This, however, is a different discussion which needs to be discussed separately in its own place.

Important Points

1. The Creation of Adam ('a)

It can be understood from this sermon that Adam was created as a human being from the very beginning and that he did not come about as a result of the process of evolution from any other species of living creatures. This is also exactly how the Holy Quran has recounted about the creation of mankind.

Of course, the Holy Quran and the Nahj al-Balāghah are not books on natural sciences, but books of guidance for human beings on their journey of self-discipline and spiritual purification. However, sometimes they would touch upon some of the facts and secrets of the natural sciences in order to draw some important moral or spiritual conclusions from them.

Today, however, the dominant theory about the emergence of various creatures on the earth, including mankind, is that of Evolution. Modern scientists and the proponents of this theory are of the belief that the living creatures that exist on the earth did not exist on the earth like this from the very beginning. They believe that the first living creatures that emerged on the earth were the single-celled organisms that first came into existence in the deep parts of the earth's oceans. According to modern scientists, these single-celled organisms then underwent several mutations as a result of which they gradually evolved into other forms of creatures which then crawled out of water and turned into land animals and birds. The supporters of the theory of evolution believe that mankind is also the result of the same process of evolution; they hold the idea that the current human beings have evolved from some human-like apes who had themselves evolved from some inferior kind of life themselves.

The proponents of this theory fall into different categories and groups themselves: some of them are the followers of Lamarck and some are the adherents of Darwin. There are also the Neo-Darwinists and the proponents of the mutation theory; all of these scientists have mounted arguments in favor of their own specific theories.

Contrary to Darwinists and other proponents of the theory of evolution, there are scientists who believe that different species of living creatures appeared the way that they are today from the very beginning. These scientists have also put forward arguments and proofs in their rebuttals of the evolution theory which are well outside the scope of this book.

However, a few necessary points need to be briefly made here:

1. The baselessness of the theory of evolution can be clearly understood from the Quran, at least with respect to mankind, though there is no clear indication in the Quran that evolution did not apply to the other living beings. Some of the proponents of the theory of evolution, who believe that it applies to human beings as well, have tried hard to justify the contents of the Quran and the Nahj al-Balāghah in a way that would be in concordance with this theory. These individuals have even cited various verses in the Quran and sermons in the Nahj al-Balāghah as evidence to substantiate their claims. In spite of this, any fair and unbiased observer will clearly admit, after studying the Quran and the Nahj al-Balāghah, that it is impossible to prove these claims unless through much skewed interpretations of the contents of these two books.

2. The issue of evolution is not something that can be proven through empirical research, experiments, tangible evidence, or logical arguments because its roots go back to millions of years ago. Therefore, whatever arguments that its proponents or opponents mount for or against it are all considered to be hypotheses, at their best, and the proofs that are presented to support them are nothing but conjecture. Therefore, no one can ever argue that any of these arguments can negate or disprove anything that is found in the Quran and the Nahj al-Balāghah regarding the creation of man.

In other words, science always follows its own path, and its theories are constantly subject to modification, revision, and change; therefore, it is considered to be incomplete at any given point in time. Therefore, it can never disprove or override religious beliefs and convictions because scientific theories and hypotheses are subject to constant change and revision, with many of them being altered, revised, or even rejected following the discovery of new proofs and evidence. Therefore, it is perfectly possible that, in the future, the anti-Darwinist theory, which is against the idea of evolution, will gain more supporters due to new discoveries that lend support to it.

In fact, the newspapers recently[1] wrote about the discovery of a human skull which dated back to two million years ago and which was no different than the skull of the current human beings. This discovery will, no doubt, severely shake the foundations of the theory of evolution as it holds that the human beings that lived a few hundred thousand years ago were not similar to current human begins at all. This clearly shows how unstable these unverifiable theories are and how easily they can be undermined by new discoveries. However, since there is no other means of research into natural sciences, these theories are formed and depended upon, until new discoveries are made to either strengthen them or reject and replace them with new ones.

Thus, a clear distinction needs to be made between theories and definitive scientific facts. Things like the fact that water is made up of Hydrogen and Oxygen are considered to be scientific facts as they can be verified through experiments in laboratories. However, theories and hypotheses are merely guesswork, albeit educated ones, which are based on a series of suspicious evidence, and they continue to be binding until some counterevidence is found against them. However, regardless of how long they continue to be binding, no one would claim that they are one hundred percent accurate and correct as they always remain theories, not facts.[2]

2. The Body/Soul Duality

It can be inferred from this section of Imam Ali's sermon, which is completely in line with the teachings of the Quran, that man has been created with two entirely different aspects; one of the aspects of his existence is associated with the material world and to the most basic elements of this world, i.e. soil and water, and the other has to do with a lofty and sublime Divinely-created spirit.

This is, in effect, the root of the conflicts that occur within man himself, with certain forces driving him toward the material world and its glitters

1. "Recently" here means around the time when this commentary was being written.

2. For more information in this regard refer to the book Darwinism va Ākharīn Farziyeh hāy-e Takāmol. An excerpt account of the discussions presented in this book has also been presented in Tafsīr-e Nemūneh, vol. 11m pp. 67-89, amid the discussions on verses 26-44 of surah al-Ḥijr.

while others push him toward the spiritual and angelic realm. This is why, on the one hand, man has carnal desires that resemble those of animals and, on the other, sublime inclinations which link him to a spiritual world.

This extremely powerful and capable body/soul existence turned man's life into a veritable continuum with one of its extremes being the highest spiritual ranks imaginable and its other extreme being a level lower than that of the vilest of beasts.

These contradictory yet amazing capabilities exist in no living being other than human beings and it is this very dual nature that makes righteous and pure human beings admirable and praiseworthy beyond compare. This is because such individuals have practiced self-restraint in the face of their lowly desires though they have been able to commit any sort of corrupt act that they liked. As a result of giving more importance to their spiritual aspect than their material one, these virtuous individuals have been able to break free of the shackles of materialism, emerge through the glass ceiling of the material world and into a world of pure spirituality which even the human imagination is unable to conjure up visions about. It is precisely this amazing aspect of man that the angels were unable to understand prior to the creation of Adam. Due to their unawareness of this curious quality inherent within mankind, they assumed that this was an unnecessary creation by Allah, as He had already created them and they were offering Him the greatest forms of glorifications and acts of worship that can ever be performed.

Therefore, they believed that the creation of this new being would be, at its best, an unnecessary repetition. It is interesting to note that in order to imply the significance of this new creation of His, Allah ascribed the sublime spiritual dimension of Adam to Himself, stating:

"... and breathed into him of My spirit [i.e. a supreme spirit]"[1]

1. Ṣād, 72.

Needless to say, Allah neither has a body nor a spirit; therefore, whenever He ascribes anything to Himself [such as "The House of Allah",
"The Month of Allah", etc.] He intends to underscore the extremely
noble, sacred, and great nature of something. Therefore, He has referred to the spirit with which He invested man with as "His" spirit in
order to emphasize the fact that it is a sacred and noble spirit which
enjoys sublime qualities with traces of Allah's Divine Attributes including Knowledge, Power, and Creation.

Thus, Allah invested man with the most noble and sublime spirit and
this was why He called Himself the best of creators at the end of the
creation of man:

$$ ثُمَّ اَنْشَاْنَاهُ خَلْقًا اٰخَرَ فَتَبَارَكَ اللهُ اَحْسَنُ الْخَالِقِينَ $$

*"... then We gave it yet another creation. So blessed is Allah, the best
of creators."*[1]

How unfortunate it is that despite possessing such immense powers
and noble spiritual qualities and potentials, man causes himself to
fall from the sublime position that is rightfully his, as the greatest of
Allah's creations, down to a lower level than the cattle:

$$ اُولٰئِكَ كَالْاَنْعَامِ بَلْ هُمْ اَضَلُّ $$

"... like cattle they are, rather, they are more astray."[2]

---

1. Al-Mu'minūn, 14.
2. Al-A'rāf, 179.

3. Mankind, the Prodigy of the Realm of Existence

Undoubtedly, Mankind is the most amazing being that has been created into this world; this is due to the extraordinary and wonderful characteristics and features of his existence, some of which have been listed in the above-mentioned remarks of Imam Ali ('a). This extraordinary being has various different limbs, body parts, and powers each of which is made up of different, and even contradictory constituents. All of these intricate systems have been gathered within him, making him a complex system and a veritable miniature version of the universe itself with all of its wonders and intricacies; he is, in fact, a miniature world within which is a larger world.

These mind-blowing characteristics allow us to appreciate the complex nature and creation of mankind on the one hand and to recognize the greatness of the Creator of mankind on the other. Therefore, we can conclude that the purpose of Imam Ali ('a) for explaining these astonishing details about the creation of man has been to underscore the amazing nature of mankind as well as the greatness of his Creator.

Part Ten
Sermon No.1

وَاسْتَأْدَى اللهُ سُبْحانَهُ الْمَلائِكَةَ وَدِيعَتَهُ لَدَيْهِمْ وَعَهْدَ وَصِيَّتِهِ اِلَيْهِمْ في
الإِذْعانِ بِالسُّجُودِ لَهُ وَالْخُنُوعِ لِتَكْرِمَتِهِ فَقالَ سُبْحانَهُ: (اسْجُدُوا لِآدَمَ
فَسَجَدُوا اِلَّا اِبْليسَ) اعْتَرَتْهُ الْحَمِيَّةُ وَغَلَبَتْ عَلَيْهِ الشِّقْوَةُ وَتَعَزَّزَ بِخِلْقَةِ النَّارِ
وَاسْتَوْهَنَ خَلْقَ الصَّلْصالِ فَأَعْطاهُ اللهُ النَّظِرَةَ اسْتِحْقاقاً لِلسُّخْطَةِ وَاسْتِتْماماً
لِلْبَلِيَّةِ وَاِنْجازاً لِلْعِدَةِ فَقالَ: (اِنَّكَ مِنَ الْمُنْظَرِينَ اِلَى يَوْمِ الْوَقْتِ الْمَعْلُومِ)

"Then Allah -glory be to Him- asked the angels for the trust that He
had reposed in them and the fulfillment of His covenant with them
that they would prostrate themselves before him and would humbly
hold him in reverence; so He- glory be to Him- said": "Prostrate
yourselves [in humble obedience] before Adam!" all prostrated themselves except Iblīs"- [who was] overtaken by indignation and vanity
and overcome by perdition; [so] he took pride in his own creation
[that was] of fire and disdained the creation [of Adam that was] of
clay.

So Allah granted him the reprieve as he had become deserving of His
Wrath and [also] to complete the test for him and fulfill His promise
to him, and He said: "Indeed, you are among the reprieved ... [But not
until the Resurrection Day; rather,] until the day of the known time"."

Commentary [Part Ten]

Iblīs's Deviation from the Right Path 🌸🌸🌸

Following a brief mention of the process of creation of man, Imam Ali ('a) begins discussing another related issue which is rather instructive and edifying in many respects.

The Imam ('a) begins this section of his speech, stating:

وَاسْتَأْدَى اللّٰهُ سُبْحَانَهُ الْمَلَائِكَةَ وَدِيعَتَهُ لَدَيْهِم وَعَهْدَ وَصِيَّتِهِ اِلَيْهِم فِي الْإِذْعانِ بِالسُّجُودِ لَهُ وَالْخُنُوعِ ١ لِتَكْرِمَتِهِ فَقَالَ سُبْحَانَهُ: اُسْجُدُوا لِادَمَ فَسَجَدُوا اِلَّا اِبْلِيسَ

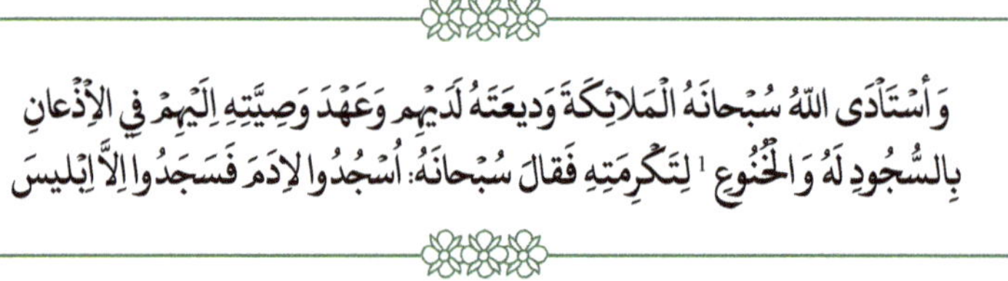

"Then Allah -glory be to Him- asked the angels for the trust that He had reposed in them and the fulfillment of His covenant with them that they would prostrate themselves before him and would humbly hold him in reverence; so He- glory be to Him- said": "Prostrate yourselves [in humble obedience] before Adam!" all prostrated themselves except Iblīs"²"

It can be clearly understood from these remarks that Allah had taken a covenant from the angels before, that when He created Adam, they would all prostrate themselves before him and this is exactly what has been explicitly mentioned in the Quran, in Surah Ṣād:

---

1. The Arabic term "خنوع", according to the Maqāyīs al-Lughah, originally means to be "humble" and "respectful" toward someone. The other dictionaries have likewise put forward similar definitions for this word.
2. Al-Baqarah, 34.

إِذْ قَالَ رَبُّكَ لِلْمَلَائِكَةِ إِنِّي خَالِقٌ بَشَرًا مِنْ طِينٍ * فَإِذَا سَوَّيْتُهُ وَنَفَخْتُ فِيهِ مِنْ رُوحِي فَقَعُوا لَهُ سَاجِدِينَ

*"[Call to mind] when your Lord said to the angels: "Indeed, I am to create a human being out of clay." * "And once I have proportioned him and breathed into him of My spirit, then fall prostrate before him.""*

The angels remembered that pledge and so when Adam was created and his creation was completed with spirit being breathed into him, turning him into a complete and perfect human being, Allah demanded the fulfillment of that pledge from the angels and commanded them all:

اسْجُدُوا لِآدَمَ فَسَجَدُوا إِلَّا إِبْلِيسَ

"Prostrate yourselves [in humble obedience] before Adam!" all prostrated themselves except Iblīs."[1]

According to some of the commentators of the Nahj al-Balāghah, the reason why Allah had taken the promise from the angels beforehand had been because if He had suddenly and abruptly ordered them to do that, they might have been shocked or even hesitated in carrying out His command. However, Allah had prepared them for that moment in advance so as to show that in order for important commands to be obeyed and carried out, one's subjects need to be briefed on them beforehand.

Then the Imam ('a) elaborates on the reasons behind Iblīs's refusal to obey Allah's command as follows:

1. Al-Baqarah, 34.

اعْتَرَتْهُ الْحَمِيَّةُ[1] وَغَلَبَتْ عَلَيْهِ الشِّقْوَةُ وَتَعَزَّزَ بِخِلْقَةِ النَّارِ وَاسْتَوْهَنَ خَلْقَ الصَّلْصَالِ

"[who was] overtaken by indignation and vanity and overcome by perdition; [so] he took pride in his own creation [that was] of fire and disdained the creation [of Adam that was] of clay."

Thus, the main reasons behind Iblīs's defiance of Allah's command were his own corrupted nature, something that the Imam ('a) refers to as "شقوه", perdition and also vanity, prejudice, arrogance, and egoism that were products of his corrupted nature. Thus, at that point, these moral vices overcame him and made him totally blind to the realities, driving him to think fire was superior to clay, though clay is the source of all sorts of great blessings for the entire world. Nevertheless, even this was not the main point here; the most important issue here is that by disobeying Allah, he openly declared that he considered his own knowledge to be superior to Allah's wisdom.

Of course, such misjudgments are not uncommon among the people who are entangled in the intricate web of moral vices which keep them from understanding the realities of things. It so happens that a selfish person whose vision and thoughts are veiled from the truth with conceit would make terrible misjudgments, considering something significant to be nothing or something insignificant to be of great importance.

Even the greatest intellectuals of the world would fall prey to grave mistakes and errors when entangled with vanity and egoism. What is meant here by "perdition" is, therefore, the inherent barriers to Iblīs's obedience to Allah, i.e. the moral vices which already existed in his heart. These barriers, or moral vices, were all acquired by him willingly and they all stemmed from his past misdeeds, not the kind of barriers and vices that were, by nature, part of him without him

1. The Arabic term "حميّه", from the root word "حمی" [pronounced "Ḥamy"], originally means the heat of sunlight, fire, human body, or any other things that generate heat. It is sometimes used to metaphorically refer to the human faculty of anger because once this faculty gives man the feeling of anger, one feels inflamed and hot.

having willingly chosen to acquire them. This is because perdition is by definition the opposite of prosperity, both of which are achieved through deeds.

Prosperity, in its religious sense, is defined as the acquisition of certain conditions for moving toward salvation and an eternal life of bliss in the Hereafter. Perdition, on the other hand, refers to the barriers which are formed on the way to salvation and prosperity. However, both of these conditions are "acquired" by human beings as well as the other responsible beings through their actions and deeds, not through some deterministic cause!

In any case, following that mortal sin and grave mistake of his, Iblīs fell from his lofty rank and was driven out of the station of nearness to Allah that he used to hold. From then on, he was considered the most hated and accursed creature in existence due to the gravity of that sin. However, even his expulsion from that lofty rank and the fact that Allah had cursed him did not cause him to be awakened and to repent of his sin, and therefore he continued to be unpardonably vain and conceited.

His refusal to admit his mistake brought him [just like all conceited, prejudiced, and stubborn individuals] to commit yet another unreasonable thing which sealed his fate and doomed him to eternal perdition. He vowed to do whatever he could to mislead Adam and his descendants in order to satisfy his feelings of anger and envy, hence taking on an even heavier burden of sins. The Quran indicates that Iblīs then asked Allah to grant him a long life and to allow him to live until the Resurrection Day:

قَالَ رَبِّ فَأَنظِرْنِي إِلَىٰ يَوْمِ يُبْعَثُونَ

""O' Lord! Reprieve me then [and let me live] until the Resurrection Day"1"

---

1. Al-Ḥijr, 36.

Amīr al-Mu'minīn ('a) then goes on to explain what happened afterwards as follows:

فَأَعْطَاهُ اللّٰهُ النَّظِرَةَ اسْتِحْقاقاً لِلسُّخْطَةِ وَاسْتِتْماماً لِلْبَلِيَّةِ وَإِنْجازاً لِلْعِدَةِ

"So Allah granted him the reprieve as he deserved the Allah's Wrath and [also] to complete the test for him and fulfill His promise to him."

However, Allah did not grant him exactly what he had asked for; He did not reprieve Iblīs until the Resurrection Day but until a specified time that was known only to Him. Imam Ali ('a) also states the following with regard to this issue:

فقال: إِنَّكَ مِنَ الْمُنْظَرِينَ إِلَى يَوْمِ الْوَقْتِ الْمَعْلُومِ

"... and He said: "Indeed, you are among the reprieved ... [But not until the Resurrection Day. Rather,] until the day of the known time""[1]

As for what the exact meaning of "the day of the known time" is, there is considerable controversy among the Quranic exegetes and the commentators of the Nahj al-Balāghah. Some are of the opinion that this is a reference made to the end of this world when religious responsibilities will be abolished and it means that although Iblīs had asked to be reprieved until the Resurrection Day, he was not reprieved until then but only until the end of this world.

Another possibility that has been mentioned with respect to this issue is that this "known time" is the lifespan of Iblīs; that is to say, Allah reprieved him until his death which is a time known to no one except

1. This is a reference made to the verses 37-38 of Surah al-Ḥijr; the original verses are as follows: قالَ فَإِنَّكَ مِنَ الْمُنْظَرِينَ • إِلى يَوْمِ الْوَقْتِ الْمَعْلُومِ

Allah. The reason why Allah did not tell him the exact deadline when his reprieve would come to an end is that in that case he would know exactly how much time he had and so he would be encouraged to commit even more transgressions and sins.

Finally, there are some experts who have put forward the possibility that this "known time" is the Resurrection Day because the term "known day" has been used in the verse 50 of surah al-Wāqi'ah to refer to the Resurrection Day:

"Indeed, the former and the later people- Shall be gathered for the appointment of a Known Day."

However, this latter possibility seems quite unlikely, because if this were true, then it should be said that Allah agreed to Iblīs's terms completely and granted him reprieve until the time that he had asked for. This is while the related verses of the Quran indicate that Allah did not agree to grant him exactly the reprieve that he had asked for. Moreover, the phrase that has been used in surah al-Wāqi'ah to refer to the Resurrection Day is different from the one used here to speak of the reprieve given to Iblīs. In surah al-Wāqi'ah, the phrase "يوم معلوم" [a Known Day] has been used, while with regard to Iblīs's reprieve the phrase "يوم الوقت المعلوم" [the Day of the known time] has been utilized. Considering these issues, it is safe to conclude that this latter interpretation is an inaccurate one and the correct interpretation is one of the first two interpretations mentioned above.

According to an Islamic Hadith, what is meant by "the Day of the known time" is the time of the advent of Imam Mahdi ('a) at which point Iblīs's life will be ended.[1] Of course, this does not mean that by Iblīs's death all temptations for sinning will be eliminated from the world, or the issue of the Divine test and obedience to Allah will be

1. Tafsīr al-'Ayāshi, vol. 2, p. 242, hadith No. 14.

no more.

This is because carnal desires which are the root cause of all sins and transgressions will remain in man's nature. It is interesting to note that Satan himself went astray because of following his own carnal desires.[1]

1. A complete description of how carnal desires and Satan's insinuations misguide mankind can be found in the second Munājāt [Munājāt al-Shākīn] of the total 15 Munājāts of Imam Ali ibn al-Ḥusayn ('a) which can be found in the book Mafātīḥ-e Novīn, p. 65.

Important Points

1. The Significance of Mankind ﷺ

One of the important reasons for man's greatness as the most noble and venerable being among Allah's other creatures is the evidence found in various verses of the Quran, indicating that the angels prostrated themselves before Adam on Allah's orders. This issue is of such great importance that it has been reiterated and emphasized in several different surahs of the Quran.[1]

These verses indicate that all of the angels, without an exception, prostrated themselves humbly before Adam, something that clearly shows man's superiority over even the angels. It appears that the Quran has repeated this fact several times in order to make human beings realize their spiritual value and worth, since this knowledge has an important role to play in man's guidance and moral training.

2. What was the Nature of the Prostration before Adam ﷺ

There is much controversy among the Quranic exegetes concerning the nature of the prostration that was commanded by Allah to be performed before Adam, as well as the question whether it is possible to prostrate before anyone except Allah. Some believe that this prostration has been performed before Allah because of his creating an amazing being like mankind and that it was only performed symbolically before Adam. Others believe that the angels did prostrate themselves before Adam but it was not the kind of prostration which is performed when worshipping Allah because this kind of prostration must be performed solely before Allah. They believe that the angels prostrated before Adam out of their humbleness to welcome him into the realm of existence or to show their respect for him.

With regard to this issue, a Hadith has been related from Imam al-Riḍā ('a) in the book 'Uyūn Akhbār al-Riḍā, which is as follows:

1. E.g.: al-Baqarah, 34; al-A'rāf, 11; al-Isrā', 61; al-Kahf, 50; and Ṭāhā, 116.

———— ❈ ————

كَانَ سُجُودُهُمْ لِلّٰهِ تَعَالى عُبُودِيَّةً وَلِاٰدَمَ اِكْرَاماً وَطَاعَةً لِكَوْنِنا فِي صُلْبِهِ

———— ❈ ————

"Their prostration before Allah was for worshipping Him and before Adam to show him their respect and reverence as we [the Ahl-al-Bayt ('a)] were to be born into his progeny."[1]

It can be inferred from this Hadith that the angel's prostration before Adam had two purposes: first they prostrated in order to worship Allah and second to show their respect for Adam ('a).

This second kind of prostration has also been referred to in the verse 100 of surah Yūsuf:

———— ❈ ————

وَرَفَعَ اَبَوَيْهِ عَلَى الْعَرْشِ وَخَرُّوا لَهُ سُجَّداً

———— ❈ ————

"And he seated his parents upon the throne, and they all fell down prostrate to him [before Allah]."

According to an Islamic Hadith about this verse, Imam al-Hādī ('a) has been quoted as saying:

———

1. 'Uyūn Akhbār al-Riḍā ('a), vol. 1, p. 263, part of hadith No. 22.

اَمَا سُجُودُ يَعْقُوبَ وَوُلْدِهِ فَإِنَّهُ لَمْ يَكُنْ لِيُوسُفَ وَإِنَّما كَانَ مِنْ يَعْقُوبَ
وَوُلْدِهِ طَاعَةً لله وَتَحِيَّةً لِيُوسُفَ كَما كَانَ السُّجُودُ مِنَ الْمَلائِكَةِ لِآدَمَ

"As for the prostration of Jacob and his sons [before Joseph], it was not an act of worship; rather, their prostration was to worship Allah and to show their respect for Joseph, and this is the same kind of prostration performed by the angels before Adam."[1]

3. Addressing the Questions Regarding the Creation of Satan

There are numerous questions surrounding the reason behind the creation of Satan, his history, his refusal to obey Allah, and Allah's reprieving him until a specified time in this world. Addressing all of these questions requires a separate book to be written on them, but we will briefly discuss some of these questions, which are related to our discussions in this section.

Question No. 1: Was Iblīs [Satan's name] an angel? If he was an angel, then why did he commit the gravest sin there is, though angels are said to be Infallible beings not prone to transgressions? And if he was not an angel, then why is he listed among the angels in the Quran?

Answer: Without a doubt, Satan was not an angel and this has been clearly and explicitly confirmed in the Quran in the following verse:

كَانَ مِنَ الْجِنِّ فَفَسَقَ عَنْ أَمْرِ رَبِّهِ

"... except Iblīs, who was one of the jinn, and transgressed against his Lord's command."[2]

---

1. Tafsīr al-Qummī, vol. 1, p. 356.

2. Al-Kahf, 50.

So Iblīs was a Jinn, not an angel; however, as he had been serving and worshipping Allah a lot before he committed that grave sin, he was also allowed in the rank of the angels and this was why he was counted as one of them. This is why in some religious texts, including the sermon of Qāṣi'ah [sermon No. 192 in the Nahj al-Balāghah] he has been referred to as "an angel". In addition to all this, the Quran indicates that Iblīs himself addressed Allah and, in justification of his disobedience, said:

"... You created me out of fire ..."[1]

It is a known fact that, among all the created beings, the Jinn have been created from fire, something that has been confirmed in the verse 15 of Surah al-Raḥmān as well:

"And He created the jinn out of a flame of a fire."

This fact has also been mentioned in the Islamic Hadiths from the Prophet's Ahl-al-Bayt as well.[2] Finally, according to the Quran, Iblīs has offspring and descendants;[3] this is while the angels do not reproduce.

1. Ṣād, 76.
2. Al-Majma' al-Bayān, vol. 1, p. 190, discussions on the verse 34 of surah al-Baqarah.
3. Al-Kahf, 50.

Question No. 2: How is it possible for Allah to give dominance to Iblīs over human beings and leave them defenseless against such a formidable enemy?! Besides, what was the point of creation of such an evil seducer? And what was the purpose of granting him a long life and respite to try hard to mislead the descendants of Adam?
Answer: Satan was initially created as a pure and righteous being who, for many long years, remained pure and righteous and worshipped Allah to the point where he was admitted into the rank of angels. However, due to his own vanity, arrogance, and conceit and also through means of the freedom of will that he had been granted [like human beings], he decided to take the path of aberration. He later followed that path until he fell to the lowest possible level of aberration and depravity.
Moreover, it is necessary to note that Satan's insinuations and temptations are not things which force human beings to commit transgressions without their knowledge or against their will. Rather, it is human beings who willingly and knowingly allow him to access their hearts and souls and to tempt them with his evil insinuations. The Quran has also clearly confirmed the fact that it is human beings themselves who give Satan permission to tempt them with evil suggestions:

""As for my servants, indeed you have no authority over them, save the perverse who follow you.""[1]

And in yet another verse, the Holy Quran has mentioned the following:

1. Al-Ḥijr, 42.

إِنَّمَا سُلْطَانُهُ عَلَى الَّذِينَ يَتَوَلَّوْنَهُ وَالَّذِينَ هُمْ بِهِ مُشْرِكُونَ

"Indeed, his authority is only over those who befriend him and those who associate him as a partner [with Allah, as they obey and serve him]."[1]

Finally, Imam Ali ('a) himself answers this question rather subtly and beautifully in his sermon, stating:

"So Allah granted him the reprieve as he deserved Allah's Wrath and [also] to complete the test for him and fulfill His promise to him,"

This means that, on the one hand, Allah granted Iblīs reprieve to be able to dole out on him a much more terrible punishment. This is because, according to the Quran, the ones who choose the path of transgressions and sins are given several warnings by Allah; if they heed the warnings and stop transgressing, they will be saved and this is in fact the very purpose of these warnings. However, if they fail to heed these warnings, Allah will leave them to plunge as deeply as they can into transgressions and vice so that their burden of sins becomes heavier and they become deserving of much more painful punishments.[2]

On the other hand, Satan and his insinuations are a great test for human beings and not only is he not a detriment to them, but he is also a means of development and growth for the believers. This is because although he is a formidable enemy for the believers, they will grow spiritually by withstanding his insinuations and rejecting his evil suggestions.

This is, in fact, how development and growth occur for human beings all throughout their life, i.e. when they are faced with a difficult situation, they will try harder to overcome that difficulty and so they grow and develop to become more powerful after solving their problems. Likewise, when human beings are faced with a powerful enemy, they

1. Al-Naḥl, 100.

2. Āl-i-'Imrān, 178; al-Rūm, 41.

use all of their intellectual and physical powers in order to overcome that enemy. The enemy, therefore, stirs them into action and forces them to try hard to increase their potentials, as a result of which they become stronger and move to higher levels of intellectual and physical capabilities.

However, the individuals whose hearts have sunk into transgressions and who have, hence, become rebellious and reckless in disobeying Allah will plunge even deeper into transgressions and become more wretched every single day that their life is extended in this world. Due to their persisting in sinning, these wicked people actually deserve such a terrible fate. This fact has also been confirmed by the Quran in the following verses:

لِيَجْعَلَ مَا يُلْقِى الشَّيْطَانُ فِتْنَةً لِّلَّذِينَ فِي قُلُوبِهِمْ مَرَضٌ وَالْقَاسِيَةِ قُلُوبُهُمْ وَلِيَعْلَمَ الَّذِينَ أُوتُوا الْعِلْمَ أَنَّهُ الْحَقُّ مِنْ رَبِّكَ فَيُؤْمِنُوا بِهِ فَتُخْبِتَ لَهُ قُلُوبُهُمْ

"This is so He may make what Satan throws in a trial for those in whose hearts is disease and for the hard-hearted ... And [also] that those who have been given knowledge may know that it is the truth from your Lord, and that they may, therefore, believe in it, and their hearts may be humbled before it ... "[1]

Question No. 3: Why did Satan consider himself to be superior to Adam and why did he object to what Allah had ordered him based on His Divine Wisdom?

Answer: It is essential to note that vanity and arrogance constitute a major obstacle and veil which prevent one from realizing the reality of things, just as they made Satan blind to the truth. Due to his arrogance and vanity, he not only rebelled against Allah and disobeyed His command, he even objected to what Allah had commanded him to do based on His Divine Wisdom. Thus, he protested that why should a noble creature like him, who had been created from fire, prostrate

---

1. Al-Ḥajj, 53-54.

himself before an inferior creature like Adam, who was made of clay. He assumed that among all elements fire was superior to soil though soil is the source of all blessings for this world and it contains all the elements necessary for sustaining life on earth. It is also this very soil which holds various kinds of treasures within itself, including all sorts of mines, jewels, and oil. Although fire and heat are also necessary for life, undoubtedly the main elements necessary for sustaining life exist in soil.

There are some Islamic Hadiths which explain that one of the lies that Iblīs told on that day was that fire is superior to soil;[1] this is while in order to start a fire, something like fuel or wood is needed, both of which come about from soil whether directly or indirectly.

Furthermore, Adam's superiority to other beings and his privilege did not lie only in his physical aspect which was from clay; rather, his greatest merit was the lofty spirit which was given to him by Allah, as explicitly mentioned in the verse [... and I breathed into him from My Spirit].

Even if we were to accept that fire is superior to soil, this would not still make Satan superior to Adam, because Adam possessed a lofty spirit given to him by Allah, which was not given to any other living being. Thus, having a body which was superior to Adam did not give Satan any right to disobey Allah's command and refrain from prostrating himself before Adam. It is possible that Satan actually knew all of this but his vanity and arrogance prevented him from acknowledging the truth.

4. The Baseless Justifications Put forward by Some Unlearned Individuals

According to the commentary of Ibn Meytham al-Baḥrānī on the Nahj al-Balāghah, some philosophers have taken the entire story of the creation of Adam, the prostration of the angels before him, and the disobedience of Iblīs to be metaphoric and not having actually happened like this.

For instance, some of them have maintained that what is meant by "the angels prostrating themselves before Adam" in this story is that

1. Tafsīr al-Qummī, vol. 2, p. 244.

the physical powers of man have been subjected to his intellectual powers [i.e. his spirit]! They have also claimed that what is meant by Iblīs in this story is man's power or faculty of imagination. Therefore, the "hosts of Iblīs" are the powerful whims and lusts [carnal desires] of man which are always at odds with man's intellectual powers. Finally, these individuals have argued that what is meant by "Paradise" from which Adam was later expelled is the lofty Divine knowledge that was made inaccessible to him after he disobeyed Allah. Needless to say, all of these justifications are unfounded and, thus, incorrect.[1]

These are clear instances of eisegesis [that is, the arbitrary interpretation of religious texts based on personal taste and interest], something that has been strictly prohibited as a terrible misdeed which would distance one far away from Allah.

The reason for such strict prohibition is rather clear: Eisegesis has been the most effective tool in the hands of deviant people, charlatans, and fabricators of religions to distort religious teachings to their own liking. These people always tried to interpret the contents of the Quran and the Islamic Hadiths based on their own opinion and in a way that has never been meant by Allah or the Ahl-al-Bayt ('a).

Therefore, if eisegesis interpretation of the Quran and the Islamic Hadiths based on personal interests becomes a common practice, there will remain no trace of the original and genuine precepts and laws of Islam, as all of them will be subjected to baseless personal opinions and meddled with by the desires of this and that. Under such conditions, the Quran and the Tradition of the Prophet (ṣ) will turn, God forbid, into a puppet in the hands of deviant individuals and unlearned people who would then change and alter them however they wish.

This is exactly why the great Muslim scholars and religious authorities insist on basing all of the interpretations of the Quran and the prophetic Hadiths on certain established principles, particularly lexicological and syntactic ones. One of these important principles is that all of the religious texts, including the contents of the Quran and the Islamic Hadiths, must be interpreted based on their apparent and literal meaning unless there are sound proofs at hand that they are

1. Sharḥ Nahj al-Balāghah Ibn Meytham, vol. 1, p. 190 on.

metaphoric. It should be noted that the proofs that are presented in order to treat some religious text as metaphoric must be considered as convincing by the common sense of the majority of the scholars and experts, and they should also be using the same proofs in their arguments as well.[1]

In any case, Imam Ali ('a) mentions the story of Iblīs and his awful fate as a lesson for all human beings so that they would know the adverse consequences of vanity, arrogance, egoism, and prejudice. Anyone who ever allows these moral vices to overcome him must remember the terrible fate of Iblīs, who was cursed by Allah for eternity and was afflicted by eternal perdition. Thus, such people have to stop allowing such evil feelings to dominate him.

Let us conclude this part with the following remarks by the late scholar, Mughnīyah, made in his commentary on the Nahj al-Balāghah:

"One can take the following lessons from the story of Adam and Iblīs:

1. If a person envies others for the virtues that they possess, or be an enemy of them because they have a good job or post that they deserve, he is considered to be a follower of Iblīs's creed and he will be one of his companions on the Resurrection Day.

2. There is but a single way toward attaining lofty moral virtues and gaining true knowledge of religion: to always submit to the truth and remain on the path of the truth irrespective of what the results would be.

3. There are many people who insist on their wrong ways, not because they do not know what they do or believe is wrong, but because of their obstinate opposition to their opponents. These people know perfectly well that their stubborn persistence in following a wrong path will entail the worst consequences for them but they still continue to follow that path.

An example of such individuals is Iblīs; if Iblīs had repented and stopped following the wrong path that he had taken, Allah would, no doubt, have accepted his repentance and forgiven him. In fact, he himself knew this and was even prepared to repent, but on condition that Allah would not order him, yet again, to prostrate himself before

1. For more information in this regard, refer to the book al-Tafsīr bī al-Ra'y, written by Ayatollah Makarem Shirazi.

Adam. This was while Allah had stipulated this same condition for the acceptance of Iblīs's repentance, i.e. that he prostrate himself before Adam."[1]

1. Fī Ẓilāl-i Nahj al-Balāghah, vol. 1, p. 51.

Part Eleven

Sermon No.1

ثُمَّ اَسْكَنَ سُبْحانَهُ آدَمَ داراً اَرْغَدَ فِيها عَيْشَهُ وَآمَنَ فِيها مَحَلَّتَهُ وَحَذَّرَهُ اِبْلِيسَ وَعَداوَتَهُ فَاغْتَرَّهُ عَدُوُّهُ نَفاسَةً عَلَيْهِ بِدارِ الْمُقامِ وَمُرافَقَةِ الأَبْرارِ فَباعَ الْيَقِينَ بِشَكِّهِ وَالْعَزِيمَةَ بِوَهْنِهِ وَاسْتَبْدَلَ بِالْجَذَلِ وَجَلاً وَبِالاِغْتِرارِ نَدَماً ثُمَّ بَسَطَ اللّهُ سُبْحانَهُ لَهُ فِي تَوْبَتِهِ وَلَقّاهُ كَلِمَةَ رَحْمَتِهِ وَوَعَدَهُ الْمَرَدَّ اِلى جَنَّتِهِ وَاَهْبَطَهُ اِلى دارِ الْبَلِيَّةِ وَتَناسُلِ الذُّرِّيَّةِ

"Thereafter Allah - glory be to Him- housed Adam in an abode where He made his life plenteous and his lodging safe, and He cautioned him against Iblīs and his enmity. Yet, [in the end] his enemy deceived him, being envious of him for his secure abode and his company of the righteous. And so he exchanged his certainty with doubt and his resolution with irresolution, and he turned his joy into fear and was enticed [by Satan] into rue.

Thereafter, Allah -glory be to Him- extended [His Mercy] to him [by granting him] the chance of repentance, inspired to him His Word of Mercy, and promised him that he would return to His Paradise [once again]. Then, He sent him down to the abode of trial and the place of procreation of progeny.

Commentary [Part Eleven]

Learning an Important Lesson from Adam's Fate ✿✿✿

In the previous sections of his speech, Amīr al-Mu'minīn ('a) discussed the tests that the angels and Iblīs underwent; in this section of his speech, however, the Imam ('a) briefly speaks about the test that Adam was put to and also Adam's fate.

It can be clearly understood from the contents of the Quran that Adam was created for life on the earth from the very beginning. For instance, the verse 30 of surah al-Baqarah reads:

اِنّى جاعِلٌ فِى الْأَرْضِ خَليفَةً

"And [call to mind] when your Lord said to the Angels: "I am to place a vicegerent [i.e. a representative] on the earth.""

There is also evidence in the Quran which proves that what is meant by "the earth" here is not Paradise [whatever paradise is taken to mean]. One piece of evidence in this regard comes from the verse 36 of surah al-Baqarah, where Allah has mentioned:

وَقُلْنَا اهْبِطُوا بَعْضُكُمْ لِبَعْضٍ عَدُوٌّ وَلَكُمْ فِى الْأَرْضِ مُسْتَقَرٌّ وَمَتاعٌ اِلَى حينٍ

"And [then to them] We said: "get down [all of you from your station], while you are enemies of one another! And for you, there will be residence on earth and means to reap the benefit for a specified term"."

Nonetheless, it was necessary for Adam to experience a period of test before being sent down to live on the earth in order to learn concepts such as Divine orders, prohibition, responsibility, obedience, disobedience, regret, and repentance. He also needed to know his enemy and what he could do to him by experience and in practice.

This was why Allah first sent him to Paradise and allowed him to enjoy the blissful bounties and blessings in it, but only prohibited him from touching the fruits of a single tree there. However, Satan's insinuations and deception were finally able to entice him into committing Tark al-Awlā [abandoning the better choice] and he ate from the forbidden tree. As soon as he did that, he was deprived of his heavenly clothes and this awakened him to the gravity of his mistake, so he turned to Allah penitently. At this point, by His Divine Grace, Allah taught Adam how to repent of his mistake, and then accepted his repentance and promised that he would return to Paradise once again. However, since the worldly consequences of that mistake could not be undone, Adam was deprived of that felicitous and blissful life in Paradise and fell to the earth to live a life full of hardship and miseries.

This was a general outlook of the contents of Imam Ali's discussions about the story of Adam, presented in this section of his sermon. Let us now consider this section of Imam Ali's sermon closely and interpret its sentences one by one.

Imam Ali ('a) begins this section of his sermon, stating:

ثُمَّ أَسْكَنَ سُبْحَانَهُ آدَمَ دَاراً أَرْغَدَ[1] فِيهَا عَيْشَهُ وَآمَنَ فِيهَا مَحَلَّتَهُ

"Thereafter Allah - glory be to Him- housed Adam in an abode where He made his life plenteous and his lodging safe."

So Adam was first lodged in a place which had both of the two most important conditions for a good life, i.e. security from harm and abun-

1. The Arabic term "ارغد", from the root word "رغد" [pronounced "Raghad"], is originally used to refer to a lavish and plenteous life and also abundance of blessings; it is used both for human beings and animals [according to al-Mufradāt and Maqāyīs al-Lughah dictionaries].

dance of blessings and bounties.
This sentence stated by Imam Ali ('a) is actually a reference made to the verse 35 of surah al-Baqarah in the Quran:

وَقُلْنا يا آدَمُ اسْكُنْ أَنْتَ وَزَوْجُكَ الْجَنَّةَ وَكُلا مِنْها رَغَداً حَيْثُ شِئْتُما

"And We said: "O' Adam! Reside, you and your wife, in Paradise and eat from the abundant [bounties] therein, whencesoever you will."

Imam Ali ('a) then explains how Allah warned Adam against the evil insinuations of Iblīs:

"... and He cautioned him against Iblīs and his enmity."

So Allah showed Adam both the way to rectitude and the way to perdition and gave him all the warnings that he needed so that he would have no argument against Allah if he slipped. These remarks by the Imam ('a) are again in reference to a verse in the Quran, namely the verse 117 of surah Ṭā Hā:

فَقُلْنا يا آدَمُ إِنَّ هذا عَدُوٌّ لَكَ وَلِزَوْجِكَ فَلا يُخْرِجَنَّكُما مِنَ الْجَنَّةِ فَتَشْقى

"So We said: "O' Adam! Indeed, this is an enemy of yours and [an enemy] of your wife. Beware not to let him expel you from Paradise or you will fall into misery."

Moreover, in order to strip Adam of any excuse, Allah showed him the tree which he had been prohibited to approach and instead He granted them permission to eat from the fruits of all other trees in Paradise

However, Adam who had just been created into this world and did not know anything of the deception and tricks of Satan, finally fell prey to Satan's evil suggestions. Amīr al-Mu'minīn ('a) has described this incident as follows:

"Yet, [in the end] his enemy deceived him, being envious of him for his secure abode and his company of the righteous."

This is basically what Satan does; he never makes an attempt to elevate himself spiritually to the rank of the righteous and the prosperous. Instead, he does whatever he can in order to strip others of their God-given blessings and to destroy their lives.

Imam Ali ('a) then continues and makes a most enlightening remark regarding the main reason behind Adam's mistake, stating:

1. The Arabic term "نفاسه" derives from the root word "نفس" [pronounced "Nafs"], which originally means "soul". Moreover, since breathing is essential for life, another derivative of this word, namely "تنفس" is used in Arabic to refer to breathing. Another derivative of this word, "منافسه", has been used in Arabic in the sense of "attempt" and "hard work" toward an important goal. The reason for this usage has been probably because when one intends to achieve an important goal, one puts himself and his soul into much trouble and hardship. In fact, due to this meaning of "hardship" inherent in this world, its other derivative, "نفاسه", has been used to refer to "envy" and "begrudging" [according to al-Mufradāt, Maqāyīs al-Lughah, and Lisān al-'Arab dictionaries].

فَباعَ الْيَقِينَ بِشَكِّهِ وَالْعَزِيمَةَ بِوَهْنِهِ[1]

"And so he exchanged his certainty with doubt, and his resolution with irresolution."

Interestingly enough, this sentence of the Imam ('a) is also in reference to a verse of the Quran which is as follows:

وَلَقَدْ عَهِدْنا إِلَى آدَمَ مِنْ قَبْلُ فَنَسِيَ وَلَمْ نَجِدْ لَهُ عَزْماً

"And We had already took a covenant [of obedience] from Adam, but he forgot; and We did not find him resolute."[2]

The Quran indicates that Satan deceived Adam and his wife by swearing to them that he is their well-wisher:

وَقاسَمَهُما إِنِّي لَكُما لَمِنَ النّاصِحِينَ

"And he swore to them: "I am indeed a well-wisher for you"."[3]

1. As regards the referent of the words "شكه" and "وهنه" ["his doubt" and "his irresolution" respectively], there is much controversy among the commentators of the Nahj al-Balāghah. Some of these experts believe that both of these words refer to Adam, meaning "Adam exchanged his certainty with his own doubt and his resolution with his own irresolution". There is another possibility in this regard that these two words refer to Satan, meaning that Adam exchanged his own certainty with Satan's uncertain words and his own resolution and determination with the irresolution and indetermination inculcated in him by Satan. Nevertheless, considering the context and the wording of this sentence, the first view mentioned above seems to be more accurate.

2. Ṭāhā, 115.

3. Al-A'rāf, 21.

In spite of this, Adam should have had certainty in Allah's promises and warnings, which are all based on sheer truth, rather than Satan's words which are all baseless conjecture and illusions. Nevertheless, because he forgot this important point, Adam entered a bargain with Satan which ended in nothing but sheer loss for him, as he undermined his own firm determination in following Allah's orders.

There is a lesson in this story for all of the descendants of Adam, as they too must only rely on whatever they are certain about in any undertaking and avoid basing their decisions on doubtful issues or uncertain things. They must all be cautious not to fall into the same trap as their father fell into and to avoid taking any course of action or path without first considering all of the aspects and facts pertaining to it. This is because Satan and his agents always cover their evil intentions in beautiful wrappings and pretend to be guiding one toward Paradise when they are in fact driving one toward Hell. These are the important lessons that all human beings in all eras must learn from the story of Adam ('a).

Imam Ali ('a) then proceeds to elaborate on the adverse consequences of that grave mistake, stating:

وَاسْتَبْدَلَ بِالْجَذَلِ[1] وَجَلاً[2] وَبِالاغْتِرارِ نَدَماً

"... and so he turned his joy into fear and was enticed [by Satan] into rue."

But what happened that awakened Adam to the grave mistake he had made and made him remorseful? Imam Ali ('a) has discussed this issue rather briefly, but a more detailed account of this incident can be found in different Surahs of the Quran. The Quran indicates that

1. According to the Ṣiḥāḥ al-Lughah Arabic Dictionary, the Arabic term "جذل" [pronounced "Jazal"] means "joy" and "happiness". According to Maqāyīs al-Lughah Dictionary, if it is pronounced as "Jizl", it would mean the root of the tree which keeps it firm in place. It appears that this word has been used to refer to "happiness" because usually a happy person stands upright and takes on a straight posture, while an unhappy person is usually slumped.

2. The term "وجل" [pronounced "Wajal"] originally means "fear" or "dread".

when Adam and his wife ate from the forbidden tree, their heavenly clothing fell off their bodies and their private parts which were covered up to that point were laid bare, which made them feel extremely ashamed in front of the angels.

However, worst of all, they were ordered to leave Paradise immediately as punishment for having disobeyed Allah's command and succumbing to the temptations of Satan. And so, degraded and humiliated, they were expelled from Paradise; nevertheless, all was not, yet, lost as there was still hope for them:

ثُمَّ بَسَطَ اللهُ سُبْحانَهُ لَهُ فِي تَوْبَتِهِ وَلَقَّاهُ كَلِمَةَ رَحْمَتِهِ وَوَعَدَهُ الْمَرَدَّ إِلَى جَنَّتِهِ[1]

"Thereafter, Allah -glory be to Him- extended [His Mercy] to him [by granting him] the chance of repentance, inspired to him His Word of Mercy, and promised him that he would return to His Paradise [once again]."

Although Adam repented of his mistake, it did not prevent his fall from Paradise as there was no reason for him to stay in Paradise any longer and he had now learned what he needed to learn and had experienced what he needed to experience there.

Imam Ali ('a) then goes on to describe what happened to Adam as follows:

1. There is much controversy among the experts with regard to the referent of the pronoun "his" in the phrase "his Paradise" in this sentence; some believe that it refers to "Allah", while others are of the opinion that it refers to Adam. If it is taken to refer to Adam, it would therefore mean that he would return to the same Paradise in which he used to live before he fell to the earth. However, if it is taken to refer to Allah, then it might not necessarily refer to the same Paradise in which Adam used to live because the Paradise that Adam used to live in could be a worldly one, while the one that he was promised entry into will be the otherworldly paradise. It appears from the context of the sentence, however, that this pronoun refers to Allah [because there are other words which refer to Allah in the same sentence, including "His Mercy"]. Some might argue that the term "مَرَدّ" indicates that Adam will be returned to the same paradise from which he was cast out, but it could also be said that going back to paradise has been said as a general sentence here; hence, it could refer to any sort of "paradise" in which he could lead a blissful life.

وَاَهْبَطَهُ اِلى دارِ البَلِيَّةِ وَتَناسُلِ الذُّرِّيَّةِ

"... and [then] He sent him down to the abode of trial and the place of procreation of progeny."

It can be clearly understood from this sentence that this world is the place created for testing mankind and that what happened in Paradise was only a necessary preliminary to the main phase of the test that mankind was to be put to. Another noteworthy point in this part of the Imam's sermon is that the issue of reproduction and the procreation of offspring only occurs in this world and not in Paradise.

Important Points

1. What Paradise did Adam Live in?

As regards the paradise where Adam was first housed, there are different and differing views. Some believe that he was lodged in the same Paradise which is promised to the righteous and the pious where they will live in the Hereafter. There are others who are of the opinion that the Paradise that Adam was first housed in was a beautiful green and woody area on the earth, a place where they have named "the worldly paradise". The latter group of experts have based their arguments for this opinion on several pieces of evidence:
They have argued that the Paradise in the Hereafter is an eternal abode for the righteous and it is impossible to exist it. They have further argued that it is not possible for a sinful creature like Iblīs to enter such a sacred and noble abode. Some might put forward a counter argument, stating that Iblīs never actually entered Paradise but waited outside it to deceive Adam at the right moment. However, this argument is in contrast to the verse 36 of Surah al-Baqarah, which reads:

"And [then to them] We said: "get down [all of you from your station], while you are enemies of one another!"

This verse clearly indicates that Allah ordered Iblīs and Adam to get down to the earth while they were enemies of one another, something which shows that they were both in the same place at that time.
Additionally, there are numerous Hadiths from the infallible Imams ('a) which indicate that the paradise where Adam was first housed was a beautiful garden on the earth. According to one such Hadith, Ḥusayn ibn Bashshār has been quoted as saying: "Once I asked Imam al-Ṣādiq ('a) about what the paradise in which Adam was first housed

had been. The Imam ('a) replied:

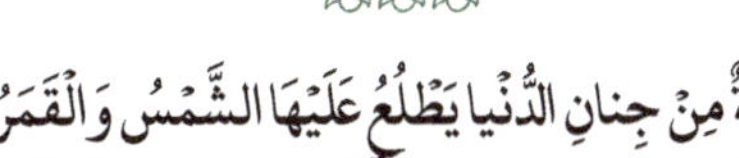

جَنَّةٌ مِنْ جِنانِ الدُّنْيا يَطْلُعُ عَلَيْهَا الشَّمْسُ وَالْقَمَرُ
وَلَوْ كانَتْ مِنْ جِنانِ الْخُلْدِ ما خَرَجَ مِنْها أَبَداً

"It was one of the [beautiful] gardens of the earth on which both the sun and the moon shone. Had it been the eternal Paradise [in the Hereafter], he would never have exited it.""[1]

The late Shaykh al-Kulaynī has likewise transmitted a similar Hadith in his book al-Kāfī, related from Imam al-Ṣādiq ('a) by Ḥusayn ibn Muyassir.[2]

The only problem that might be raised here is with regard to the following part of Imam Ali's remarks about the place where Adam was first housed:

نَفاسَةً عَلَيْهِ بِدارِ الْمُقامِ

"... being envious of him for his secure abode and his company of the righteous."

It might be argued that this sentence means that Adam had been housed in the eternal Paradise because it is only that place which is a truly secure lodging. However, this sentence might be merely indicative of the fact that had Adam not made that mistake, he might have been allowed to live in that beautiful earthly garden for much longer, before being sent to live his normal life on earth. However, the mistake that he made caused him to be sent to the life of trial and test on

1. 'Ilal al-Sharāyi', vol. 2, p. 600, hadith No. 55.

2. Al-Kāfī, vol. 3, Bāb Jannah al-Dunyā, p. 247, hadith No. 2.

the earth much sooner.

It could also be argued that this sentence means that Iblīs deceived Adam, hoping to be able to deprive him of a blissful life in the eternal Paradise of the afterlife because if Adam had been completely obedient to Allah, he would have been admitted into the eternal Paradise in the Hereafter.

2. Did Adam Commit a Sin?

The people who believe that even Divinely-sent prophets are prone to sins have no problem claiming that what made Adam fall from Paradise was a sin that he committed. However, the followers of the school of the Ahl-al-Bayt ('a) believe that the Divinely-sent prophets are infallible and not prone to sins or transgressions whether in regard to convictions, the promotion of religious laws and teachings, or everyday actions and deeds. They further believe that the Divinely-sent prophets have always been infallible, both before they were sent as prophets and after that.

Based on this belief, the Shi'a Muslims believe that Adam never committed any sins and that the fact that Allah had forbidden him from approaching that tree had not been a strict prohibition from an unlawful act, but a prohibition from an abominable act [Makrūh]. However, since prophets, particularly Adam before whom all the angels had prostrated themselves, enjoy high ranks with Allah, it does not befit them to do even a single abominable act.

Therefore, if prophets do something that is considered abominable, they will be severely rebuked by Allah [though ordinary people will not receive any sort of punishment for doing abominable acts] because as it has been said "the good deeds of the righteous are considered sins for those closest to Allah"!

Put differently, there are two kinds of sins: absolute sins and relative sins. Absolute sins are evil actions that are absolutely prohibited for all people; these include lying, stealing, and drinking wine, etc. Relative sins, on the other hand, are actions which are not considered to be sins when done by ordinary people; rather, some of these actions might be even rewarded by Allah as recommendable acts when done by ordinary people. However, some of these recommendable or permissible actions are considered not befitting for those who are closest to Allah and so if these actions are done by the chosen servants of Allah, they will be considered transgressions on their part. However, these are not absolute transgressions which are evil by nature, but only actions which do not befit chosen servants of Allah, and this is the exact meaning of Tark al-Awlā [abandoning the better choice].

Moreover, some experts have argued that the prohibition that Adam received with regard to eating from the fruits of that tree had not been a Divinely-issued prohibition which must necessarily be followed; rather, it had been a kind of advice, much like the advice that a doctor gives his patients, telling them not to eat some food because it would prolong their illness.

Evidently, disobeying the advice of a doctor is neither disrespecting the doctor nor a serious sin, and nor does it constitute an instance of disobeying his command. Rather, the only result of such disobedience would be prolonged illness and pain which the patient himself has to suffer and endure.

There are some indications as to this fact in some of the verses of the Quran concerning the story of Adam; one of such verses is the following:

فَقُلْنا يا آدَمُ إِنَّ هذا عَدُوٌّ لَكَ وَلِزَوْجِكَ فَلا يُخْرِجَنَّكُما مِنَ الْجَنَّةِ فَتَشْقى

"So We said: "O' Adam! Indeed, this is an enemy of yours and [an enemy] of your wife. Beware not to let him expel you from Paradise or you will fall into misery."[1]

According to some Islamic Hadiths, Adam never actually wanted to eat from that specific tree; however, since he had been using the fruits of some similar trees, Satan told him about that forbidden tree: "Allah did not prohibit this tree for you [meaning it was another tree that Allah made prohibited for him]."[2] So, according to these Hadiths, Satan deceived Adam by making him unknowingly eat from that forbidden tree.

1. Ṭāhā, 117.

2. وَقالَ ما نَهيكُما رَبُّكُما عَنْ هذِهِ الشَّجَرَةِ ['Uyūn Akhbār al-Riḍā ('a), vol. 1, p. 195, hadith No. 1]; al-A'rāf, 20.

Another point which needs to be kept in mind is that, according to the Quran, Iblīs swore to Adam and his wife Eve that he was their well-wisher and meant to do them good by encouraging them to eat from that tree. Obviously, he was lying but neither Adam nor his wife Eve had ever heard anyone lie before and this was actually why they fell for his temptations:

"And he swore to them: "I am indeed a well-wisher for you"."[1]

Of course, if they had been a little more careful, they would have realized that Iblīs was lying because they had been warned before about that by Allah that Iblīs was their sworn enemy. Therefore, it was rather unwise to listen to such a spiteful enemy and easily accept that he intended good things for them.

3. What was the Forbidden Tree?

There is considerable controversy among Quranic exegetes and the commentators of the Nahj al-Balāghah concerning what that forbidden tree actually was. Some are of the opinion that it was an actual and ordinary tree, while others believe that it was not an actual tree but a spiritual or moral virtue and privilege, metaphorically referred to as a tree.

At any rate, whether it was an actual tree or a spiritual virtue, the question remains as to what kind of tree or spiritual virtue it exactly was. Although Imam Ali ('a) has not elaborated on this issue in his sermon, it seems necessary to complete our discussion of the story of Adam and his being deceived by Iblīs here by presenting a short discussion about this issue here. The Holy Quran has referred to the forbidden tree in a general way in six different instances without elaborating on the nature of that tree or its specifications. However, there is a wealth of information about it in the Islamic Hadiths as well as the writings of the Quranic exegetes and the

1. Al-A'rāf, 21.

commentators of the Nahj al-Balāghah. Some of these Hadiths and interpretations indicate that the forbidden food was wheat [note that the Arabic term "شجره" [translated into English here as "tree"] can be used to refer to trees as well as other plants; this different usage can be seen in the Quran in the story of prophet Jonah, where the Quran has referred to a squash plant as "شجره"].[1] There are other pieces of evidence suggesting that it was a vine tree, a fig tree, a palm tree, or a camphor tree.[2]

On the other hand, the people who believe that this "tree" has been something spiritual have interpreted it to have been "the knowledge of the Ahl-al-Bayt ('a)"; some of the other proponents of this view hold that it had been "envy" or "knowledge" in general.

According to an Islamic Hadith, once Imam al-Riḍā ('a) was asked about the reason behind so many different views about the nature of that forbidden tree; the Imam ('a) is narrated to have said the following in response to this question:

"All of these views are, in fact, correct because the trees in Paradise are different from the trees of this world. There are some trees in Paradise which yield, not a single fruit, but different fruits. In addition, when Adam received so much respect from Allah and even the angels prostrated before him, and after he was housed in Paradise, he wondered whether Allah has created any beings that are superior to him in spiritual rank. It was at that point that Allah showed him the lofty rank of prophet Muḥammad (ṣ) and his Ahl-al-Bayt ('a), and so Adam wished in his heart that he enjoyed the same rank as them."[3]

An interesting point about the current version of the Torah which we have access to is the view that it puts forward regarding the nature of the forbidden tree. According to the current Torah, eating from the fruit of the forbidden tree would give the person knowledge [apparently knowledge of good and evil] and also an eternal life. Therefore, according to the Torah, Allah prohibited Adam and Eve from eating from that tree lest they should become knowledgeable and eternal beings, much like gods!!![4]

---

1. وَأَنْبَتْنَا عَلَيْهِ شَجَرَةً مِنْ يَقْطِينٍ : "And We made a gourd bush grow above him [for him to rest in its cool shade]." [al-Ṣāffāt, 146].

2. Al-Tibyān, vol. 1, p. 158; Al-Durr al-Manthūr, vol. 1, pp. 52-53, the interpretation of the verse 35 of Surah al-Baqarah.

3. Ma'ānī al-Akhbār, p. 124, hadith No. 1 [with some excerption].

4. Genesis, 2:17.

Such contents are clear and undeniable proofs of the fact that the current Torah is a distorted book, made by unlearned human beings, and that it is undoubtedly not the real and genuine Torah. It is rather unbelievable how the Torah considers the acquisition of knowledge by Adam a sin punishable by expulsion from Paradise, as if Paradise is no place for knowledgeable and learned human beings! It seems that the Islamic Hadiths which indicate that the forbidden tree had been knowledge are also fabricated Hadiths which have been forged based on the distorted contents of the Torah.

4. What were the Words Which were Taught to Adam to Repent with?

In his discussion of the story of Adam, Imam Ali ('a) has only made a passing mention of the words that Allah taught Adam by means of which he repented of his mistake; however, the Imam ('a) has not elaborated any further on this issue and has not mentioned what those words exactly were.

The Holy Quran has likewise made a brief mention of this fact and only indicates that Adam received certain words from Allah with which he repented of his mistake, but again, there is no mention of what those words had actually been. Nevertheless, Imam Ali's remarks with respect to this issue as well as the related contents of the Quran indicate that they have been extremely important words with significant meanings.

Some experts have maintained that what is meant by these "words" has been Adam's admitting his mistake before Allah, something which has also been mentioned in the verse 23 of surah al-A'rāf:

رَبَّنَا ظَلَمْنَا أَنْفُسَنَا وَإِنْ لَمْ تَغْفِرْ لَنَا وَتَرْحَمْنَا لَنَكُونَنَّ مِنَ الْخَاسِرِينَ

"They said: "O' Lord! we have wronged ourselves, and if You do not forgive us and have mercy upon us, we will certainly be among the losers"."

There are some Islamic Hadiths which have mentioned the same kind of penitent words, spoken by Adam in acknowledgment of his mistake, with different wordings:

لا إِلَهَ إِلَّا أَنْتَ سُبْحَانَكَ وَبِحَمْدِكَ عَمِلْتُ سُوءاً
وَظَلَمْتُ نَفْسِى فَاغْفِرْلِى إِنَّكَ خَيْرُالْغَافِرِينَ

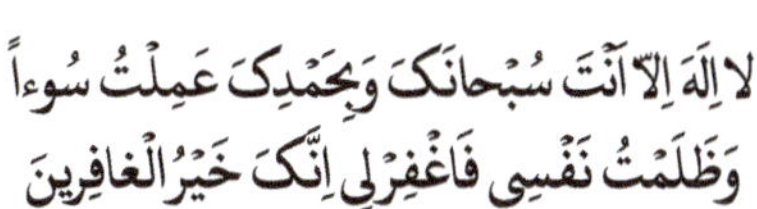

"There is no deity but You [O' Lord!] Glory to You and all praise be to You! I have erred and wronged myself, so forgive me, for You are the best of forgivers."[1]

Likewise, there are a number of Islamic Hadiths, narrated from Imam al-Ṣādiq ('a) or Imam al-Bāqir ('a), which indicate similar things about this issue.[2]

In spite of this, most of the Islamic Hadiths indicate that the words that Adam was taught were the sacred names of the Pure Five, i.e. Muḥammad (ṣ), 'Alī ('a), Fāṭimah ('a), Ḥasan ('a), and Ḥusayn ('a); according to these Hadiths, Adam adjured Allah by these sacred names to forgive him and so Allah forgave him.

For instance, according to an Islamic Hadith transmitted in the book al-Khiṣāl, Ibn 'Abbās has been quoted as saying: "Once I asked the Prophet (ṣ) what were the words which Adam received from Allah [and repented with]. The Prophet (ṣ) answered:

1. Biḥār al-Anwār, vol. 11, p. 181, hadith No. 35.

2. Al-Kāfī, vol. 8, p. 304, hadith No. 427 [Hadith fī kalemāt talaqqā Ādam min rabbeh].

سَأَلَهُ بِحَقِّ مُحَمَّدٍ وَعَلِيٍّ وَفاطِمَةَ وَالْحَسَنِ وَالْحُسَيْنِ
إلّا تُبْتَ عَلَيْهِ فَتابَ اللّٰهُ عَلَيْهِ إِنَّهُ هُوَ التَّوابُ الرَّحيمُ

"He adjured Allah by Muḥammad, 'Alī, Fāṭimah, Ḥasan and Ḥusayn to accept his apology and repentance, and so Allah accepted his repentance, for He is Ever-Relenting, the Ever-Merciful""[1]

It is noteworthy that the same concept with minor differences has been transmitted in the famous Hadith-based Sunni Quranic exegesis, Al-Durr al-Manthūr.[2]

Another similar Hadith, found in Imam al-Ḥasan al-'Askarī's book of Quranic exegesis reads: "When Adam made that mistake and wanted to ask Allah's forgiveness for it, he said to Allah, "O' Lord! Accept my apology and my repentance, for I now know the adverse consequences of transgression and the humiliation that it entails!"

Allah replied, "Do you not remember that I had ordered you to adjure Me by Muḥammad and his pure Ahl-al-Bayt in times of distress and tribulation?" Adam said, "Yes, O' Lord!"

Allah said, "Then adjure Me by Muḥammad, 'Alī, Fāṭimah, Ḥasan and Ḥusayn and pray to Me to forgive you for their sake so that I may answer your prayer and give you more than what you pray for!"""[3]

Based on yet another Hadith, 'Āyishah has quoted the Prophet (ṣ) as saying that the words that Adam repented with were the following:

1. Al-Khiṣāl, vol. 1, p. 270, hadith No. 8.

2. Tafsīr al-Durr al-Manthūr, vol. 1, p. 60 [amid the interpretation of the verse 37 of surah al-Baqarah].

3. The Book of Quranic exegesis attributed to Imam al-Ḥasan al-'Askarī ('a), p. 225.

اَللّهُمَّ اِنَّکَ تَعْلَمُ سِرّي وَعَلانيَتي فَاقْبَلْ مَعْذِرَتي وَتَعْلَمُ حاجَتي فَاَعْطِني سُؤْلي وَتَعْلَمُ ما في نَفْسي فَاغْفِرْلي ذَنْبي اَللّهُمَّ اِنّي اَسْاَلُکَ ايماناً يُباشِرُقَلْبي وَ يَقيناً صادِقاً حَتّى اَعْلَمَ اَنَّهُ لا يُصيبُني اِلّا ما کَتَبْتَ لي وَارْضِني بِما قَسَمْتَ لي

"O' Lord! Indeed You know whatever I conceal and whatever I reveal, so accept my apology; and You know, O' Lord, what I need, so grant me what I implore of you; and you know what lies in my heart, so forgive me my sin. O' Lord! I ask You for a faith that would guide my heart, and true certitude so that I may know that nothing would befall me except what You have ordained for me, and to be content with what you have ordained for me."[1]

Although it might seem at first glance that completely different views of this issue have been put forward in these Hadiths, there is no contradiction between their contents, as it is possible that Adam adjured Allah by the Pure Five ('a) and he also implored Allah using these supplications.

There are also some who believe that the words in question were not actually anything spoken verbally, but a sort of spiritual rapture that Adam experienced; but again, there is no contradiction between this view and what was discussed above, as all of the supplications that were mentioned in the Islamic Hadiths could have been recited by Adam amid the spiritual rapture that he experienced.

It should be noted, however, that the fact that there is no contradiction between Adam not having known the names of the Pure Five ('a) before Allah teaching him those names with Adam's possession of the knowledge of the Names. This is because the knowledge of the Names probably refers to the knowledge of the secrets of creation, but the ways to engage in self-discipline and self-purification as well as the way to make up for one's past mistakes and try to attain nearness to Allah is far different from the knowledge of the secrets of creation.

1. Tafsīr al-Durr al-Manthūr, vol. 1, p. 59.

Therefore, the issue of the knowledge of the Names is completely unrelated to the names of the Pure Five (‘a) which were later taught to Adam.

Part Twelve
Sermon No.1

وَاصْطَفَى سُبْحَانَهُ مِنْ وَلَدِهِ أَنْبِيَاءَ أَخَذَ عَلَى الْوَحْيِ مِيثاقَهُمْ وَعَلَى تَبْلِيغِ الرِّسالَةِ أَمانَتَهُمْ
لَمّا بَدَّلَ أَكْثَرُ خَلْقِهِ عَهْدَ اللهِ إِلَيْهِمْ فَجَهِلُوا حَقَّهُ وَاتَّخَذُوا الأَنْدادَ مَعَهُ وَاجْتالَتْهُمُ
الشَّياطِينُ عَنْ مَعْرِفَتِهِ وَاقْتَطَعَتْهُمْ عَنْ عِبادَتِهِ فَبَعَثَ فِيهِمْ رُسُلَهُ وَواتَرَ إِلَيْهِمْ أَنْبِياءَهُ
لِيَسْتَأْدُوهُمْ مِيثاقَ فِطْرَتِهِ وَيُذَكِّرُوهُمْ مَنْسِيَّ نِعْمَتِهِ وَيَحْتَجُّوا عَلَيْهِمْ بِالتَّبْلِيغِ وَيُثِيرُوا
لَهُمْ دَفائِنَ الْعُقُولِ وَيُرُوهُمْ آياتِ الْمَقْدِرَةِ: مِنْ سَقْفٍ فَوْقَهُمْ مَرْفُوعٍ وَمِهادٍ تَحْتَهُمْ مَوْضُوعٍ
وَمَعايِشَ تُحْيِيهِمْ وآجالٍ تُفْنِيهِمْ وَأَوْصابٍ تُهْرِمُهُمْ وَأَحْداثٍ تَتابَعُ عَلَيْهِمْ. وَلَمْ يُخْلِ اللهُ
سُبْحانَهُ خَلْقَهُ مِنْ نَبِيٍّ مُرْسَلٍ أَوْ كِتابٍ مُنْزَلٍ أَوْ حُجَّةٍ لازِمَةٍ أَوْ مَحَجَّةٍ قائِمَةٍ. رُسُلٌ لا
تُقَصِّرُ بِهِمْ قِلَّةُ عَدَدِهِمْ وَلا كَثْرَةُ الْمُكَذِّبِينَ لَهُمْ. مِنْ سابِقٍ سُمِّيَ لَهُ مَنْ بَعْدَهُ أَوْ غابِرٍ
عَرَّفَهُ مَنْ قَبْلَهُ. عَلى ذلِكَ نَسَلَتِ الْقُرُونُ وَمَضَتِ الدُّهُورُ وَسَلَفَتِ الأَباءُ وَخَلَفَتِ الأَبْناءُ

"And [thereafter] Allah -glory be to Him- chose prophets from among Adam's progeny and took their pledge on [safeguarding His] Revelations and on the task of delivering the Message which was entrusted to them. [This was] at a time when most of Allah's servants had perverted their covenant with Him, were ignorant of His rights, and took equals beside Allah [for worship], and also the devils had turned them away from knowing Him and had hindered them from worshiping Him.

So He raised up His Messengers among them[people] and kept sending His prophets to them, one after the other, to appeal to them for the fulfillment of the pledge of His [created] nature [that is inherent within them], and to remind them of His long-forgotten bounties, to deprive them of any excuses by delivering His edicts to them, to uncover to them the hidden treasures of wisdom, and to show them the Sings of [His] Power, from the sphere lifted high above them, the cradle laid down beneath them, the livelihood that sustains them, the moments of death that end their lives, the lingering pains and strains that age them, and the incidents that chase after them.

And never did Allah - glory be to Him- abandon His servants without a Divinely-sent prophet or Book, [or without] an adequate proof or an established path. "[Allah sent] such [men as] prophets as would never be impeded by their small numbers or the great numbers of their impugners, and among whom were predecessors who would name the one who follows, or successors who had been introduced by one before them. And so centuries unfolded and ages went by; fathers passed and sons succeeded them."

Commentary [Part Twelve]

Divinely-sent Prophets and Their Important Mission

In this section of his sermon, Amīr al-Mu'minīn ('a) focuses on the sending of prophets by Allah, which is the next phase of human life on earth that followed the creation of Adam and his descension to the earth. The Imam ('a) begins his discussion in this section by explaining the reason behind the sending of the prophets and then goes on to explain the nature and the purpose of their mission. He then continues to elaborate on the teachings of the prophets and finally ends this section, touching upon some of the most prominent characteristics and attributes of the prophets and their steadfastness in facing the problems and difficulties and their relations with one another throughout the history of mankind.

At the beginning of this section of his speech, Imam Ali ('a) states:

وَاصْطَفَى سُبْحانَهُ مِنْ وَلَدِهِ أَنْبياءَ أَخَذَ عَلى الْوَحْيِ ميثاقَهُمْ [1] وَعَلى تَبْليغِ الرِّسالَةِ أَمانَتَهُم

"And [thereafter] Allah -glory be to Him- chose prophets from among Adam's progeny and took their pledge on [safeguarding His] Revelations and on the task of delivering the Message which was entrusted to them..."

So, upon their selection as Divinely-sent messengers, all of the prophets took solemn vows and gave Allah their most solemn pledges that they would safeguard Divine Revelations and deliver that weighty Divinely-given trust to mankind with extra care. Thus, although they

1. The Arabic term "ميثاق", according to the Arabic dictionary Ṣiḥāḥ al-Lughah, derives from the root word "وثوق", which means "to trust someone with something valuable or important". Therefore, the word "ميثاق" is used to refer to the pledges or pacts made with someone which makes one trust them with important things. [The original spelling of the word "ميثاق" had been "موثاق" and it turned into its current form over time.]

were granted the greatest honor there is and became Divinely-sent prophets, they took on the most enormous and heaviest responsibility as well.

There are certain questions including why Allah picked out certain individuals among human beings to become prophets, what the nature of the Divine Revelation is, and why prophets received Divine Revelations while other people do not, which need to be addressed in their due place.[1]

This section of Imam Ali's sermon is, in fact, a reference made to the following verse in the Quran:

وَإِذْ اَخَذْنَا مِنَ النَّبِيِّينَ مِيثَاقَهُمْ وَمِنْكَ وَمِنْ نُوحٍ وَإِبْرَاهِيمَ
وَمُوسَى وَعِيسَى بْنِ مَرْيَمَ وَاَخَذْنَا مِنْهُمْ مِيثَاقًا غَلِيظًا

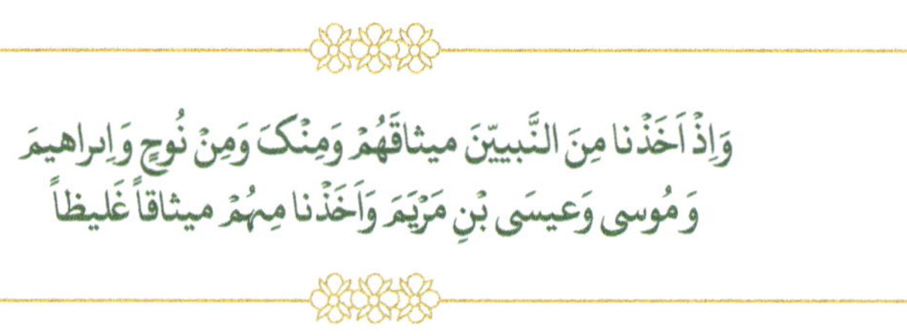

"And [call to mind] when We took a pledge from the prophets and from you [as well] and from Noah and Ibrāhīm and Moses and Jesus son of Mary; and We took from them an assured pledge [that they would not flag or fail in their duty]."[2]

The Imam ('a) then continues and sheds light on the main reason behind the sending of prophets to mankind:

---

1. For a thorough discussion of these questions and their answers, refer to the book Payām-e Quran, vol. 7, p. 317.

2. Al-Aḥzāb, 7.

لَمّا بَدَّلَ اَكْثَرُ خَلْقِهِ عَهْدَ اللهِ اِلَيْهِمْ فَجَهِلُوا حَقَّهُ وَاتَّخَذُوا الْأَنْدادَ[1] مَعَهُ
وَاجْتالَتْهُمُ[2] الشَّياطِينُ عَنْ مَعْرِفَتِهِ وَاقْتَطَعَتْهُمْ عَنْ عِبادَتِهِ

"[This was] at a time when most of Allah's servants had perverted their covenant with Him, were ignorant of His rights, and took equals beside Allah [for worship], and also the devils had turned them away from knowing Him and had hindered them from worshiping Him."

Therefore, many among the descendants of Adam fell into the terrible abyss of polytheism due to their unawareness and lack of knowledge of Allah, something which caused the devils to bring them under their own influence and prevent them from worshipping the one true God, i.e. Allah.

As regards the notion of "the covenant of Allah" in this section of Imam Ali's sermon, many of the commentators of the Nahj al-Balāghah believe that it is in reference to the covenant that Allah took from mankind in the world of Dharr.[3] It could also be argued that it is in reference to man's original nature which, by nature, guides him toward Allah.

In fact, the next remarks made by the Imam ('a) reinforce this view as he makes mention of this God-given nature of mankind. Put simply, Allah has created man with a pure nature upon which He bestowed

---

1. The word "انداد" is the plural of "ند" [pronounced "Nid"], which means "equal" and "like". The original meaning of this word, however, according to the Arabic dictionaries, had been "separation", "escaping", and "defying". This is, in fact, why the Arabic lexicologists believe that the term "ند" is not used for just any equals, but for equals that are someone's opposites as they take the exact opposite course and route as the person in question takes. In this sense, this term can be taken to be synonymous with the English words "rival" and "adversary".

2. The Arabic word "اجتال", from the root word "جولان", means "rotation" or "turning". Moreover, since Imam Ali ('a) has used it with the preposition "عن" [meaning "from"] here, it means to "turn someone away from someone else". It could also be argued that it means that in order to turn people away from Allah, the devils would constantly turn them in different directions, keeping them busy and unmindful of Allah.

3. As regards the concept of the "world of Dharr", it has been argued by the experts that it could be in reference to man's original nature and the capabilities that Allah has bestowed inherently within mankind. For more information in this regard, refer to Tafsīr-e Nemūneh, vol. 7, p. 4, the interpretation of the verse 172 of Surah al-A'rāf.

the basic drive knowledge of Tawḥīd and a drive toward the worship of the One and Only God. It is due to this pure original nature that mankind is, by nature, averse to evil and loves virtuousness.

If all human beings could protect their original nature against impurity and contamination, it would automatically guide them toward spiritual development and growth as well as toward the perfection that they were created to attain, albeit by Allah's Grace. Under such circumstances, the Divinely-sent prophets would have had a rather easy job as they would only give people a little help in their process of spiritual development and growth.

However, due to their deviation from their original nature and perverting it, many people gradually swerved away from the path of monotheism whose manifestation in their beliefs was their inclination toward polytheism and idolatry and whose manifestation in practice was that they succumbed to the temptations of Satan.

Since these terrible man-made problems were destroying mankind, Allah sent prophets to mankind with the extremely heavy responsibility of reforming various human communities. These responsibilities, as well as the qualities and attributes of the prophets, have been later touched upon by Amīr al-Mu'minīn ('a).

Imam Ali ('a) then goes on and mentions the philosophy behind the sending of prophets to mankind as follows:

فَبَعَثَ فِيهِمْ رُسُلَهُ وَوَاتَرَ إِلَيْهِمْ أَنْبِيَاءَهُ[1] لِيَسْتَأْدُوهُمْ مِيثَاقَ فِطْرَتِهِ وَيُذَكِّرُوهُمْ مَنْسِيَّ نِعْمَتِهِ وَيَحْتَجُّوا عَلَيْهِمْ بِالتَّبْلِيغِ وَيُثِيرُوا لَهُمْ دَفَائِنَ الْعُقُولِ

"So He raised up His Messengers among them and kept sending His prophets to them, one after the other, to appeal to them for the fulfillment of the pledge of His [created] nature [that is inherent within them], to remind them of His long-forgotten bounties, to deprive them of any excuses by delivering His edicts to them, to uncover to them the hidden treasures of wisdom ..."

In this section of his sermon, Amīr al-Mu'minīn ('a) lists four major purposes of the sending of prophets:

First, to ask people to fulfill the pledge that is inherent within their original nature with which they have been created. Allah has placed the basic knowledge of monotheism and Tawḥīd within every human being and if they let it grow within them in its natural process of growth, it will bring all human beings to be, by nature, monotheist believers.

Once this basic nature has fully grown into a true monotheist soul, people will be committed to goodness, the truth, and justice without needing anyone to guide them to these moral virtues. However, if, instead of growing this sacred nature, people pervert it with their misdeeds and misbeliefs or if the polytheist parents contaminate and spoil it in their children, the resulting human beings will be said to have been misled or gone astray. This is, in fact, where the Divinely-sent prophets enter the picture, as a part of the mission of the prophets has always been guiding the misled and the astray people back to their original monotheistic nature.

The second reason for the sending of prophets, according to Imam Ali

1. The Arabic verb "واتر", from the root word "وتر" [meaning "odd"] and the opposite of "شفع" [meaning "even"], means "one". It means that Allah sent prophets to mankind one after the other in order to guide his servants to the right path. Some experts believe that this word means "arranged successively with some interval". For instance, the sentence "واترما عليه من الصوم", means "he fasted every other day". In this sense, this word is the opposite of "consecutive", which refers to things which are arranged successively without intervals.

('a), is to remind mankind of the forgotten bounties of Allah. This is because man has been invested with myriads of physical and spiritual blessings and bounties by Allah and if he makes use of these bounties correctly, he can build a prosperous life for himself.

However, if he forgets these blessings and bounties for too long, this might result in their total destruction and he might lose them forever. This issue is like the case of a person who owns a beautiful garden, but he neither uses the abundant water that he has to water his garden nor does he pick the fruits of his trees on time. It goes without saying that if he goes on like that, he would destroy his garden and anyone who comes forward to remind him of his great blessings has done him the greatest service possible. This is exactly what the Divinely-sent prophets attempted to do for mankind.

The third aim of the prophets, as explained by Imam Ali ('a), is to give people the final proof and deprive them of any excuse [of not following the path of monotheism] through sound rational arguments and by delivering heavenly teachings and Divine edicts to them.

The fourth purpose of the prophets is to uncover the amazing intellectual powers that human beings possess. Allah the Almighty has invested man with great intellectual treasures which, if discovered and utilized correctly, will allow him to make an enormous leap in science and knowledge.

However, things like ignorance, destructive teachings, sins, and moral vices function as veritable veils and hindrances for these great human potentials and prevent them from flourishing. So another aim of the prophets is to take the cover off of these potentials and guide human beings to discover and make correct use of these great treasures within them.

The Imam ('a) then deals with the fifth purpose of the sending of Divinely-sent prophets, explaining that another reason that Allah sent prophets to man is to show him the great Signs of Allah in the entire world:

"... and to show them the Sings of [His] Power ..."

And then he lists these Sings of Allah's power as follows:

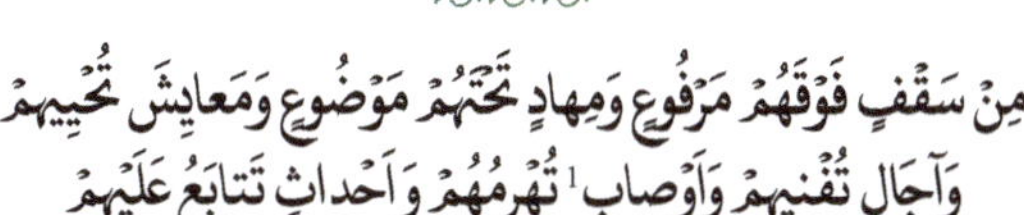

مِنْ سَقْفٍ فَوْقَهُمْ مَرْفُوعٍ وَمِهادٍ تَحْتَهُمْ مَوْضُوعٍ وَمَعايِشَ تُحْيِيهِمْ
وَآجَالٍ تُفْنِيهِمْ وَأَوْصابٍ[1] تُهْرِمُهُمْ وَأَحْداثٍ تَتابَعُ عَلَيْهِمْ

"... from the sphere lifted high above them, the cradle laid down beneath them, the livelihood that sustains them, the moments of death that end their lives, the lingering pains and strains that age them, and the incidents that chase after them."

All of these are, in fact, secrets of Allah's creation in the heaven and the earth as well as the means of man's livelihood and the causes of his suffering, all of which can remind him of Allah. There are also various events and incidents which happen to everyone in this world and which serve as lessons for them to learn and to be awakened by. So another responsibility of the prophets is to draw people's attention to these Signs of Allah, teaching them things which would increase their knowledge of Allah's creation and raise their awareness regarding the purpose of life and the spiritual aspect of their life.

Imam Ali ('a) then continues his sermon, stressing the following:

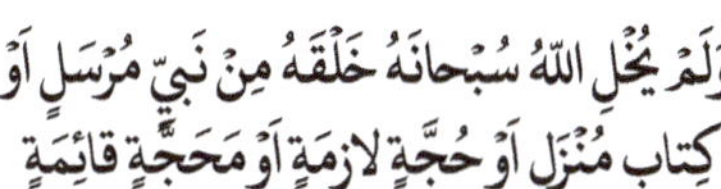

وَلَمْ يُخْلِ اللهُ سُبْحانَهُ خَلْقَهُ مِنْ نَبِيٍّ مُرْسَلٍ أَوْ
كِتابٍ مُنْزَلٍ أَوْ حُجَّةٍ لازِمَةٍ أَوْ مَحَجَّةٍ قائِمَةٍ

"And never did Allah - glory be to Him- abandon His servants without a Divinely-sent prophet or Book, [or without] an adequate proof or an established path."

1. According to al-Mufradāt Arabic dictionary, the Arabic term "اوصاب", which derives from the root word "وصب", originally means "chronic illness". Its other derivative, namely "واصب" is used to refer to anything lingering or perpetual. It appears that the Imam ('a) has used this word here to refer to the kinds of problems, difficulties, and pains that people constantly face in the life of this world.

In this part of his sermon, Amīr al-Mu'minīn ('a) refers to four means of guidance, at least one of which has always existed in all nations so that they might be deprived of any excuses [for not taking the right path].

First is the Divinely-sent prophets- whether those who had scriptures of their own or promoted the religion of another Arch-prophet; the existence of a Divinely-sent prophet among any nation is enough for them to be awakened and guided to the right path as long as they decided to do so. In any case, the existence of a prophet in a community is enough for them to be deprived of all excuses for not following the path of guidance.

Second is the Divinely-sent Scriptures which still exist to the day, even though the prophets who brought them have passed away. Third are the Infallible Imams, who are the rightful successors of prophets and have been referred to as "an adequate proof" here. As regards this phrase, some experts believe that it might be in reference to the human intellect and reason. However, since intellect and reason alone are insufficient for guiding man to the right path, it seems unlikely that this has been what the Imam ('a) meant by this phrase. Nevertheless, there is no problem with interpreting it as referring both to the Infallible Imams ('a) and human reason at the same time.

Finally, the fourth means of guidance which has been referred to by Imam Ali ('a) here is the "established path" which is an implicit reference made to the sacred tradition of the prophets and their successors, i.e. the Infallible Imams ('a). It is noteworthy that the Arabic term "محجه" has been defined as a clear "path" or "way" which can lead one to the desired destination, whether it is an actual physical destination or a spiritual goal.[1]

So, as Imam Ali ('a) mentions, Allah has never withheld the means of guidance from any peoples or nations during any eras, and by providing them with some means of guidance, He took away from them all excuses for not having faith or taking the right path.

Following this section of his speech, Imam Ali ('a) begins discussing the qualities, attributes, and characteristics of the prophets:

1. Al-Taḥqīq fī Kalamāt al-Quran al-Karīm, vol. 2, p. 169, the entry "Ḥajj".

رُسُلٌ لا تُقَصِّرُ بِهِمْ قِلَّةُ عَدَدِهِمْ وَلا كَثْرَةُ الْمُكَذِّبِينَ لَهُمْ

"[Allah sent] such [men as] prophets as would never be impeded by their small numbers or the great numbers of their impugners ..."

The Divinely-sent prophets were such brave men that they would sometimes stand up to thousands and thousands of enemies alone. They would enter huge fires, putting their trust solely in Allah, and emerged from them unharmed. They would fearlessly go to idol temples, break down all of the idols of idol-worshipping nations, and would stand before the angry idol-worshippers and make them ashamed of their aberrant creeds through sound and powerful arguments.

At times, they would walk fearlessly into the sea from one side, trusting in Allah to protect them, and emerge unharmed from the other side by His Will, and at other times, they would stand up bravely to large numbers of enemies with drawn swords, ready to strike and finish them off. It is rather interesting that, among all of the qualities and attributes of the prophets, Imam Ali ('a) focuses on their courage, steadfastness, and fortitude.

The Imam ('a) then goes on and further describes the Divinely-sent prophets as follows:

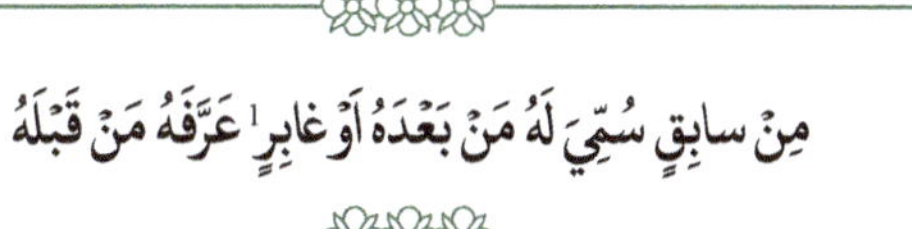

مِنْ سابِقٍ سُمِّيَ لَهُ مَنْ بَعْدَهُ أَوْ غابِرٍ[1] عَرَّفَهُ مَنْ قَبْلَهُ

"Among them were predecessors who would name the one who follows, or successors who had been introduced by one before them."

1. The Arabic word "غابر", from the root words "غبار" and "غبور", is used to refer to anything that remains like residue somewhere. Its other derivatives, "غبره" [pronounced "Ghobrah"] and "غبار" are used to refer to the residual milk that remains in the breasts and the small amount of dust that remains floating in the air respectively. This word is also used to refer to past times or individuals. [For more information in this regard, refer to the Maqāyīs al-Lughah, al-Mufradāt, and Lisān al-'Arab Arabic dictionaries].

In this part of his sermon, Imam Ali (‘a) points out one of the most important ways in which real Divinely-sent prophets were identified and recognized: true prophets would inform their followers of the arrival of the next prophet and would describe him completely to them, and the later prophets were recognized through the descriptions of their predecessors.[1]

Finally, Imam Ali (‘a) concludes this part of his speech by stating the following:

عَلى ذلِکَ نَسَلَتِ[2] الْقُرُونُ وَمَضَتِ الدُّهُورُ وَسَلَفَتِ الْآباءُ وَخَلَفَتِ الْأَبْناءُ

“And so centuries unfolded and ages went by; fathers passed and sons succeeded them.”

1. In some other manuscripts of the Nahj al-Balāghah, the word “سمّی” has been used as a passive verb and our interpretation of this section of this sermon is based on this same usage of this word. However, there are certain other manuscripts in which the active voice of the same verb has been used, in which case, this sentence needs to be translated as follows: “Prophets who were named by the next prophets.” However, the first version and interpretation of this sentence seem to be more accurate.

2. The word “نسلت”, from the root word “نسل”, is used to refer to the unfolding of generations one after the other. This is a rather beautiful literary description of the centuries, as they have been likened to different generations that are born, one to the other as they succeed each other.

Important Points

1. Prophets as the Gardeners of the Orchard of Humanity

It can be inferred from the beautiful and precisely calculated remarks made by Imam Ali ('a) in this section of his sermon that Allah has invested human beings with all the capabilities and potentials that they need in their quest for a prosperous and fulfilling life.

He has placed within human beings many valuable treasures and He has planted in their very nature all sorts of lofty seeds which can grow into sublime moral virtues and valuable human traits. He has then sent His prophets to them as veritable gardeners to help those valuable seeds in mankind to grow and flourish. These Divinely-sent experts also showed man the long-forgotten treasures that are within them and they also taught them how to make use of those treasures to their own benefit; these facts have been mentioned by Imam Ali ('a) rather succinctly in the following sentences:

"… to appeal to them for the fulfillment of the pledge of His [created] nature [that is inherent within them], and to remind them of His long-forgotten bounties … and to uncover to them the hidden treasures of wisdom."

As it is completely apparent in these remarks, the Divinely-sent prophets did not bring human beings anything that was not already inherent within their very nature; rather, they would only try to help them develop and grow based on the great potentials that was already in them. In a sense, it can be said that the prophets had only been sent to mankind to take the veil off of his inner jewel and to allow that jewel to shine on his life.

Some experts even believe that all of the teachings that were brought to human beings by prophets were mere reminders for them because the seeds of knowledge already existed within their nature and they needed only to be uncovered to them. Therefore, all of the teachers of mankind, including the Divinely-sent prophets and their righteous followers, only tried to show human beings the valuable potentials that were already within them so that they would act to actualize

them. This issue can be likened to the underground water which is brought to the surface in order to be used for drinking and agriculture through digging wells. The water already exists under the ground and the digging of wells is a mere means of bringing it to the surface.
There is a large number of verses in the Quran which indicate that much of the teachings sent down by Allah are meant as "admonition" or "reminder" to mankind, something that is in line with the above-mentioned view. However, since this is a very deep and long discussion, requiring its own place to be dealt with, we will stop it here.

2. Awakening Incidents

In another section of the above-mentioned remarks made by Imam Ali ('a), it has been mentioned that in addition to teaching Divinely-sent knowledge to mankind and showing them the Sings of Allah's greatness in the world, Divinely-sent prophets are also duty-bound to draw people's attention to awakening incidents.
Incidents like the end of the life of this world, the destruction of material gains and blessings, as well as great pains, tragedies and adversities are all lessons for mankind. It is clear that had it not been for these incidents which occur every now and then, human beings would long have been engulfed in deep ignorance and unawareness, a state from which it would have been almost impossible for them to awaken.[1]

3. The Role of Religion in Human Life

Another important point which is learned from this part of Imam Ali's sermon is the role of religion in human life. Imam Ali ('a) explained rather eloquently that if it had not been for the Divinely-sent prophets and their hard work, polytheism and idolatry would have permeated the entire world and the devils would prevent mankind from gaining any knowledge of Allah or worshipping Him.
One reason behind this is that human reason and intellect are not enough for him to be able to discern good from bad and to recognize all the necessary conditions for prosperity in all its forms. Although

1. For more information in regard to this important issue, refer to the book Payām-e Quran, vol. 4, p. 546 on.

intellect is like a lamp which sheds some light on the path ahead of mankind, it is rather incomplete without the great light of Divine Revelation which could shed light on the entire road ahead of him. Therefore, without having access to revealed teachings, mankind will be unable to find the correct path toward prosperity and growth.

This clearly shows how wrong the Brahmans were as they rejected the sending of Divinely-sent prophets. If human intellect were able to reach all of the secrets within man and in his outside world as well as the knowledge of the past, present, and future all at the same time, it might be possible for it to make correct judgments at all times, and so it might be a complete means for securing human prosperity both in this world and the Hereafter.

However, considering the major limitations of human intellect in perceiving realities and the fact that its unknowns are always more than what is known to it at any given point in time, it is obvious that it cannot be trusted as the sole means of making correct judgments and finding the correct ways.

Of course, this is not to understate human intellect, as it has been emphasized as one of the proofs of Allah in various Islamic references, including this same sermon by Imam Ali ('a). Its importance has also been underscored in various Islamic Hadiths, with some of them even calling it the "prophet within" to emphasize its great importance. For instance, a famous Hadith from Imam al-Kāẓim ('a) reads:

إن لله على الناس حجتين: حجة ظاهرة وحجة باطنة فأما الظاهرة فالرسل والأنبياء والأئمة: وأما الباطنة فالعقول

"Allah has provided human beings with two proofs [so that they may believe in Him and follow His commands]: one visible proof and one invisible proof. His visible proofs are the Divinely-sent Messengers, prophets, and Infallible Imams, and His invisible proofs are human intellect and reason."[1]

1. Al-Kāfī, vol. 1, Kitāb al-'Aql wa al-Jahl, p. 16, hadith No. 12.

Nevertheless, although this inner proof is important, it is rather limited in its scope and capability to guide mankind. On the other hand, the visible proof of Allah in the outside world, i.e. the Divinely-sent prophets, has no limitation in the scope of the guidance that it can offer to mankind. This is because the guidance that the prophets offer originates from the unlimited source of Allah's knowledge.

Based on the discussion presented above, let us present our rebuttal of the sophistry of the Brahmans. The Brahmans argue that the knowledge and guidance that the Prophets bring us from the Creator are either of the following two kinds: either they are intelligible to our intellects or they are unintelligible. They further argue that if this knowledge is intelligible to our minds, then it means that our intellects had already had the power to perceive that knowledge and so there had basically been no need for prophets to bring that knowledge for us. However, if that knowledge is unintelligible, it means that the human mind is unable to perceive it; hence, it is irrational information and of no value whatsoever, because no human being would embrace anything that is in contrast to his sound mind.

The clear flaw in this argument is that the Brahmans have not made a distinction between "irrational" and "unknown" things; they have done this as if they assumed that the human intellect is an omnipotent means of gaining knowledge and it has the power to perceive everything that exists without any help.

However, the correct view regarding the knowledge that is ever presented to us is to divide it into three categories: first is the knowledge that is consistent with human reason and intellect; second is the knowledge that is inconsistent with human reason and intellect, and third is the knowledge that had been unknown to human intellect up until the first time it was offered to human beings.

Most of the knowledge that there is in this world is arguably of the third type, i.e. what mankind does not know and needs to get his hands on, and this is exactly where the Divinely-sent prophets enter the picture. Additionally, we are constantly grappling with the concern that our perceptions of things might be wrong or mistaken; this is also another instance where prophets can come to our aid and verify our perceptions, telling us which of them are correct and which are wrong.

4. Mankind Needs Some Conclusive Proof in All Times and Eras

Another noteworthy point made by Imam Ali ('a) in this section of his sermon is that Allah has never left human beings, in any eras and epochs, without proofs to guide them to the correct path. These proofs could be prophets who were sent to them, the Divinely-sent scriptures which were delivered to them, infallible Imams who succeeded prophets and guided them, or their traditions and teachings which showed mankind the right way.

Interestingly, Imam Ali ('a) mentioned "Divinely-sent prophets" and "scriptures" together and then "proofs of Allah" [meaning Infallible Imams] and the authentic traditions of the prophets together. This shows that the Imam ('a) meant to emphasize the fact that for any scripture to be effective it needs to be accompanied by a prophet to implement its teachings and for the traditions of prophets to be useful to people, they need to be safeguarded and put into practice by the Infallible successors of the prophets.

This is exactly what we, the Shi'as, believe in and something that has evidently been corroborated in the following Hadith by Imam al-Ṣādiq ('a):

لَوْلَمْ يَبْقَ فِي الْأَرْضِ إِلَّا اثْنَانِ لَكَانَ أَحَدُهُمَا الْحُجَّةَ

"If no one except two individuals remain on the earth, one of them will indeed be the proof of Allah [and the Imam and leader of the other one]."[1]

Similarly, one of the aphorisms narrated from Imam Ali ('a) reads:

1. Al-Kāfī, vol. 1, Bāb Annahu law Lam Yabqa fī al-Arḍ ..., p. 179, hadith No. 1.

اَللَّهُمَّ بَلى لا تَخْلُوا الأَرْضُ مِنْ قائِمٍ لِلّهِ بِحُجَّةٍ إِمّا ظاهِراً
مَشْهُوراً وَإِمّا خائِفاً مَغْمُوراً لِئَلاّ تَبْطُلَ حُجَجُ اللهِ وَبَيِّناتُهُ[1]

5. The Qualities and Characteristics of Prophets

The prophets who were sent by Allah to guide mankind were not ordinary individuals; they enjoyed all of the qualities and characteristics required for carrying out their important mission. These included great courage to stand up to ignorant and stubborn people in order to deliver their Message to them, and also steadfastness in carrying out their mission even if it led to their martyrdom at the hands of their adversaries.

This specific characteristic of the prophets has been referred to by Imam Ali ('a) in the following section of his sermon:

"[Allah sent] such [men as] prophets as would never be impeded by their small numbers or the great numbers of their impugners ..."

The history of prophets [particularly that of the Prophet of Islam (ṣ)] is the best witness that no danger or obstacle could prevent them from making all the attempts that they could toward delivering their message and carrying out their mission.

This specific characteristic of the Divinely-sent prophets has also been mentioned in the Quran in the following verse:

اَلَّذِينَ يُبَلِّغُونَ رِسالاتِ اللهِ وَيَخْشَوْنَهُ وَلا يَخْشَوْنَ اَحَداً اِلاّ اللهَ

"[The past prophets were] those who delivered the messages of Allah and feared Him and did not fear anyone but Allah;"[2]

1. Nahj al-Balāghah, words of wisdom, No. 147.
2. Al-Aḥzāb, 39.

According to the author of the book Minhāj al-Barā'ah, it can be clearly understood from this part of Imam Ali's remarks that dissimulation had been impermissible for Divinely-sent prophets. This clearly refutes the accusations leveled at Shi'a Muslims by al-Fakhr al-Rāzī who wrote in one of his books: "... they [meaning Shi'a Muslims] believe that pretending to be a disbeliever as a way of dissimulation is permissible even for the Divinely-sent prophets."[1]

It should be noted that the Shi'a beliefs are much more sensitive to the issue of religion: according to the Shi'a convictions, when the religion itself is in a serious danger, dissimulation is not only impermissible for Infallible Imams, it is even impermissible for ordinary people! Dissimulation, according to the Shi'a beliefs, is obligatory under certain conditions and prohibited under some others. For instance, dissimulation is obligatory under conditions where making one's true beliefs and ideas manifest will entail some unnecessary loss. An example of this is when a group of Muslims are captivated by some atrocious enemies of Islam and, if they reveal their true beliefs, they will all be executed by the enemy and so the Muslim army will lose a substantial number of its forces and become weak.

Under such conditions, it is necessary for Muslims to dissimulate their beliefs so as to prevent an unnecessary loss of lives and strength of the Muslim front. Conversely, there are conditions where, if one conceals one's true beliefs, it will result in one's humiliation and abjection. Under such conditions, one must bravely reveal their true beliefs and patiently tolerate the consequences that follow, whatever they may be. One of the most outstanding examples of this lack of dissimulation [when dissimulation is not permissible] is what was done by Imam al-Ḥusayn ('a) and his companions in Karbala.

Therefore, since the Divinely-sent prophets constantly operated under conditions in which if they had dissimulated their beliefs, their efforts toward carrying out their mission would have be thwarted, they were ordered never to dissimulate their beliefs.

One point which needs to be made here is that the belief in the necessity of dissimulation under certain circumstances neither belongs exclusively to Shi'a Muslims nor even to Muslims in general. Rather,

1. Minhāj al-Barā'ah [by al-Khū'ī], vol. 2, p. 160.

it is one of the basic rational things that needs to be done whenever revealing the true beliefs will result in useless and unnecessary loss of lives or resources.[1]

1. For a complete discussion of the issue of dissimulation and the five rulings concerning it [i.e. the conditions under which it is obligatory, prohibited, recommendable, and abominable] as well as the related Quranic verses and Islamic Hadiths about it, refer to the book Al-Qawā'id al-Fiqhīyah, vol. 1, p. 383, the section on "Qā'idah al-Taqīyah".

Part Thirteen
Sermon No.1

اِلَى اَنْ بَعَثَ اللّٰهُ سُبْحَانَهُ مُحَمَّداً رَسُولَ اللّٰهِ صَلَّى اللّٰهُ عَلَيْهِ وَآلِهِ لِاِنْجَازِ عِدَتِهِ وَاِتْمَامِ
نُبُوَّتِهِ مَأْخُوذاً عَلَى النَّبِيِّينَ مِيثَاقُهُ مَشْهُورَةً سِمَاتُهُ، كَرِيماً مِيلَادُهُ، وَاَهْلُ الْاَرْضِ يَوْمَئِذٍ
مِلَلٌ مُتَفَرِّقَةٌ وَاَهْوَاءٌ مُنْتَشِرَةٌ وَطَرَائِقُ مُتَشَتِّتَةٌ، بَيْنَ مُشَبِّهٍ لِلّٰهِ بِخَلْقِهِ اَوْ مُلْحِدٍ فِي اسْمِهِ
اَوْ مُشِيرٍ اِلَى غَيْرِهِ. فَهَدَاهُمْ بِهِ مِنَ الضَّلَالَةِ وَاَنْقَذَهُمْ بِمَكَانِهِ مِنَ الْجَهَالَةِ. ثُمَّ اخْتَارَ
سُبْحَانَهُ لِمُحَمَّدٍ صَلَّى اللّٰهُ عَلَيْهِ وَآلِهِ وَسَلَّمَ لِقَاءَهُ، وَرَضِيَ لَهُ مَا عِنْدَهُ، وَاَكْرَمَهُ عَنْ دَارِ
الدُّنْيَا وَرَغِبَ بِهِ عَنْ مَقَامِ الْبَلْوَى، فَقَبَضَهُ اِلَيْهِ كَرِيماً صَلَّى اللّٰهُ عَلَيْهِ وَآلِهِ، وَخَلَّفَ
فِيكُمْ مَا خَلَّفَتِ الْاَنْبِيَاءُ فِي اُمَمِهَا اِذْ لَمْ يَتْرُكُوهُمْ هَمَلاً بِغَيْرِ طَرِيقٍ وَاضِحٍ وَلَا عَلَمٍ قَائِمٍ

"[And so it was] until Allah _ glory be to Him_ sent Muḥammad
_ may Allah bless him and his progeny_ as His Messenger to fulfill His promise and complete prophethood with him. [he was sent
as a prophet while] a pledge had been taken from all the prophets
concerning him [that they would all have faith in him and give glad
tidings of his advent to their followers], his signs and characteristics
were well known, and he was of noble and blessed birth.

The people of the earth were, at that time, divided nations with differing creeds, dispersed ideas, and diverse ways, with some likening
Allah to His creation, some calling idols by His Name, and others
turning to [deities] other than Him. So Allah saved them from error
by means of him [i.e. Prophet Muḥammad] and delivered them from
ignorance by the blessing of his standing [with Him].

And then Allah _ glory be to Him_ chose for Muḥammad _ may Allah
bless him and his progeny_ the meeting with Him, and He preferred
for him what was with Him, so He ennobled him [by taking him away]
from the abode of this world for He disliked for him [to remain in] this
place of tribulations.

Thus, He took him away honorably- may Allah bless him and his *progeny- and he [the Prophet (ṣ)] left among you what the [other] prophets had left among their nations, for they would not leave them stranded without a clear path and a standing standard."*

Commentary [Part Thirteen]

The Advent of Islam

In this part of his sermon, Imam Amīr al-Mu'minīn ('a) focuses on the following four points:

1. The sending of the Prophet of Islam (ṣ) to mankind and the advent of Islam, some of the Prophet's sublime character qualities and virtues, and some of the signs of his prophethood;

2. The conditions of the people of the world at that time, the deviant beliefs and convictions that they held at that time, and how they were saved from those terrible conditions and dark times by the advent of Prophet Muḥammad (ṣ);

3. The demise of the Prophet of Islam (ṣ);

4. The most important legacy of the Prophet (ṣ), i.e. the Quran.

Imam Ali ('a) begins this section of his sermon with the following remarks:

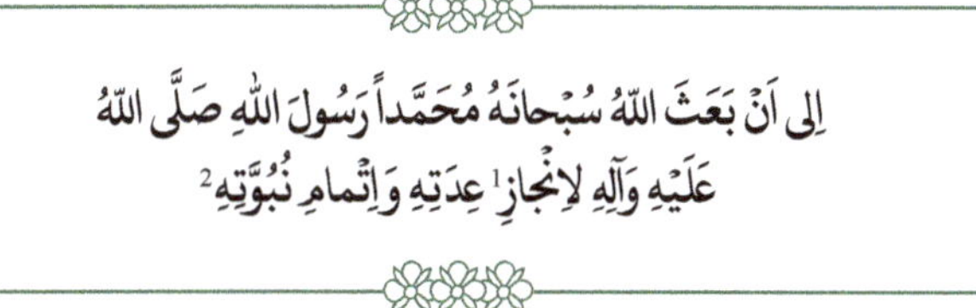

$$\text{اِلى اَنْ بَعَثَ اللّٰهُ سُبْحانَهُ مُحَمَّداً رَسُولَ اللّٰهِ صَلَّى اللّٰهُ عَلَيْهِ وَآلِهِ لاِنْجازِ عِدَتِهِ وَاِتْمامِ نُبُوَّتِهِ}^2$$

"[And so it was] until Allah _ glory be to Him_ sent Muḥammad _ may Allah bless him and his progeny_ as His Messenger to fulfill His promise and complete prophethood with him."

The Imam ('a) then continues and mentions some of the God-given privileges of the Prophet of Islam (ṣ) as follows:

---

1. The Arabic word "اِنْجاز", from the root word "نجز" [pronounced "Najaz"], means "to end" or "to fulfill".

2. The pronoun in the word "نبوته" refers to the Prophet of Islam (ṣ) but the pronoun in "عدته" can be interpreted in two ways: it can be taken to refer to Allah or to the Prophet of Islam (ṣ). However, it is more accurate to take it to refer to Allah because the sending of the Prophet of Islam (ṣ) was a promise made by Allah and announced to all of the past prophets including Prophet Abraham ('a). Another view with regard to these two pronouns is that both of them refer to Allah.

مَأْخُوذاً عَلَى النَّبِيِّينَ مِيثَاقُهُ

"[Muḥammad was sent as a prophet while] a pledge had been taken from all the prophets concerning him [that they would all have faith in him and give glad tidings of his advent to their followers] ..."

مَشْهُورَةً سِمَاتُهُ[1]، كَرِيماً مِيلَادُهُ

"... his signs and characteristics were well known, and he was of noble and blessed birth."

The last phrase of this sentence might be in reference either to the noble ancestry of the Prophet of Islam (ṣ) or the fact that his birth entailed lots of blessings for the entire world. Based on historical accounts, upon the birth of Prophet Muḥammad (ṣ), all of the idols placed within the Ka'bah in Mecca collapsed, the thousand-year-old fire in the fire temples of Iran died out, the Sāveh Lake which was worshipped by some people dried out overnight, and a part of the palace of Iranian kings collapsed. All of these strange incidents heralded the advent of a new era of fighting polytheism and establishing the monotheistic faith.

Imam Ali ('a) then adds:

وَأَهْلُ الْأَرْضِ يَوْمَئِذٍ مِلَلٌ مُتَفَرِّقَةٌ وَأَهْوَاءٌ مُنْتَشِرَةٌ وَطَرَائِقُ مُتَشَتِّتَةٌ

"The people of the earth were, at that time, divided nations with differing creeds, dispersed ideas, and diverse ways ..."

1. The Arabic term "سماته", which is the plural of the word "سمة", means "signs" or "characteristics".

بَيْنَ مُشَبِّهٍ لِلّٰهِ بِخَلْقِهِ أَوْ مُلْحِدٍ فِي اسْمِهِ أَوْ مُشِيرٍ إِلَى غَيْرِهِ

"... with some likening Allah to His creation, some calling idols by His Name, and others turning to [deities] other than Him."

The term "ملحد", from the root word "لحد" [pronounced "Laḥd"], is used to refer to a hole that is on the side of something. Its other derivative, "الحاد", is used to refer to any undertaking that deviates the course of moderation and goes to extremes, and this is why this word is used to refer to polytheism, idolatry, or any other similar deviant creeds.
Moreover, what is meant by the phrase "مُلْحِدٍ فِي اسْمِهِ" in this part of the sermon is what was suggested above: some people would use the Name of Allah to address idols. For instance, the idol-worshippers of Mecca had named three of their idols "اللات" [pronounced "al-Lāt"], "العزى" [pronounced "al-'Uzzā"], and "منات" [pronounced "Manāt"] after the Divine Names "الله", "العزيز", and "المنان" respectively.
This phrase could also mean that the polytheists ascribed the attributes of the created beings to Allah and that they did not exactly refer to Allah the way He truly deserved. Nevertheless, both of these views are correct and can be both what is meant by this phrase.
The Imam ('a) then continues with his sermon, stating:

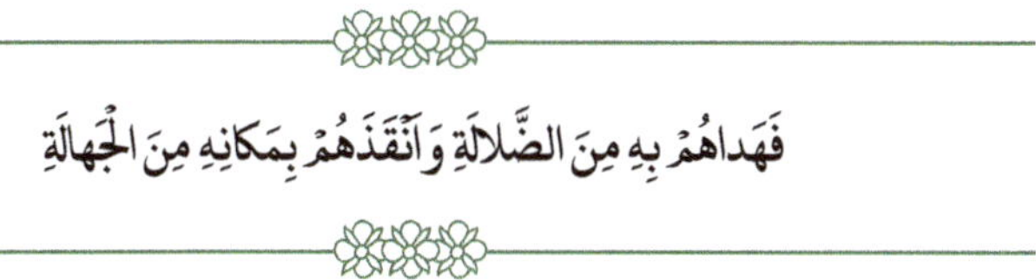

فَهَدَاهُمْ بِهِ مِنَ الضَّلَالَةِ وَأَنْقَذَهُمْ بِمَكَانِهِ مِنَ الْجَهَالَةِ

"So Allah saved them from error by means of him [i.e. Prophet Muḥammad] and delivered them from ignorance by the blessing of his standing [with Him]."

Then the Imam ('a) goes on:

ثُمَّ اخْتارَ سُبْحانَهُ لِمُحَمَّدٍ صَلَّى اللهُ عَلَيْهِ وَآلِهِ وَسَلَّمَ لِقاءَهُ، وَرَضِيَ لَهُ
ما عِنْدَهُ، وَأَكْرَمَهُ عَنْ دارِ الدُّنْيا وَرَغِبَ بِهِ عَنْ مَقامِ الْبَلْوى[1]

"And then Allah - glory be to Him- chose for Muḥammad - may Allah bless him and his progeny- the meeting with Him, and He preferred for him what was with Him, so He ennobled him [by taking him away] from the abode of this world for He disliked for him [to remain in] this place of tribulations."

فَقَبَضَهُ إِلَيْهِ كَرِيماً صَلَّى اللهُ عَلَيْهِ وَآلِهِ وَخَلَّفَ فِيكُمْ ما خَلَّفَتِ الْأَنْبِياءُ
فِي أُمَمِها إِذْ لَمْ يَتْرُكُوهُمْ هَمَلاً[2] بِغَيْرِ طَرِيقٍ واضِحٍ وَلا عَلَمٍ قائِمٍ

"And so, He took him away honorably_ may Allah bless him and his progeny_ and he left among you what the [other] prophets had left among their nations, for they would not leave them stranded without a clear path and a standing standard [to find their way]."

Obviously, these latter remarks by Imam Ali ('a) are in keeping with the famous hadith of Thaqalayn, according to which the Prophet of Islam (ṣ) has been quoted as saying: "I am departing you while leaving among you two weighty things: The Book of Allah and my Ahl-al-Bayt; if you adhere to them both, you shall never go astray, and these two shall never separate from each other until they come to me by the Ḥawḍ al-Kawthar [Pond of Abundance] ."[3]

1. The Arabic term "رغب", when used with the preposition "في", becomes a transitive verb and means to "like" or "adore" something. However, if it is used with the preposition "عن", it will mean "hate" or "dislike". Therefore, the meaning of this sentence is that Allah did not like the Prophet (ṣ) to tolerate the adversities and tribulations of this world any longer and so He took him away from this lower world to the spiritual higher world.

2. The Arabic word "هَمَل" [pronounced "Hamala"], from the root word "همل" [pronounced Haml], means to forsake someone or something unattended or to leave them stranded.

3. For more information regarding the chains of narrators of the Hahith of Thaqalayn as well as the

In the subsequent sections of his sermon, Imam Ali ('a) presents a comprehensive discussion of one of these two weighty things, namely the Quran, but he does not mention anything about the other weighty thing, the Prophet's Ahl-al-Bayt ('a) in this sermon. In spite of this, as it will be discussed later on, Imam Ali ('a) attends to the important issue of the Ahl-al-Bayt in some of the other sermons that he delivers. Finally, some believe that the phrase "علم قائم" in this part of the sermon is in reference to the "al- Awṣiyā'" [the true successors] of the Prophet (ṣ), the Ahl-al-Bayt ('a).

In any case, these remarks indicate that the prophets cared for the fate of their people much more than a father is worried about the fate of his children after his death. Therefore, the Divinely-sent prophets not only cared a lot for their people during their lives, they also took measures to ensure the well-being and prosperity of their nations after their demise. This is why it is virtually impossible to assume that any of them passed away without having appointed a worthy successor with clear instructions to lead his people after him, so as to prevent the results of a lifetime of efforts for guiding those people from being destroyed after him.

discussion of its authenticity as a widely transmitted tradition [Mutawātir] by both the Sunni and Shi'a scholars, refer to the book Payām-e Quran, vol. 9, pp. 61-78.

Important Points

1. The Religions and Faiths That Existed before the Advent of the Prophet of Islam (ṣ)

In this section of his sermon, Imam Ali (‘a) has made some rather profound references to the various religions and creeds, both in the Arabian Peninsula and elsewhere, which existed during the pre-Islamic dark era and before the advent of the Prophet of Islam (ṣ).

According to historians and other experts, at the time of the advent of Islam, there were countless different deviant creeds in all corners of the world including the Arab community of the Arabian Peninsula. For instance, Ibn Abī al-Ḥadīd, the famous commentator of the Nahj al-Balāghah has made the following remarks regarding the various creeds of the Arab people before the advent of Islam:

… they [meaning the Arabs] fell into two distinct categories: The Mu‘aṭṭilah and the non-Mu‘aṭṭilah. A faction of the Mu‘aṭṭilah people were atheists and did not believe in Allah at all. These were the people who were referred to in the Holy Quran as follows:

ما هِيَ إِلَّا حَيَاتُنَا الدُّنْيَا نَمُوتُ وَنَحْيَا وَمَا يُهْلِكُنَا إِلَّا الدَّهْرُ

“They say: “There is nothing beyond the life of this world; we live and we die, and nothing destroys us but time [i.e. the transient nature of this life].”[1]

Another faction of them believed in Allah but disbelieved in the Hereafter and Resurrection; these people would say:

1. Al-Jāthiyah, 24.

$$\text{مَنْ يُحْيِ الْعِظَامَ وَهِيَ رَمِيمٌ}$$

" "Who shall bring the bones back to life when they have decayed?"[1]

There was also a third group of them who believed in Allah and the Resurrection, but they rejected the idea of prophets being sent to mankind by Allah, and so they would engage in idol-worshipping.

The idolaters themselves also fell into different categories and were different factions and groups: some of them would consider their idols to be Allah's equals, and this was why they named their idols "شريك" [meaning "equals"]. During the Ḥajj pilgrimage, these people would chant the following phrase which reflected this polytheistic belief of theirs:

$$\text{لَبَّيْكَ اللّهُمَّ لَبَّيْكَ لَا شَرِيكَ لَكَ اِلَّا شَرِيكاً هُوَ لَكَ}$$

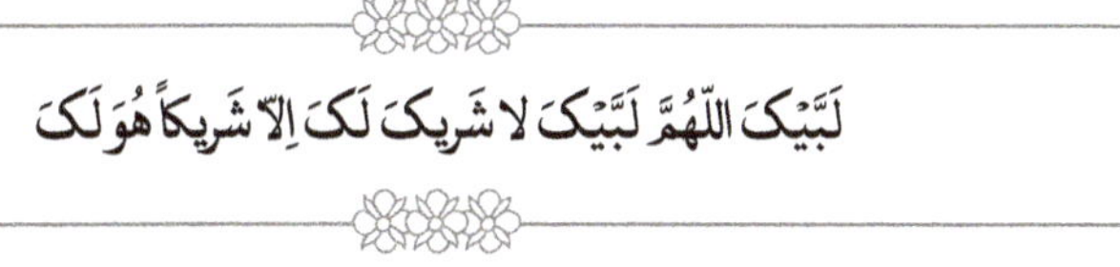

There was another faction of idolaters whose members believed that the idols could act as intercessors and that they could intercede with Allah on their behalf. According to The Quran, these people would say of their convictions:

$$\text{مَا نَعْبُدُهُمْ اِلَّا لِيُقَرِّبُونَا اِلَى اللّهِ زُلْفَى}$$

"We only worship them in order that they may bring us near to Allah."[2]

1. Yāsīn, 78.
2. Al-Zumar, 3.

There were others among these polytheists who believed in the corporeality of Allah; these people believed that Allah had a physical body with limbs, qualities, and attributes like those of human beings. Some of these people, like Umayyah ibn Abī al-Ṣalt would claim: "Allah is sitting on the throne stretching down his legs and resting them on the seat"!!

[Unfortunately, the remnants of these deviant beliefs lingered and lived on through the Islamic era in some backward and unlearned people. This went to the point where some of these people preached the belief that Allah will descend from the heavens one day in the form of a beautiful young man, wearing gold shoes, and a huge butterfly will be circling around his face!! There were plenty of these ridiculous beliefs and baseless ideas at that time]."[1]

He then continues: "The other group of people among the Arab people were the non-Mu'aṭṭilah; these were a small minority in the Arab community who truly believed in Allah and were pious and righteous monotheists. Among these people were 'Abd al-Muṭṭalib, his sons; 'Abdullāh and Abū Ṭālib, Quss ibn Sā'idah, and a few others."[2]

Some of the commentators of the Nahj al-Balāghah have categorized the pre-Islamic Arab scholars into the following categories:

- The people who only specialized in genealogy;
- The individuals who interpreted dreams;
- The scholars of Anwā' [a kind of astrological school of thought which was mostly based on superstitions];
- The pagan priests who supposedly had the power of foresight and predicted the future or knew secret things.

Outside the Arabian Peninsula, there were also various creeds and faiths which had their own followers. In India, for instance, there were the Brahmans who believed only in the authority of the human intellect and rejected all other religions as baseless. There were also others who worshipped stars, the sun, the moon, or other sorts of idols and false gods.

In addition to all of these, there were the Jewish, Christians, and Zoroastrians whose faiths were originally monotheistic but became dis-

1. Sharḥ Nahj al-Balāghah Ibn Abī al-Ḥadīd, vol. 3, p. 227.

2. Ibid, vol. 1, p. 117 on.

torted and perverted as time went by. For instance, the Zoroastrian faith had been altered to the point where its priests would promote the worship of a dual god at that time, believing in the god of goodness and god of evil.

This creed, which might have been a monotheistic creed in the beginning and brought by some Divinely-sent prophets, had been mixed with superstitions and baseless thoughts to the extent that, according to some experts, its adherents came to believe in the following ridiculous story:

The god of goodness and the god of evil had a fierce battle with each other and they kept fighting until some angels reconciled them. In the end, they agreed that the lower world would be ruled by the god of evil for seven thousand years [and the higher world by the god of goodness for the same span of time]!![1]

At the same time, the Christians had fallen into the polytheistic belief of the Trinity just as the Jews were following a scripture which had long been distorted with rather strange ideas.

In this section of his sermon, Imam Ali ('a) rather succinctly discusses all of these deviant groups and their beliefs, categorizing them into three general factions:

- The people who likened Allah to His created beings and associated partners with Him; examples of these are the Zoroastrians and Christians. Another group within this faction would ascribe the attributes of the created beings to Allah; an example of these is the majority of the Jews.
- The second were the people who used Allah's name for other than Him. These included many of the idol-worshippers who used Allah's names for their idols, believing that they were intermediaries between them and Allah.
- The third group consisted of people who referred to other than Allah as their god. These included the followers of the Dahrīyah School, who believed that the nature was the creator of the world. Other people who fell into this category were the people who worshiped idols, stars, the moon, or any other celestial body, as they considered their idols or certain celestial bodies to be gods.

1. Sharḥ Nahj al-Balāghah Ibn Meytham, vol. 1, pp. 205-206.

It was under such conditions that the Prophet of Islam (ṣ) was sent as a prophet to let the light of the Quran shine on humanity. It was through the sacred teachings brought by the Prophet (ṣ) for all human beings that the loftiest monotheistic notions and the most accurate teachings regarding the Creator of the world, Allah, and His Divine Attributes were revealed to humanity.

In addition, the achievements of the past prophets which had been terribly tarnished by superstitions and polytheistic notions were once again presented by the Prophet of Islam (ṣ) to the entire world in their pure and unaltered form. He brought for mankind the laws which supported the oppressed and the less fortunate, and which meant to establish justice and order all throughout the world.

What the Prophet of Islam (ṣ) did for mankind delivered them from what the Holy Quran has described as "manifest error". He then continued his efforts to give them proper moral training and teach them to engage in self-discipline and self-purification through teaching them the Quran and other Islamic teachings:

هُوَالَّذِى بَعَـثَ فِى الأُمِّيِّينَ رَسُولاً مِنْهُمْ يَتْلُوا عَلَيْهِمْ آيَاتِهِ وَيُزَكِّيهِمْ وَ يُعَلِّمُهُمُ الْكِتَابَ وَالْحِكْمَةَ وَإِنْ كَانُوا مِنْ قَبْلُ لَفِى ضَلالٍ مُّبِينٍ

"It is He who has sent to the unlettered people a prophet from among themselves to recite His Āyāt to them and to edify and purify them and instruct them in the Book and wisdom, though they had been before that in manifest error."[1]

It was by the advent of this great Prophet that the tarnished and distorted face of Allah's religion was cleansed and purified once more and a new chapter of human history began. This is a reality which has been acknowledged and confirmed even by non-Muslims.

For instance, George Bernard Shaw, the famous Irish scholar and author, has written the following in this regard:

---

1. Al-Jumu'ah, 2.

I have always held the religion of Muḥammad in high estimation because of its wonderful vitality. It is the only religion which appears to me to possess that assimilating capability to the changing phase of existence which can make itself appeal to every age … [Muḥammad] must be called the Saviour of Humanity. I believe that if a man like him were to assume the leadership of the modern world he would succeed in solving its problems in a way that would bring it the much-needed peace and happiness. Muḥammad was the most perfect human being among the past and the present-day people and no likes of him can be imagined to come into being in the future.[1]

2. Farsightedness of the Prophets

It can be clearly understood from Imam Ali's above-mentioned remarks that the Divinely-sent prophets not only cared about their nations and their fate during their lifetimes but they worried about what would happen to the future generations of their nations as well. This was why they would not only plan for the guidance of their people during their own lifetime, but they also had rather long term plans to ensure the guidance of their people in the future as well. This was why they did all they could to make their teachings and the line of the prophets live within their society.

Undoubtedly, the Prophet of Islam (ṣ) was no exception in this regard and, like all other prophets, he took measures to ensure that the line of guidance would live on after him. But since some people believe that the Prophet of Islam (ṣ) did not appoint a successor for himself to lead his people after his demise, let us put the following question to anyone who believes that:

Is it possible that, despite what all the Divinely-sent prophets had done [and on Allah's orders], the great Prophet of Islam (ṣ) would leave his people stranded and wandering in confusion after his demise?!! Is it even possible to assume that he passed away, forsaking his people without a learned and competent guardian to guide them and a clear path to follow?!!

Without a doubt, this is not what the Prophet (ṣ) actually did, and the Hadith of Thaqalayn, which is an authentic widely-transmitted Hadith

1. Fī Ẓilāl-i Nahj al-Balāghah, vol. 1, p. 63.

related both in the Sunni and Shi'a references, is a living proof of that. According to this tradition, the Prophet (ṣ) has been quoted as making the following enlightening remarks before his demise: "I am leaving among you two weighty things: The Book of Allah and my Ahl-al-Bayt ..." Is this not a clear and undeniable proof of the Prophet's foresight and his plan to ensure that his people would be well-guided after him?!

Part Fourteen
Sermon No.1

كِتابَ رَبِّكُمْ فيكُمْ: مُبَيِّناً حَلالَهُ وَحَرامَهُ و فَرائِضَهُ وَفَضائِلَهُ وَناسِخَهُ وَمَنْسُوخَهُ وَرُخَصَهُ
وَعَزائِمَهُ وَخاصَّهُ وَعامَّهُ وَعِبَرَهُ وَأَمْثالَهُ وَمُرْسَلَهُ وَمَحْدُودَهُ وَمُحْكَمَهُ وَمُتَشابِهَهُ، مُفَسِّراً
مُجْمَلَهُ وَمُبَيِّناً غَوامِضَهُ، بَيْنَ مَأْخُوذٍ ميثاقُ عِلْمِهِ وَمُوَسَّعٍ عَلَى الْعِبادِ فِي جَهْلِهِ وَبَيْنَ
مُثْبَتٍ فِي الْكِتابِ فَرْضُهُ وَمَعْلُومٍ فِي السُّنَّةِ نَسْخُهُ وَواجِبٍ فِي السُّنَّةِ أَخْذُهُ وَمُرَخَّصٍ
فِي الْكِتابِ تَرْكُهُ وَبَيْنَ واجِبٍ بِوَقْتِهِ وَزائِلٍ فِي مُسْتَقْبَلِهِ وَمُبايَنٌ بَيْنَ مَحارِمِهِ مِنْ كَبيرٍ
أَوْعَدَ عَلَيْهِ نيرانَهُ أَوْ صَغيرٍ أَرْصَدَ لَهُ غُفْرانَهُ وَبَيْنَ مَقْبُولٍ فِي أَدْناهُ وَمُوَسَّعٍ فِي أَقْصاهُ

"Left among you is the Book of your Lord which sets forth what He has sanctioned as lawful and unlawful, [what He has ordained as] obligatory and recommendable, its abrogating [laws] and abrogated [ones], its [laws of what is] permissible and impermissible, its exclusive and inclusive laws, its edifications and parables, its absolute and conditional rules, and its unequivocal and allegorical verses.
He [the Prophet (ṣ)] detailed its compendious verses and expounded on its inscrutable ones. In it, there are [important] parts regarding the knowledge thereof pledge had been taken [from all people] and parts the lack of knowledge thereof has been made permissible for the servants [of Allah, such as the Disjoined Letters in the Quran which are mysterious teachings not intended for all the believers].
There were also rules which had been established in the Book [of Allah] as obligatory to follow [for a limited time] but were signified as abrogated in the Tradition [of the Prophet (ṣ)], and things which had been made obligatory to follow in the Tradition [of the Prophet (ṣ)] but were later permitted by the Book [of Allah] to abandon.
And there are also things [in it] which had been obligatory at their due time but were not so afterward, and it has made clear-cut distinctions between its prohibitions_from [prohibitions regarding] mortal sins for which Allah has promised His hell [as punishment] to the

lesser sins for which He has appropriated His pardon.

[Finally] there are laws [therein] regarding acts of which even a small portion will be accepted [by Allah] though people are free to perform greater portions of them. [This was the comprehensive Scripture Allah sent down to His prophet and this was the Book that he left among his people as his legacy]."

Commentary [Part Fourteen]

The Characteristics of the Quran

Imam Ali ('a) repeatedly spoke of the significance and importance of the Quran in many of his speeches and sermons, many of which can be found in the Nahj al-Balāghah, each time focusing on a different aspect of this Holy Scripture.

In this sermon, the Imam ('a) discussed the comprehensive nature of the Quran, and he did that with a specific purpose. Imam Ali's purpose here was to emphasize that although the Prophet of Allah ('a) had passed away, he had left among his people a comprehensive Book which could perfectly guide them in their material, spiritual, personal, and social lives. This is because this Book contains all the instructions, laws, regulations, and teachings that human beings need in order to find the way toward the prosperous spiritual and material life on both personal and social levels.

Imam Amīr al-Mu'minīn ('a) begins this section of his speech, stating:

كِتابَ رَبِّكُمْ فيكُمْ

"Left among you is the Book of your Lord..."

The Imam ('a) then continues and lists fourteen important points regarding the comprehensive scope and all-encompassing nature of the Quran:

مُبَيِّناً حَلالَهُ وَحَرامَهُ وفَرائِضَهُ وَفَضائِلَهُ

"... which sets forth what He has sanctioned as lawful and unlawful, [what He has ordained as] obligatory and recommendable..."

This sentence is a reference made to the five basic laws of Islam, i.e. things that are considered obligatory duties of every Muslim, things which are enjoined on them as recommendable acts, things which have been made prohibited to them, things which have been made lawful for them, and things which were declared as abominable.

وَناسِخَهُ وَمَنْسُوخَهُ

"... its abrogating [laws] and abrogated [ones]..."

What is meant here by "the abrogating and the abrogated" are the verses in which new laws or rules were revealed which abrogated some older laws. This was what occurred only during the time of the Prophet of Allah (ṣ) when Divine Revelations were still being sent down to mankind, but after the Prophet's demise no such thing can occur ever again.

The reason behind this was that even though some of the laws sent down seemed to be final and unchanging, they were, in fact, for some transitional stage during the early years of Islam, and after that stage was over those laws were also abrogated and replaced by new ones which were called "the abrogating" laws.

An example of such laws was the one which required the Muslims to pay some money for charity before meeting the Prophet (ṣ) to have private talks with him:

يَا أَيُّهَا الَّذِينَ آمَنُوا إِذَا نَاجَيْتُمُ الرَّسُولَ فَقَدِّمُوا بَيْنَ يَدَيْ نَجْوَاكُمْ صَدَقَةً

"O' you who believe! When you seek to whisper [something] to the Prophet, pay something for charity [in the Way of Allah]."[1]

This was merely a test for the Muslim people at that time and no one passed the test except one man, Imam Ali ('a), as no one except him actually acted based on it. So, a short while after that, the abrogating law was revealed in the following verse of the Quran:

أَأَشْفَقْتُمْ أَنْ تُقَدِّمُوا بَيْنَ يَدَيْ نَجْوَاكُمْ صَدَقَاتٍ فَإِذْ لَمْ تَفْعَلُوا وَتَابَ اللَّهُ عَلَيْكُمْ
فَأَقِيمُوا الصَّلَاةَ وَآتُوا الزَّكَاةَ وَأَطِيعُوا اللَّهَ وَرَسُولَهُ وَاللَّهُ خَبِيرٌ بِمَا تَعْمَلُونَ

"Did you fear to pay something for charity before your whispering [lest you should become poor]?! Now, seeing that you did not do it and Allah has accepted your repentance, uphold Ṣalāt and pay Zakāt and obey Allah and His Prophet, and [know that] Allah is ever Aware of what you do."[2]

وَرُخَصَهُ وَعَزَائِمَهُ

"... its [laws of what is] permissible and impermissible ..."

This sentence might be a reference made to one of the principles of

1. Al-Mujādalah, 12.
2. Al-Mujādalah, 13.

Islamic jurisprudence [Fiqh] according to which when a law which prohibits something or makes it obligatory is abolished, sometimes it is replaced by a law which declares it generally permissible, such as the law explained in the following verse of the Quran:

"But when you exit the state of Ihram, then hunting for game will be permissible for you."[1]

Clearly, "hunting for game" does not become "obligatory" after exiting the state of Ihram; it only becomes permissible after that.
And sometimes a prior prohibition or obligation is abolished only to be replaced by its opposite law; an example in this regard is the following verse of the Quran:

"And when you travel in the land, there is no sin upon you that you shorten the prayer if you fear sedition [and threat] on the part of the disbelievers, for the disbelievers are to you a manifest enemy."[2]

In this case, it is clear that shortening the prayer during travel is an obligatory ruling and not merely permissible or a choice.
Technically speaking, the first of the above-mentioned laws is called "permission" as either doing or not doing the act in question is permitted. The second law, however, is called "departure" as one must necessarily depart from the previous law and act upon the second.

1. Al-Mā'idah, 2.
2. Al-Nisā', 101.

Another possibility that has been put forward regarding these two words is that what is meant by "رخصت" is the laws which prohibit something or declare something as obligatory, but which have been subject to exceptions under certain conditions. An example of such laws can be found in the following verse of the Quran:

$$\text{فَمَنِ اضْطُرَّ غَيْرَ بَاغٍ وَلَا عَادٍ فَلَا إِثْمَ عَلَيْهِ}$$

"But whoever is constrained, without being disobedient or a transgressor, there will be no sin upon them,"[1]

On the other hand, the term "عزائم" refers to laws which have no exception; an example of such laws is found in the following verse:

$$\text{وَاعْبُدُوا اللّٰهَ وَلَا تُشْرِكُوا بِهِ شَيْئاً}$$

"And worship Allah and do not associate any partners with Him;"[2]

$$\text{وَخَاصَّهُ وَعَامَّهُ}$$

"... its exclusive and inclusive laws..."

The "exclusive" laws of the Quran do not include all of the Muslims; an example of such laws is the laws of the Ḥajj pilgrimage which apply only to individuals who can afford it and are able to go on the pilgrimage:

---

1. Al-Baqarah, 173.
2. Al-Nisā', 36.

وَلِلَّهِ عَلَى النَّاسِ حِجُّ الْبَيْتِ مَنِ اسْتَطَاعَ إِلَيْهِ سَبِيلًا

"... and [an obligatory] duty owed to Allah by the people is that they make pilgrimage to [His] House, those who can afford to make it."[1]

An inclusive law, on the other hand, is the one that applies to all Muslims without exception, and example of which is the following verse of the Quran:

وَأَقِيمُوا الصَّلَاةَ

"And uphold Ṣalāt..."[2]

Another possibility regarding the word "خاص" in this part of the Imam's sermon is the verses which seem to be general in scope at first glance but actually refer to specific individuals; an example of such laws can be found in the verse of Wilāyah:

إِنَّمَا وَلِيُّكُمُ اللَّهُ وَرَسُولُهُ وَالَّذِينَ آمَنُوا الَّذِينَ يُقِيمُونَ الصَّلَاةَ وَيُؤْتُونَ الزَّكَاةَ وَهُمْ رَاكِعُونَ

"Your Guardian and Protector is none other than Allah, His Prophet, and the believers who uphold Ṣalāt and pay Zakāt while bowing down (in Ṣalāt)."[3]

1. Āl-i-'Imrān, 97.
2. Al-Baqarah, 43.
3. Al-Mā'idah, 55.

It is a known fact that this verse referred to Allah, His Prophet, and only one of the believers, namely, Imam Ali ('a).
On the other hand, inclusive verses of the Quran are the ones that apply generally to all of the mentioned referents without exception; an example of these verses is the following:

"The thief, man or woman, cut off [four fingers of] their hands as a recompense for what they have committed!"[1]

"... its edifications and parables ..."

The Arabic word "عبر" derives from the root words "عبرة" and "عبور" [meaning "to pass"], and this is why when one has passed a certain incident, one takes a lesson from it for later similar experiences.
The Holy Quran is full of edifying lessons which are based on the history of the past prophets and nations and what they did and what happened to them. All of these edifying stories have been put forward in the Quran so that people would learn the lessons in them for their own lives at any point in time.
Moreover, the term "امثال" can be in reference to the parables which have been presented in the Quran in large numbers. An example of these parables is the following:

1. Al-Mā'idah, 38.

أَلَمْ تَرَ كَيْفَ ضَرَبَ اللَّهُ مَثَلًا كَلِمَةً طَيِّبَةً كَشَجَرَةٍ طَيِّبَةٍ

"Have you not regarded how Allah has set forth a parable, likening a good [and pure] word to a good tree ..."[1]

Or it can be references made to specific individuals whose life stories have been presented as examples or parables in the Quran. An example of such cases is the following verse:

وَضَرَبَ اللَّهُ مَثَلًا لِلَّذِينَ آمَنُوا امْرَأَتَ فِرْعَوْنَ إِذْ قَالَتْ رَبِّ ابْنِ لِي عِنْدَكَ
بَيْتًا فِي الْجَنَّةِ وَنَجِّنِي مِنْ فِرْعَوْنَ وَعَمَلِهِ وَنَجِّنِي مِنَ الْقَوْمِ الظَّالِمِينَ

"And Allah sets forth an example for the believers: the wife of Pharaoh, when she said: "O' Lord! Build me a house near You in Paradise and save me from Pharaoh and what he does and save me from the wrongdoing people!""[2]

وَمُرْسَلَهُ وَمَحْدُودَهُ

"... its absolute and conditional rules..."

The absolute laws are the ones which have been laid down in the Quran without any conditions, like the following:

1. Ibrāhīm, 24.

2. Al-Taḥrīm, 11.

"... Allah has permitted trade..."[1]

Conditional laws are the ones which are mentioned together with certain conditions under which they will begin to apply. An example of these laws is the following:

"Do not eat up one another's property inadmissibly [and unlawfully] amongst yourselves, except when business is conducted by mutual consent."[2]

Needless to say, when there are two laws regarding the same issue with one of them being absolute in exposition and the other containing certain conditions, we must conclude that the law in question applies under the conditions set out. For instance, take the example of the rules presented above; according to these two rules and the condition that has been laid down in the second one, trade or business is legitimate and permissible only when it is conducted by both parties' consent.

"... and its unequivocal and allegorical verses."

1. Al-Baqarah, 275.
2. Al-Nisā' 29.

The unequivocal verses of the Quran are the ones whose contents and exposition are completely clear, leaving no doubt about what they intend to communicate. An example of these is the following verse:

قُلْ هُوَ اللّٰهُ اَحَد

"Say: "He is Allah, the One"."[1]

Allegorical verses of the Quran are the ones which seem, at the first glance, to be ambiguous though they too can be interpreted with the help of the contents of some other verses in the Quran. An example of such verses is the following:

اِلى رَبِّها ناظِرَة

"Looking at [the bounties of] their Lord."[2]

مُفَسِّراً مُجْمَلَهُ وَمُبَيِّناً غَوامِضَهُ

"He [the Prophet (ṣ)] detailed its compendious verses and expounded on its inscrutable ones."

The "compendious verses" of the Quran are the ones which explain some laws or rituals in a very general way without giving any de-

1. Al-Ikhlāṣ, 1.

2. Al-Qiyāmah, 23.

tails regarding them. An example of such verses are the ones which have enjoined performing prayers on Muslims; these verses contain the general law but they have not presented any details of how the prayers are to be performed, or how many Rak'ahs of them are to be performed. As regards these verses, it was the job of the Prophet (ṣ) to present the necessary details pertaining to them.

The "inscrutable" verses of the Quran are the ones that cannot be understood at all without the explanations of the Prophet (ṣ) or the other Infallibles. An example of these is "Al-ḥurūf al-muqaṭṭa'ah" [disjoined letters] which exist in the beginning of a number of Surahs in the Quran and which have been explained and demystified in the Islamic Hadiths.

The difference between "allegorical" and "inscrutable" parts of the Quran is that the allegorical parts have an apparent meaning that even at the first glance can be understood by most people. Conversely, the inscrutable ones are the ones that are virtually incomprehensible to most people at the first glance.

بَيْنَ مَأْخُوذٍ مِيثَاقُ عِلْمِهِ وَمُوَسَّعٍ عَلَى الْعِبَادِ فِي جَهْلِهِ

"... In it there are [important] parts regarding the knowledge thereof pledge had been taken [from all people] and parts the lack of knowledge thereof has been made permissible for the servants [of Allah, such as the Disjoined Letters in the Quran which are mysterious teachings not intended for all the believers]."

Examples of the first kind of teachings of the Quran include the ones which are about Tawḥīd [Oneness of Allah] and the Attributes of Allah; these are the teachings which all the believers are required to have knowledge of. Examples of the second part of the teachings of the Quran are the ones regarding the Essence of Allah, which cannot be known by anyone, and also the nature of the Resurrection and the afterlife which the believers need to generally believe in but are not required to have full knowledge of their details.

وَبَيْنَ مُثْبَتٍ فِي الْكِتَابِ فَرْضُهُ وَمَعْلُومٍ فِي السُّنَّةِ نَسْخُهُ

"There were also rules which had been established in the Book [of Allah] as obligatory to follow [for a limited time] but were signified as abrogated in the Tradition [of the Prophet (ṣ)],"

An example of such rules is the penal code regarding the punishment of adultery; the Quran indicates that the punishment for an adulterer or an adulteress is life imprisonment [al-Nisā', 15], while, according to the Islamic tradition, this rule was later abrogated and replaced with stoning by the Prophet (ṣ).

وَوَاجِبٍ فِي السُّنَّةِ أَخْذُهُ وَمُرَخَّصٍ فِي الْكِتَابِ تَرْكُهُ

"... and things which had been made obligatory to follow in the Tradition [of the Prophet (ṣ)] but which were later permitted by the Book [of Allah] to abandon."

This sentence refers to the parts of the Prophetic Tradition which were later abrogated by certain verses of the Quran. An example of these laws was the law of fasting during the early years of Islam. At that time, Muslims were allowed to break their fast only at the beginning of the night, so if someone overslept and then woke up after that time, it was impermissible for them to do anything that would invalidate their fasting.

However, later on, this rule was abrogated by the following verse of the Quran:

وَكُلُوا وَاشْرَبُوا حَتَّى يَتَبَيَّنَ لَكُمُ الْخَيْطُ الْأَبْيَضُ مِنَ الْخَيْطِ الْأَسْوَدِ مِنَ الْفَجْرِ

"And eat and drink, until the white thread of the dawn becomes discernible from the dark thread [of the night] to you."[1]

وَبَيْنَ واجِبٍ بِوَقْتِهِ وَزائِلٍ في مُسْتَقْبَلِه

"And there are also things [in it] which had been obligatory at their due time but were not so afterward,"

These remarks by the Imam ('a) are in relation to certain laws which make certain things obligatory for a period of time but then stop to apply after that. Timed obligatory duties like the obligatory fasting during the month of Ramadan are examples of these duties. The laws regarding these duties stop to apply once the specific time for that duty is up [for instance when the month of Ramadan finishes, the law of obligatory fasting no longer applies].

Unlike these temporary duties, there are other religious duties which are permanent, meaning that they always and at all times need to be carried out. These include enjoining what is good and forbidding what is bad in the society and promoting justice and whatever is considered good. These duties are absolutely obligatory to carry out at all times.[2]

Some experts are of the opinion that this sentence concerns obligatory acts such as the Ḥajj pilgrimage, which becomes obligatory for one to perform only once during one's life time. Some other scholars believe that it is in reference to the issue of Hijrah [emigration in the way of

1. Al-Baqarah, 187.

2. This sentence needs another phrase to complete it because the second sort of laws, i.e. those concerning acts which are always obligatory to perform, has not been mentioned here. The completing sentence would have been the following: "وَ بَيْنَ ما يَكُونُ واجِباً دائماً".

Allah]. According to historical accounts, since Muslims were under tremendous pressure from the polytheists in Mecca during the first years
of Islam, it had been made obligatory upon them to immigrate to other
regions. However, after the Conquest of Mecca, this law was annulled.
Nevertheless, this law still applies to the places which are like Mecca
during the early years of Islam, meaning that when Muslims are under
pressure in a certain place, they are required to immigrate to other regions to save themselves.

وَمُبَايَنٌ بَيْنَ مَحارِمِهِ مِنْ كَبِيرٍ اَوْعَدَ عَلَيْهِ نِيرَانَهُ اَوْ صَغِيرٍ اَرْصَدَ لَهُ غُفْرانَهُ

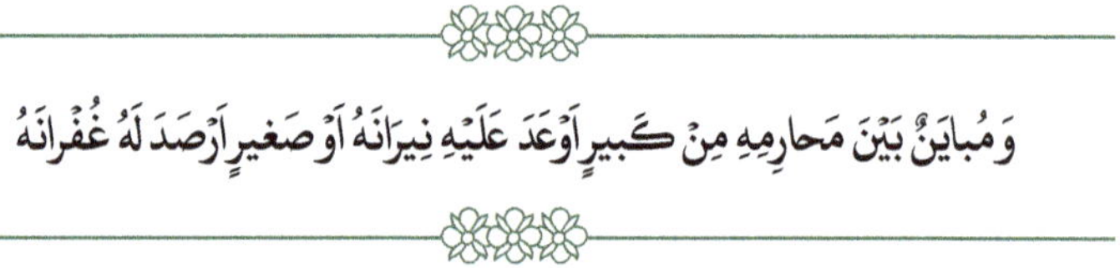

*"... and it has made clear-cut distinctions between its prohibitions,
from [prohibitions regarding] mortal sins for which Allah has promised His hell to the lesser sins for which He has appropriated His
pardon."*

This section of the Imam's remarks is with respect to certain cardinal
sins, including polytheism and murder, which have been explicitly
referred to in the Quran as sins which will be met with the most horrendous of punishments.[1]

Moreover, the Imam ('a) also mentioned lesser sins which are minor
misdeeds referred to in the verse 32 of surah al-Najm as "اللَّمم":

---

1. To learn more about the Islamic law regarding polytheism refer to the verse 72 of Surah al-
Mā'idah, which is as follows:
مَنْ يُشْرِكْ بِاللهِ فَقَدْ حَرَّمَ اللهُ عَلَيْهِ الْجَنَّةَ وَ مَأْوَاهُ النَّارُ [whoever associates partners with Allah, Allah will indeed
forbid him Paradise, and his refuge is the Hellfire.]
Also, to learn about the Islamic laws regarding murder, refer to the verse 93 of Surah al-Nisā',
which mentions:
وَمَنْ يَقْتُلْ مُؤْمِناً مُتَعَمِّداً فَجَزَاؤُهُ جَهَنَّمُ خَالِداً فِيها [for he who slays a believer intentionally, his recompense is
Hell, therein he shall remain forever].

الَّذِينَ يَجْتَنِبُونَ كَبَائِرَ الْإِثْمِ وَالْفَوَاحِشَ إِلَّا اللَّمَمَ

"Those who avoid the mortal sins and indecent acts, excepting lesser offenses [which they occasionally perpetrate]."

Some Quranic exegetes have interpreted the word "لمم" to mean having the intention of sinning without actually committing the sin, or committing rather minor sins.

وَبَيْنَ مَقْبُولٍ فِي أَدْنَاهُ، وَمُوَسَّعٍ فِي أَقْصَاهُ

"[Finally] there are laws [therein] regarding acts of which even a small portion will be accepted [by Allah] though people are free to perform greater portions of them. [This was how comprehensive Scripture Allah sent down to His prophet and this was the Book that he left among his people as his legacy]".

These remarks are in relation to the kinds of religious duties and acts which are required to be done in small amounts but people are free to do more than the required amount if they wish. As regards what these acts exactly are, some Quranic exegetes have maintained that one of the examples of these acts is the recitation of the Quran, as evidenced by the following verse of the Quran:

فَاقْرَءُوا مَا تَيَسَّرَ مِنَ الْقُرْآنِ

"So now recite the Quran as much as is feasible."[1]

So people are recommended to recite a little of the Quran whenever they can but if they can recite more of it, they are free to do so [and this is what the final verses of surah al-Muzzammil clearly suggest]. By contrast, there are laws regarding certain duties which must be done exactly as the Quran indicates. For instance, the obligatory fasting during the month of Ramadan must be performed by all Muslims who are of age and they must all fast every day of the month of Ramadan [according to verses 183-185 of Surah al-Baqarah].

1. Al-Muzzammil, 20.

Important Points

1. The Comprehensive Nature of the Quran

The most salient point discussed in this part of the sermon by Imam Ali ('a) is the comprehensiveness of the Quran or what is called the miraculous nature of the contents of the Quran.

Through these fourteen points which the Imam ('a) makes about the Quran, he discusses some of the subtleties of the laws and teachings which have been included in this Divinely-sent scripture. The Imam ('a) explains how the diversity of the teachings of the Quran could meet all of the needs of human beings, from their religious needs to their practical and moral issues to their religious obligatory duties and things which are prohibited for them to do.

The Imam ('a) then deals with the relation between the Quran and the tradition of the Prophet (ṣ), explaining the differences between permanent and temporary laws, exclusive and inclusive rules, absolute and conditional regulations, as well as abrogating and abrogated verses in the Quran.

A careful examination of these points clearly shows how carefully planned and calculated the contents of the Quran are, as they were arranged so that they would meet all the needs of mankind. As we have discussed in Tafsīr-e Nemūneh, amid our discussion of the verse 23 of Surah al-Baqarah, these calculated, profound, diverse, and comprehensive contents of the Quran constitute one of the aspects of the miraculous nature of the Glorious Quran.

In other words, how could an illiterate individual, who came from such a dark society of ignorance and nescience, possibly present to humanity such a weighty Book, which is of such comprehensive scope, without being inspired its contents from the Divine source of knowledge?! There is no doubt, whatsoever, that no human being could bring such a grand Scripture which is full of edifying lessons, instructive parables, deep moral teachings, and comprehensive laws without receiving revelations from the Source of creation.

Another interesting point regarding these succinct yet profound remarks is that the Imam ('a) presented a complete outline of the sci-

ence of Principles of Islamic Fiqh in them in a rather brief and summarized manner. Today, centuries after the Imam ('a) presented this amazing outline, the field of Principles of Islamic Fiqh has become a vast scientific field but its blueprints are still the ones outlined by Imam Ali ('a) all those centuries before, which are as follows:
Laws pertaining to the lawful and the unlawful, the abrogating and abrogated laws, the laws of permission and departure, exclusive and inclusive rules, absolute and conditional laws, unequivocal and allegorical laws, compendious and elaborate rules, temporary and permanent laws, and the laws of obligatory duties, extremely recommendable acts, and ordinary recommendable acts.
The Imam ('a) gives a brief outline of all of these important principles succinctly and draws the attentions to them so as to lay the foundation for a huge field of knowledge that would come into being in the future.

2. Who Possesses the Complete Knowledge of the Quran

It can be understood from Imam Ali's remark in this section of his sermon that the Prophet of Islam (ṣ) had the duty of interpreting some of the complicated and concise parts of the Quran to people so that nothing ambiguous would remain regarding them for anyone. This is, in fact, why the Holy Quran has ordered all the people the following:

"Take whatever the Prophet gives you [and obey him]."[1]

Some might ask the following questions at this point: why does the Quran need to be interpreted and, basically, why does it have intricacies and complicated parts requiring interpretation if it has been revealed for the use of the whole of mankind?

1. Al-Ḥashr, 7.

In order to understand the answer to these questions, the following points need to be taken into consideration:

The first point is that the Quran is, in effect, the constitution of the religion of Islam and, naturally, it could not contain all of the details of the laws and regulations of Islam elaborately. Therefore, it laid down the most important principles and left the explanation of their details to the Prophet (ṣ).

For instance, the Quran has explained that such religious rites as daily prayers, the Ḥajj pilgrimage, and fasting during the month of Ramadan are obligatory for all Muslims. However, each of these rites has their own specific regulations, instructions, and rulings which can fill several books, so they could not all have been included in the Quran. Similarly, the laws of trade and commerce, the issue of judgment and judicial system, the laws of giving testimony, the ordained punishments, and generally the penal code of Islam all have their own countless details which also need several volumes of books to contain. Obviously, then, it had been impossible to include all of these laws along with their every detail into a single scripture, namely the Quran.

The second point is that the fact that the people needed the Prophet (ṣ) to explain the details of these laws to them caused them to become closely related to and familiar with the tradition of the Prophet of Allah (ṣ), a connection which is rather helpful for them for a variety of reasons.

Simply put, the Quran is like the course book of Islam and the Prophet (ṣ) was like the teacher who taught its contents; though the course book contains all the lessons that the students need, there needs to be a teacher to help them understand the complex parts of this book. Therefore, the relation of the students with the teacher helps them to understand much of the complex and intricate parts of their course book.

The question that arises here is whether a Divinely-sent leader is still living among mankind on the earth now that the Prophet of Allah (ṣ) has passed away.

The answer is that there must always be such a teacher among mankind, otherwise problems will begin to overwhelm them. It is exactly due to this issue that we believe that an infallible Imam necessarily exists on the earth during every time period and that it is these infallible leaders who possess the complete knowledge of the Quran. These Infallibles are the ones who have been referred to as the "'Itrah" [the Ahl-al-Bayt ('a)] by the Prophet (ṣ) himself in the famous Hadith of Thaqalayn; based on this tradition, the Prophet (ṣ) explained to his people that the Infallible Imams would always live on the earth and that the bond between them and the Quran would remain unbreakable until the Resurrection Day:

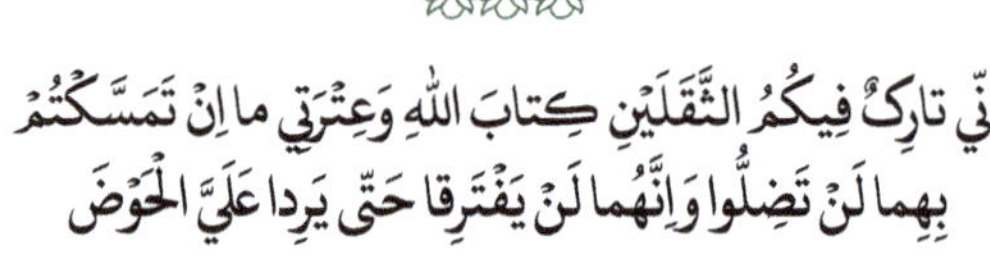

إنّي تارِكٌ فيكُمُ الثَّقَلَيْنِ كِتابَ اللهِ وَعِتْرَتي ما إنْ تَمَسَّكْتُمْ
بِهِما لَنْ تَضِلُّوا وَإنَّهُما لَنْ يَفْتَرِقا حَتّى يَرِدا عَلَيَّ الْحَوْضَ

"I am leaving among you two weighty things, the Book of Allah and my 'Itrah [the Ahl-al-Bayt]; so long as you adhere to them and follow them, you shall not be misguided, and these two will not be separated from one another until they come to me by the Ḥawḍ al-Kawthar [Pond of Abundance] on the Resurrection Day]."[1]

3. The Criteria for Recognizing Mortal Sins from Lesser Sins

There is a great deal of controversy among Muslim theologians over what sins are considered mortal and what sins are lesser misdeeds. Some believe that this dichotomy is a relative one and that sins will fall into each category when compared with one another in terms of their seriousness. That is to say, when different sins are compared with one another, the more serious offenses are counted as mortal sins and the less serious ones are regarded as lesser sins. [The late Shaykh al-Ṭabarsī has attributed this view, in his book al-Majma' al-Bayān[2], to Shi'a scholars; apparently what he meant was that this was the

1. This specific version of this famous Hadith is based on the different narratives regarding it which are found in the Shi'a and Sunni Hadith references. For more information regarding this hadith, refer to the books Iḥqāq al-Ḥaqq, vol. 9, pp. 309-375; Biḥār al-Anwār, vol. 23, p. 118, 132-134, and 155; and Payām-e Quran, vol. 9, pp. 61-78.

2. Al-Majma' al-Bayān, vol. 2, p. 555.

view of only some of the Shi'a scholars and not all of them because, as we will discuss below, many Shi'a scholars have another view regarding this issue].

There are other scholars who believe that mortal sins, just as their name suggests, are rather serious offenses which are considered to be grave misdeeds both by the religious law and the sound mind. These scholars have then cited sins such as murder, usurpation of other people's property and rights, dealing in usury and adultery as examples of mortal sins. They have also argued that it is due to the seriousness of these sins that the Islamic Hadiths indicate that they will be punished by the most severe of penalties in the Hereafter.

For instance, according to a famous Islamic Hadith, Imam al-Bāqir ('a), Imam al-Ṣādiq ('a) and Imam al-Riḍā ('a) have been quoted as saying the following in this regard:

اَلْكَبائِرُ الَّتِي أَوْجَبَ اللهُ عَزَّوَجَلَّ عَلَيْها النّارَ

"Mortal sins are the ones for which Allah has [explicitly] legislated the punishment of Hellfire."[1]

Therefore, the lesser sins are the ones which are not so serious as to be punished by such a severe punishment.

There are some other Islamic Hadiths which have listed seven, twenty, and seventy mortal sins, and this difference in number might be indicative of different subsets of major categories of mortal sins.

1. Nūr al-Thaqalayn, vol. 1, p. 473, hadith No. 207.

4. The Abrogating and Abrogated Laws and the Philosophy behind the Abrogation of Certain Laws

The concept of the "Abrogating and Abrogated" laws in the Quran is one of the most controversial issues within the field of Islamic theology. Some might be even surprised to realize that there are "abrogating" and "abrogated" verses in the Quran, wondering how it is possible for laws to be abrogated in a scripture. [It should be noted that this concept refers to the instance of a new law regarding a certain matter abrogating an older law about that same matter and replacing it; an example of such an abrogation is the law which was sent down in the Quran, requiring Muslims to perform their prayers in the direction of the Masjid al-Ḥarām and the Ka'bah, abrogating a prior law which required them to perform their prayers in the direction of Al-Aqṣā Mosque in Jerusalem al-Quds].

The existence of new laws to abolish older versions in human laws is completely normal and understandable; this is because human minds and intellects are constantly undergoing development and so they might create certain rules today and later find out some flaws in them and draft new and improved ones to replace them with. However, the question which is raised here is: How is it possible for Divinely-legislated laws to be abrogated?!

The answer to this question is easy; Allah's Knowledge is unlimited and it never undergoes development or change. However, things might change in this material world over time, so they need to be treated differently than before. For instance, a certain medicine might work on a certain illness today, but it might lose its effect over time, or even be detrimental for the patients suffering from that specific illness due to their different conditions. Therefore, a physician might prescribe a certain medicine today and might cancel his prescription a while later and forbid his patients from taking that specific medicine. This is very much the reason why some laws were abrogated and replaced by new ones in the Quran. For instance, performing prayers in the direction of Jerusalem al-Quds and Masjid al-Aqṣā might have been quite beneficial in the early years of Islam. This was particularly because the Ka'bah was full of idols at that time and it had turned into a means of ethnic hegemony and supremacy; therefore, if the Muslims had chosen to perform their prayers in its direction, it could have create several problems.

Consequently, they performed their prayers in the direction of Masjid al-Aqṣā for thirteen years so as to prevent Islam to be associated with idols and idol-worshipping centers of that day. However, after they emigrated to Medina, they were ordered by the new law to perform their prayers in the direction of the Ka'bah as they were no longer under pressure from the polytheists of Mecca; hence, performing prayer in the direction of that House of monotheism would entail plenty of good for them and no detriments.

There are, of course, several issues and discussions surrounding the concept of the abrogating and abrogated laws in the Quran which cannot all be contained here; however, what was discussed here was meant as a hint to shed some light on the philosophy behind the abrogation of certain laws in the Quran.[1]

5. Historical Stories and Beautiful Parables in the Quran

A large portion of the Quran has been dedicated to the discussion of the history of the past peoples, particularly the discussion of the efforts of the great Divinely-sent prophets in guiding their people to the right path. These stories are replete with edifying lessons and instructive points which are all valuable information for all human beings wherever and whenever they live, particularly because these lessons are all based on the real-life experiences of their fellow human beings. This is, in fact, why the Holy Quran has discussed these stories, relating some of them [particularly the stories of prophets such as Ibrāhīm, Noah, Moses, and Jesus] repeatedly in several different Surahs. However, it does not repeat the same story exactly in different Surahs but views the same historical incident or event from different perspectives. The Quran itself has mentioned the following regarding the stories of the past peoples that it relates:

1. For more information in this regard, refer to Tafsīr-e Nemūneh, vol. 1, p. 388, the commentary on the verse 106 of surah al-Baqarah.

لَقَدْ كَانَ فِي قَصَصِهِمْ عِبْرَةٌ لِّأُولِي الْأَلْبَابِ

"Indeed, there was in their stories an edifying lesson for the possessors of sound mind."[1]

Sometimes, the Quran even goes further than merely relating the history of the past nations and speaks of the ruins of their ancient civilizations and cities, encouraging the present-day people to go on and visit those ruins as living proofs of who those past people were and what their fates were:

قُلْ سِيرُوا فِي الْأَرْضِ فَانظُرُوا كَيْفَ كَانَ عَاقِبَةُ الَّذِينَ مِن قَبْلُ

"Say: "Travel on the earth; then behold how was the end of those who were before you.""[2]

In addition to these historical stories, the Quran has also employed several different parables and examples to guide mankind. For instance, it sometimes cites real-life examples or incidents which actually befell some individuals, and at other times, it employs parables containing similes from the natural world, whether from plants or animals. These parables and similitudes are so attractive and at the same time eloquent and deep that they are actually considered one of the miraculous aspects of the Quran.

The Quran itself suggests that contemplating these parables and reflecting deeply on them will awaken the minds to take the lessons intended in them:

1. Yūsuf, 111.

2. Rūm, 42.

وَلَقَدْ ضَرَبْنَا لِلنَّاسِ فِي هَٰذَا الْقُرْآنِ مِنْ كُلِّ مَثَلٍ لَعَلَّهُمْ يَتَذَكَّرُونَ

"And We have indeed set forth for mankind in this Quran from every parable [and every kind of teaching], so that they may take heed."[1]

Imam Ali ('a) also particularly focuses on this function of the Quran in this section of his speech so as to highlight the comprehensive nature of the Quran and draw the attention of all Muslims to it as an issue of prime importance.

1. Al-Zumar, 27.

Part Fifteen
Sermon No.1

وَفَرَضَ عَلَيْكُمْ حَجَّ بَيْتِهِ الْحَرَامِ الَّذِي جَعَلَهُ قِبْلَةً لِلْأَنَامِ يَرِدُونَهُ وُرُودَالْأَنْعَامِ وَيَأْلَهُونَ إِلَيْهِ وَلُوهَ الْحَمَامِ وَجَعَلَهُ سُبْحَانَهُ عَلَامَةً لِتَوَاضُعِهِمْ لِعَظَمَتِهِ وَإِذْعَانِهِمْ لِعِزَّتِهِ وَاخْتَارَمِنْ خَلْقِهِ سُمَّاعاً أَجَابُوا إِلَيْهِ دَعْوَتَهُ وَصَدَّقُوا كَلِمَتَهُ وَوَقَفُوا مَوَاقِفَ أَنْبِيَائِهِ وَتَشَبَّهُوا بِمَلَائِكَتِهِ الْمُطِيفِينَ بِعَرْشِهِ، يُحْرِزُونَ الْأَرْبَاحَ فِي مَتْجَرِ عِبَادَتِهِ وَيَتَبَادَرُونَ عِنْدَهُ مَوْعِدَ مَغْفِرَتِهِ جَعَلَهُ سُبْحَانَهُ وَ تَعَالى لِلْإِسْلَامِ عَلَماً وَلِلْعَائِذِينَ حَرَماً فَرَضَ حَقَّهُ وَأَوْجَبَ حَجَّهُ وَكَتَبَ عَلَيْكُمْ وِفادَتَهُ فَقالَ سُبْحَانَهُ: وِللهِ عَلَى النَّاسِ حِجُّ الْبَيْتِ مَنِ اسْتَطَاعَ إِلَيْهِ سَبِيلاً وَمَنْ كَفَرَفَإِنَّ اللهَ غَنِيٌّ عَنِ الْعَالَمِينَ

"Allah has made obligatory upon you the pilgrimage to His sacred House which He made a Qiblah [and a polestar] for people and which they enter as thirsty cattle [enter their drinking place] and take refuge in like enthralled doves.

And Allah - glory be to Him- made it a token of their humility before His Greatness and their submission to His Might. And He chose from among His servants some who would keep an ear out for His call to answer Him, to believe in His Words, to stay at the place of the Divinely-sent prophets, and to become like the angels who circumambulate His Throne.

"[And in so doing] they reap much profit in the marketplace of worship of Allah, and rush toward Him for His promised forgiveness. And Allah - the Glorified, the Most High- made it an emblem [and a symbol] for Islam and a sanctuary for the refugees. He made what is due for it incumbent [upon all], the pilgrimage to it obligatory [for all], and prescribed visiting it for you all, and He_ glory be to Him_ said:

"and [an obligatory] duty owed to Allah by the people is that they make pilgrimage to [His] House, those who can afford to make it"

Commentary [Part Fifteen]

The Last Part of the Sermon: Focusing on the Immense Significance of the Ḥajj Pilgrimage

Following a discussion of the great significance of the Quran, Imam Ali (ʻa) focuses on the Ḥajj pilgrimage in the last section of his sermon, emphasizing its importance within the framework of Islamic rites and rituals. It is not clear whether the Imam (ʻa) spoke of any other religious laws or rituals after his discussion of the significance of the Quran because, as it was discussed earlier, al-Sayyid al-Raḍī did not mean to collect all parts of the Imam's sermons in the Nahj al-Balāghah; he only included a collection of Imam Ali's words, particularly the most eloquent ones.

Nevertheless, the fact that the Imam (ʻa) focused specifically on the Ḥajj pilgrimage, following his discussion of the creation of the cosmos and the various stages of the creation of man and the advent of the Prophet of Islam (ṣ), shows that the Ḥajj is of unparalleled importance in Islam. This is probably because the Ḥajj pilgrimage is, in a way, a display of the essence and the gist of of Islam and a manifestation of the religion's personal, social, ethical, political, and instructive aspects.

God-willing, we will touch upon these multiple aspects of the Ḥajj pilgrimage at the end of our discussions in this section. Let us now begin taking a closer look at the remarks made by Imam Ali (ʻa) in this section of his speech.

Imam Amīr al-Mu'minīn (ʻa) begins this part of his speech, concentrating first on the law of the Ḥajj as an obligatory religious ritual for all Muslims and then encourages all Muslims to perform this important obligatory ritual, using a beautiful and emotive language:

وَفَرَضَ عَلَيْكُمْ حَجَّ بَيْتِهِ الْحَرَامِ

"Allah has made obligatory upon you the pilgrimage to His sacred House ..."

Then he continues and describes the Ka'bah as follows:
"... which He made a Qiblah [and a polestar] for people ..."[1]
It is the center and the polestar in whose direction all Muslims perform prayers several times a day, gathering around it in huge circles and taking it as the token of their unity; this is, in effect, one of the secrets behind the unity of Muslim people.
The Imam ('a) then goes on to present another evocative description of this sacred sanctuary and the rituals which are performed by its side every year by thousands and thousands of fervent devotees of Allah:

1. Some experts have maintained that the Arabic term "انام" means "mankind"; there are other experts who believe that it is used to refer to any intelligent being that lives on the earth, including the Jinn and mankind. Based on the first view, the Ka'bah would be the Qiblah of human beings only, while based on the second view, it is a Qiblah and a polestar for both the Jinn and mankind. There is a third group of experts who are of the opinion that it derives from the root word "ونام", which means "voice"; they have argued that it is used to refer to any being that has a "soul", i.e. mankind and the Jinn [Tāj al-'Arūs, the entry "انم"].

يَرِدُونَهُ[1] وُرُودَ الْأَنْعامِ وَيَأْلَهُونَ[2] إِلَيْهِ وَلُوهَ الْحَمامِ[3]

"...and which they enter as thirsty cattle [enter their drinking place] and take refuge in like enthralled doves."

Undoubtedly, those who truly appreciate the philosophy of the Ḥajj move toward the House of Allah like thirsty people rushing toward water and like enthralled doves arriving in their safe refuge. They would make this pilgrimage in order to purify their hearts and souls and to elevate their souls through the unparalleled spirituality found in the vicinity of the sacred House of Allah. They would go there, seeking refuge with Allah from the evils of the devils, their own carnal desires, and sins, circumambulating around the Ka'bah and running between Mounts Ṣafā and Marwah with all their hearts devoted solely to their Lord.

The reason why the Ḥajj pilgrims have been likened to thirsty creatures or cattle here is that they enter the sanctuary of Allah for visiting His sacred House in an extremely humble and modest manner. This could also be in reference to their restlessness and their longing when they first arrive to visit the Ka'bah and perform their circumambulation around it. It should be noted that although such similitudes are quite common in the Arabic literature and they have positive connotations, in other languages they might have negative ones.

Moreover, the reason why the Ḥajj pilgrims are likened to doves in this part of the Imam's sermon is that doves are a symbol of peace, love,

1. The Arabic word "يردون", from the root word "ورود", has been originally used to refer to the thirsty animals entering a drinking place to drink. It has later come to be used to refer to entering any place.

2. Some lexicologists believe that the term "يألهون" derives from the root words "اله" and "ألوه", which mean "worship". According to this view, the term "يألهون" in this sentence means "they worship ...". There are other experts who have suggested that it means "bewilderment" or "enthrallment" because when man thinks about the Essence and Attributes of Allah, he becomes both bewildered and enthralled with their grandeur. There is still another group of experts who are of the opinion that it derives from the root word "وَلَهَ" whose "و" letter has been turned to the letter "ء" over time. Based on this viewpoint, this word means "taking refuge" and "supplicating" while being enthralled.

3. The Arabic word "حَمام" [pronounced "Ḥamām"] means "dove" or "pigeon"; its other derivative "حِمام" [pronounced "Ḥimām"] means "death"; in this sentence, however, the first word, i.e. "dove" is intended.

security, and kindness, and their sound is that of serenity and enthusiasm. Interestingly enough, the beginning of the Ḥajj pilgrimage is marked by entering the state of Ihram and chanting the Talbiyah, which consists of certain phrases chanted by the Ḥajj pilgrims in order to show that they have come to answer Allah's call to Ḥajj.

So the Ḥajj pilgrimage is essentially a great feast to which Allah has invited all of His servants, and so whoever is able to go on it travels to Allah's sanctuary every year during the Ḥajj season. These pilgrims will then recite the Talbiyah to show their longing and enthusiasm to be part of Allah's spiritual feast held by the side of His sacred House. The result of this pilgrimage is the spiritual elevation and a spirit of piety that the Ḥajj pilgrims experience after finishing the rituals.

Imam Ali ('a) then continues his speech focusing on the philosophy of the Ḥajj pilgrimage. He states:

وَجَعَلَهُ سُبْحانَهُ عَلامَةً لِتَواضُعِهِمْ لِعَظَمَتِهِ وَإذْعانِهِمْ لِعِزَّتِهِ

"... And Allah _ glory be to Him_ made it a token of their humility before His Greatness and their submission to His Might."

The Ḥajj pilgrimage consists of a series of rituals which are done as acts of worship offered to Allah in a state of complete humbleness and modesty. There are no other acts of worship which are done in such states of humility and submission before Allah.

In order to begin the Ḥajj pilgrimage, the Ḥajj pilgrims must enter the state of Ihram. This means that they must take off all of their beautiful clothes, expensive jewels, and their accessories, and cover their bodies merely with two simple strips of seamless fabric. They must then perform the ritual circumambulation around the Ka'bah and the ritual running between the Mounts Ṣafā and Marwah in those same clothes. They must then stay in the desert of 'Arafāt, then go to Mash'ar and Mena and perform the stoning of Satan and finally end their rituals by getting a complete head shave. These are all rituals and acts of worship done to show the Ḥajj pilgrims' complete submission to Allah and their humbleness before Him. These acts also serve to eliminate the spirits of arrogance, vanity, and egotism in the believer, liberating him from the shackles of these moral vices.

Imam Amīr al-Mu'minīn ('a) then proceeds to mention how great an honor Allah bestows on some people by granting them the chance to be in the rank of the Ḥajj pilgrims:

$$ \text{وَاخْتَارَ مِنْ خَلْقِهِ سُمَّاعاً أَجَابُوا اِلَيْهِ دَعْوَتَهُ وَصَدَّقُوا كَلِمَتَهُ} $$

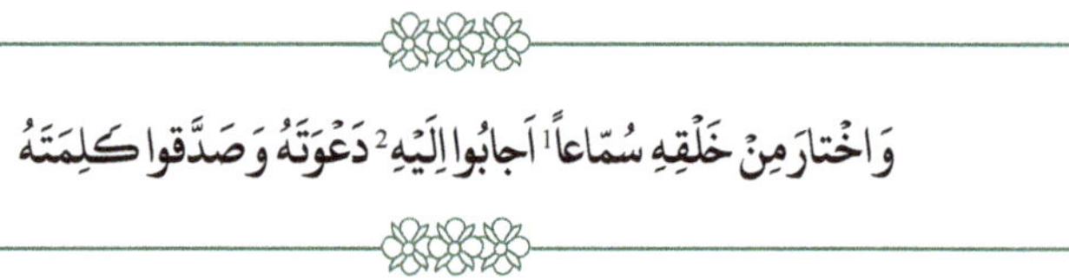

"And He chose from among His servants some who would keep an ear out for His call to answer Him, to believe in His Words…"

According to the Islamic Hadiths, when Ibrāhīm and Ismail finished building the Ka'bah on Allah's orders, Allah ordered them to call out to people loudly so that they would all come there to perform the Ḥajj pilgrimage. When Ibrāhīm received that order, he said, "But my voice is not loud enough for all the people to hear."

Allah replied, "You call out for them and I will deliver it to them." So Ibrāhīm went up to the place which is known today as the Station of Ibrāhīm in the Masjid al-Ḥarām to carry out Allah's orders. As soon as he had mounted that place, it began rising up to the sky until it was higher than the mountains. Then, Ibrāhīm placed his hands on his ears, and called out loudly toward the east and the west:

$$ \text{أَيُّهَا النَّاسُ كُتِبَ عَلَيْكُمُ الْحَجُّ اِلَى الْبَيْتِ الْعَتِيقِ فَأَجِيبُوا رَبَّكُمْ} $$

"O' Mankind! The Ḥajj pilgrimage to the House of Allah has been prescribed for you, so answer your Lord's call!"

---

1. The Arabic term "سُمَّاع" [pronounced "Summā'"] is the plural of "سامع" [meaning "listener"].

2. The pronoun "اليه" can be in reference either to Allah or the Ka'bah; either case, it does not make a major difference in the meaning of this sentence.

According to these Hadiths, Ibrāhīm's call reverberated all throughout the world, and all the people to the east and west of the world, and even those who had not yet been born into this world, heard his call, and all answered: "لَبَّيْکَ اللّهُمَّ لَبَّيْک" [Here I am, o' Lord, here I am, at Your service!].[1]

According to some Islamic Hadiths, the ones who responded to Ibrāhīm's call with "لبيک" on that day, will be able to perform the Ḥajj pilgrimage as many times as they said "لبيک" on that day; however, those who failed to respond to that call with a "لبيک" on that day, will be unable to make the Ḥajj pilgrimage.[2]

Imam Ali ('a) then goes on to focus once again on the philosophy of the Ḥajj and its constructive role in the moral and spiritual training of mankind, stating the following:

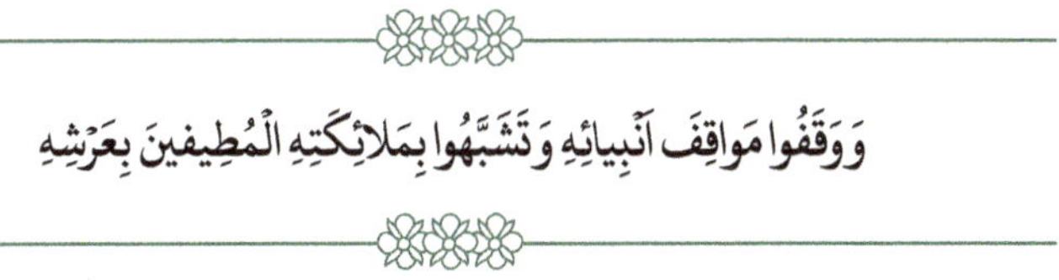
وَوَقَفُوا مَوَاقِفَ أَنْبِيائِهِ وَتَشَبَّهُوا بِمَلائِكَتِهِ الْمُطِيفِينَ بِعَرْشِهِ

"... to stay at the place of the Divinely-sent prophets, and to become like the angels who circumambulate His Throne."

The reason why the Imam ('a) stated here that those who make the Ḥajj pilgrimage will stay where the Divinely-sent prophets stood is that many prophets after Ibrāhīm, and according to some Islamic Hadiths even before him, went on pilgrimages to this sacred House.[3] Moreover, the reason why the Imam ('a) called the Ḥajj pilgrims "like angels" is that, according to Islamic teachings, there is a house, high in the heavens, located right above the Ka'bah, around which the an-

1. Tafsīr al-Qummī, vol. 2, p. 83.

2. Al-Kāfī, vol. 4, bāb Ḥajj Ibrāhīm wa Ismail wa Binā'ihimā al-Bayt, p. 206, hadith No. 6; Biḥār al-Anwār, vol. 96, p. 187, hadith No. 18.

3. According to some Islamic Hadiths, the great Prophet of Islam (ṣ), Adam, Noah, Ibrāhīm, Moses, Jesus, Jonah, and Suleiman are among the prophets who went on pilgrimages to the center of monotheism, the Ka'bah. [Al-Khū'ī, Minhāj al-Barā'ah, vol. 2, p. 252].

gels circumambulate as an act of worship offered to Allah.[1]
Following his discussion of the significance of the Ḥajj, the Imam (ʻa) explains the enormous blessings that the Ḥajj pilgrims can reap from this spiritual journey of theirs, stating the following:

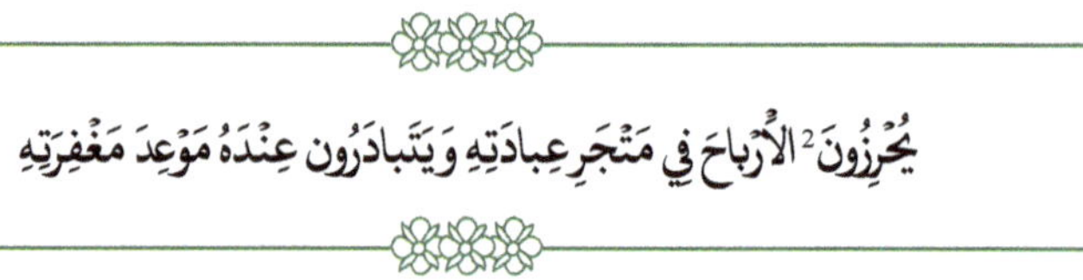

يُحْرِزُونَ[2] الْأَرْبَاحَ فِي مَتْجَرِ عِبَادَتِهِ وَيَتَبَادَرُونَ عِنْدَهُ مَوْعِدَ مَغْفِرَتِهِ

"[And in so doing] they reap much profit in the marketplace of worship of Allah, and rush toward Him for His promised forgiveness."

Words such as "reap", "profit" and "marketplace" are beautiful metaphors used here to bring the great benefits of this spiritual journey close to mind through concrete concepts that people are already familiar with. The Imam (ʻa) likened the Ḥajj to a lucrative trade, and what trade is more lucrative than the forgiveness of one's entire sins through a single act of worship, i.e. the Ḥajj pilgrimage?! Based on the Islamic Hadiths, when a Ḥajj pilgrim completes his Ḥajj rituals, he comes out like the day he/she was born.
The Imam (ʻa) further adds the following:

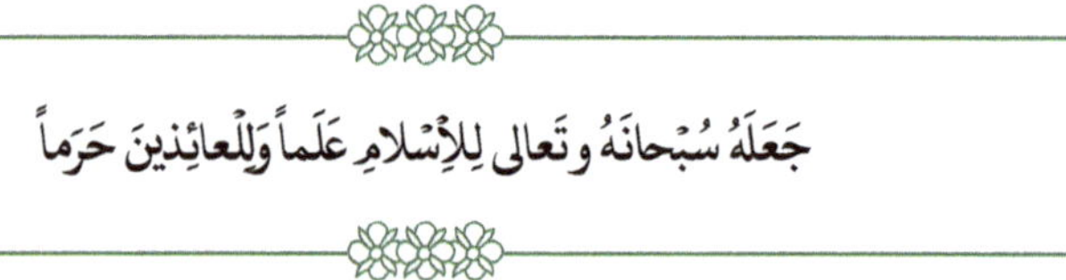

"And Allah - the Glorified, the Most High- made it an emblem [and a symbol] for Islam and a sanctuary for the refugees."

Without doubt, the Kaʻbah is the great emblem of Islam and a symbol which is always standing. It is a banner around which all Muslims

1. Tafsīr al-ʻAyāshi, vol. 1, p. 159, amid discussing the hadith No. 530.

2. The Arabic word "يحرزون", from the root word "احراز", means "to save" and "to hoard". This is why the term "حرز", another derivative of this word, is used for a well-protected place such as a vault, a safe, or a storehouse.

gather and a sign with which they preserve their independence from other faiths. It is also a sign and display of their greatness and glory, as every year during the Ḥajj season, it is visited by thousands and thousands of Muslims, which imbues the religion of Islam with a new vitality.

After discussing the significance and the secrets of the Ḥajj pilgrimage, Imam Ali ('a) further emphasizes that the Ḥajj pilgrimage is an obligatory religious duty:

فَرَضَ حَقَّهُ وَأَوْجَبَ حَجَّهُ وَكَتَبَ عَلَيْكُمْ وِفَادَتَهُ١ فَقَالَ سُبْحَانَهُ: وَلِلَّهِ عَلَى النَّاسِ
حِجُّ الْبَيْتِ مَنِ اسْتَطَاعَ إِلَيْهِ سَبِيلاً وَمَنْ كَفَرَ فَإِنَّ اللَّهَ غَنِيٌّ عَنِ الْعَالَمِينَ

"He made what is due for it incumbent [upon all], the pilgrimage to it obligatory [for all], and prescribed visiting it for you all, and He_ glory be to Him_ said: "and [an obligatory] duty owed to Allah by the people is that they make pilgrimage to [His] House, those who can afford to make it."²"

---

1. The Arabic term "وفادة" originally means "to rise" and "become manifest". It has later come to be used to mean to arrive or visit a place. Its other derivative "وفد" is used to refer to political "delegations" which are sent from one country to another in order to visit the ruler or some important authorities in that country.

2. Āl-i-'Imrān, 97.

Important Points

Given the significance of the issue of the Ḥajj pilgrimage, there are countless important issues to be discussed about it and different aspects of it to be explored and explained, issues about which a separate book needs to be written. Here, however, we will settle for a number of most important points pertaining to the issue of the Ḥajj.

1. The History of the Ka'bah

The Ka'bah, which is also known as the sacred House of Allah, has a long history which, based on the Islamic Hadiths,[1] dates back to the time of Adam ('a). According to the Islamic Hadiths, it was Adam ('a) who first built the Ka'bah and circumambulated it as an act of worship offered to Allah.

According to historical accounts, upon the occurrence of the Great Deluge which happened during the time of Noah ('a), the Ka'bah was also destroyed. But then, as explicitly mentioned in the Quran[2], it was later rebuilt by Ibrāhīm ('a) together with his son Ismail ('a), and together they made the Ḥajj pilgrimage to the House of Allah.

The Quran demonstrates that the first sacred sanctuary of monotheism that was ever built on the earth was the Ka'bah, which was built in the city of Mecca:

إِنَّ أَوَّلَ بَيْتٍ وُضِعَ لِلنَّاسِ لَلَّذِي بِبَكَّةَ مُبَارَكًا

"Indeed, the first house established for the people [in which to worship Allah] was the one at Mecca, a source of blessing ..."[3]

Moreover, as it was mentioned before, there are Islamic Hadiths which indicate that right above where the Ka'bah is located on the

1. Biḥār al-Anwār, vol. 12, p. 86.
2. Al-Baqarah, 127.
3. Āl-i-'Imrān, 96.

earth there is a temple high in the heavens around which the angels circumambulate just as people do around the Ka‘bah on the earth. There are some Islamic Hadiths which suggest that the first part of land that emerged from under water on the earth was the place where the Ka‘bah is located[1]; in fact, the story of the "Daḥw al-Arḍ" is indicative of the same fact. According to this story, the surface of the earth was covered in water in the beginning of its creation due to heavy rains. But then water began to recede and different patches of land began to emerge with the first patch of land emerging from under water being the place where the Ka‘bah is located.

There is a plethora of facts pertaining the great significance of the Ka‘bah, mentioned both in the Nahj al-Balāghah and the Islamic Hadiths related from the other Infallible Imams (‘a). For instance, according to one of such Hadiths, Imam al-Bāqir (‘a) has been quoted as saying:

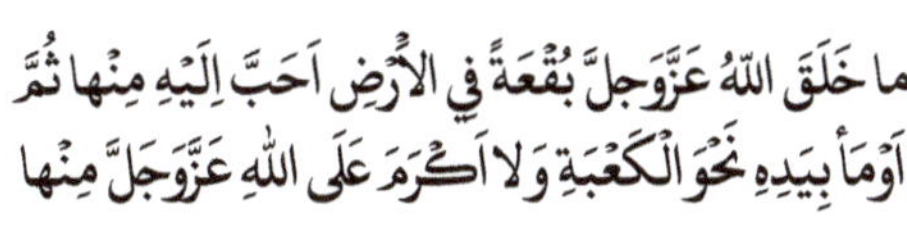

ما خَلَقَ اللهُ عَزَّوَجَلَّ بُقْعَةً فِي الأَرْضِ أَحَبَّ إِلَيْهِ مِنْها ثُمَّ
أَوْمَأَ بِيَدِهِ نَحْوَ الكَعْبَةِ وَلا أَكْرَمَ عَلَى اللهِ عَزَّوَجَلَّ مِنْها

"Allah the Almighty has not created any patch of land on the earth that is more pleasing to Him than this [and then the Imam (‘a) pointed his hand in the direction of the Ka‘bah, and then continued:] and no place on the earth is more venerable in the sight of Allah than this."

According to the same Hadith, the Imam (‘a) also says the following regarding the Ka‘bah:

1. Al-Kāfī, vol. 4, p. 188, bāb anna Awwala Mā Khalaqa Allah min al-Arḍīn Mawḍi‘ al-Bayt; Minhāj al-Barā‘ah [by al-Khū’ī], vol. 2, p. 235.

إِنَّ النَّظَرَ إِلَيْهَا عِبَادَةٌ

"... even looking at it constitutes an act of worship."[1]

The Ka'bah is considered as an emblem of and a center for the unity of Muslims, and it is located in the middle of the large circle around which Muslims, from all around the world, perform their congregational prayers several times every day. It is also the largest center for the annual gatherings of Muslims and it always stands as a sign of their greatness as a nation. Every year, a large number of Muslims arrive in the city of Mecca to spend a few days in its vicinity in order to benefit from its great spiritual and material blessings.

Let us take a look, at this point, at an interesting issue which has been narrated by Zurārah, one of the greatest companions of Imam al-Bāqir ('a) and Imam al-Ṣādiq ('a), with regard to the Ḥajj pilgrimage. According to a historical narrative, once Zurārah said to Imam al-Ṣādiq ('a):

جَعَلَنِيَ اللهُ فِدَاكَ، أَسْأَلُكَ فِي الْحَجِّ مُنْذُ أَرْبَعِينَ عَاماً فَتُفْتِينِي

"May I be sacrificed for you! It is now forty years that I am constantly asking you about the laws of the Ḥajj pilgrimage and you keep giving me answers [and there are still more laws about the Ḥajj pilgrimage!!!]"

In response, Imam al-Ṣādiq ('a) said:

1. Al-Kāfī, vol. 4, Bāb Faḍl al-Naẓar ilā al-Ka'bah, p. 240, hadith No. 1.

يا زُرَارَةَ بَيْتُ يُحَجُّ إِلَيْهِ قَبْلَ آدَمَ بِأَلْفَيْ عامٍ تُرِيدُ اَنْ تَفْنَى مَسَائِلُهُ في اَرْبَعينَ عاماً

"O' Zurārah! How do you expect the explanation of the laws of pilgrimage to this House to finish in forty years seeing as it has been constantly visited by pilgrims since two thousand years before the creation of Adam?!!"[1]

It can be inferred from this tradition that even before the creation of man this sacred sanctuary had been frequently visited by the angels or other beings that lived on the earth before mankind.

2. The Philosophy of the Ḥajj Pilgrimage ⊛

In this section of his sermon, the Imam Ali ('a) has made enlightening remarks regarding the philosophy of the Ḥajj pilgrimage and the secrets behind its rituals. When considered together with the related Islamic Hadiths regarding the issue of the Ḥajj pilgrimage, these remarks indicate that this great act of worship enjoys four major aspects: a moral and devotional aspect, a sociopolitical aspect, a cultural aspect, and an economic aspect.

As regards their moral and devotional aspect, the Ḥajj rituals function as a means of moral training and self-purification for people. Through its amazing and symbolic rituals, it guides one to fortify the foundations of piety and sincerity within oneself.

The following remark is a famous phrase, used in several Islamic traditions, which captures this specific aspect of the Ḥajj pilgrimage:

---

1. Man Lā Yaḥḍuruh al-Faqīh, vol. 2, Bāb Nawādir al-Ḥajj, p. 519, hadith No. 3111.

... يَخْرُجُ مِنْ ذُنُوبِهِ كَهَيْئَةِ يَوْمَ وَلَدَتْهُ أُمُّهُ

"Anyone who makes the pilgrimage to the House of Allah [with sincere devotion, complete attention to its rituals to perform them correctly, together with the knowledge of the secret behind them] will be cleansed of their sins like the day they were born."[1]

This is clear proof as to the amazing effect of the Ḥajj pilgrimage on human heart and soul, as it has the potential of purifying people of all the effects of the sins that they have committed. In fact, what greater benefit can the Ḥajj pilgrims possibly expect to gain from any acts of worship other than to be cleansed of the adverse effects of a lifetime of sins and transgressions which have tarnished their souls?!

If the Ḥajj pilgrims perform their Ḥajj rituals attentively, with every step they take during their pilgrimage, they will come one step closer to Allah, and they can feel the presence of their One and Only Lord everywhere as they go through their rites. This is, in effect, what makes the Ḥajj pilgrimage a second birth for those who make it!

People who truly benefit from the spiritual blessings of the Ḥajj pilgrimage carry these blessings with them until the end of their lives and they constantly feel this unparalleled feeling of spirituality in their lives. It is probably due to this amazing effect that the Ḥajj pilgrimage is obligatory upon every individual only once in their lifetime.

As for its sociopolitical aspect, if the Ḥajj pilgrimage is made as prescribed by the Islamic law and called to by Prophet Ibrāhīm ('a), it will be a means of dignity and grandeur for Muslims. It is also a means of fortifying the foundations of the religion, the unity of the Muslim people as well as a source of power and glory for the Muslim nation which instills fear in the hearts of the enemies of Islam. Additionally, the Ḥajj pilgrimage is a display of the monotheists' repudiation of the polytheists.

This great religious convention which is held annually in the vicin-

1. Biḥār al-Anwār, vol. 96, p. 26, hadith No. 111.

ity of the House of Allah provides the best opportunity for Muslims to reinvigorate themselves, replenish their energy, and strengthen the ties of brotherhood amongst themselves. This way, they can prepare themselves against the plots of the enemies and withstand their invasion. Such a huge convention with such great spiritual dimensions and such enthusiastic participants is truly unequalled in the world.

It is rather unfortunate that Muslims have not yet realized the great power the Ḥajj pilgrimage gives them, or else they would have used this great opportunity every year in order to advance the cause of Islam and deliver devastating blows to the foundations of disbelief in the world.

The importance of the Ḥajj pilgrimage is to such a great extent that it has been described as follows in some Islamic Hadiths:

لا يَزالُ الدِّينُ قائِماً ما قامَتِ الْكَعْبَةُ

"The religion [of Islam] will stand as long as the Ka'bah stands."[1]

It seems that some of the sworn enemies of Islam have realized the great power of the Ḥajj in regard to political issues, and therefore they have taken aggressive stances against it. For instance, William Gladstone, one of the British prime ministers of the late 19th century, once stated the following in his address to the House of Commons: "As long as the name of Muḥammad is celebrated on the minarets [in the mornings and the evenings] and the Quran is the way of life of Muslims and the Ḥajj is held [so majestically every year], the Christian world is in great danger and we will be unable to reform the world [albeit in the imperialistic sense of the word, as done by the British imperialist, which means nothing more than imperialism!]"[2]

There are some other narratives which indicate that Gladstone also

1. Al-Kāfī, vol. 4, Bāb Annahū law Taraka al-Nās al-Ḥajj la Jā'a hum al-'Adhāb, p. 271, hadith No. 4.

2. Rāhnamāy-e Ḥaramayn-e Sharīfayn, vol. 1, p. 54 [cited from the Goftār-e Māh].

said the following in his address: "It is imperative that you, the Christian politicians, remove the name of Muḥammad from the Muslim call-to-prayer, pass it into oblivion, burn the Quran, and demolish the Ka'bah!"

Similarly, the following remarks have been made by a western Christian figure: "Woe to the Muslims if they do not understand the meaning of the Ḥajj and woe to others if Muslims understand the meaning of the Ḥajj!"

Obviously, the enemies of Islam will never try to actually burn all of the copies of the Quran and they will never be able to destroy the Ka'bah; however, they can use the negligence of Muslims to pass the laws of Islam into oblivion and strip the Ḥajj pilgrimage of all of its meaning and function.

The cultural aspect of the Ḥajj is that, as it has also been confirmed by the Islamic Hadiths, it constitutes a means through which the message of the Prophet of Islam (ṣ) and the Infallible Imams ('a) can be disseminated all throughout the world. Moreover, since every year a large number of great religious scholars, scientists, speakers, and authors from different Muslim countries make the Ḥajj pilgrimage, it is the best opportunity for the exchange of opinions and information among them and also the greatest chance for them to revive the message of the Prophet (ṣ) and the Infallible Imams ('a).

Finally, there is the economic aspect of the Ḥajj pilgrimage, which has also been mentioned in the Islamic traditions as one of the important aspects of this great event. According to these traditions, the Ḥajj pilgrimage can help strengthen Muslims financially and help them exit financial hardship.

The question might arise at this point as to what financial function the Ḥajj pilgrimage could possibly have. In response, it should be pointed out that one of the most dangerous problems of the Muslim world today is their economic dependence on the foreign powers, most of whom are the enemies of Islam.

So, it behoves Muslims to hold seminars and conferences during the Ḥajj season and invite prominent Muslim economists to draw up plans, as a great act of worship offered to Allah, in order to save their fellow Muslim brothers and sisters from poverty and economic dependence on non-Muslim powers. These experts could arrange meetings on the sidelines of the Ḥajj pilgrimage, speak about the economic problems of the Muslim world, and work out sound plans to eliminate those problems.

This issue should be pursued not as a personal issue and for personal gain, but with the purpose of strengthening the Muslim nation as a whole, saving them from poverty, and helping them restore their former glory.[1]

From what was discussed above, the deep nature of the remarks made by Imam Ali ('a) about the Ḥajj pilgrimage is further revealed. It is now clear why the Imam ('a) likens the Ḥajj pilgrims to the angels who are circling around Allah's Throne, calling the Ḥajj pilgrimage a "lucrative business" from which people can reap a great deal of profit. It is perhaps due to the immense benefits of the Ḥajj pilgrimage that the Imam ('a) focuses only on this specific act of worship in this part of his sermon, as it is a collective act of worship which has worldly, otherworldly, moral, spiritual, and even political dimensions.

There are many more issues surrounding the Ḥajj pilgrimage as well as other countless facts pertaining to it that need to be discussed. However, since Imam Ali ('a) has discussed these other issues in detail in his other sermons, which have also been included in the Nahj al-Balāghah, we will present our discussions regarding them while presenting commentaries on those sermons.

1. According to an Islamic tradition, narrated by Hishām ibn Ḥakam from Imam al-Ṣādiq ('a), the Imam ('a) referred to all of these aspects of the Ḥajj pilgrimage in a general manner [Wasā'il al-Shi'a, vol. 8, p. 8]. For more information on the philosophy of the Ḥajj, refer to Tafsīr-e Nemūneh, vol. 14, p. 75.

www.ingramcontent.com/pod-product-compliance
Lightning Source LLC
Chambersburg PA
CBHW052108030426
42335CB00025B/2887